Praise for *Out of Silence*

"A little boy prey to obscure, uncontrollable forces, and his family, whose bravery and hope in the face of overwhelming odds somehow exalts them to a realm that is not an exaggeration to call heroic."
  —*The New York Times Book Review*

"From time to time a special book is written that changes one's way of perceiving the self and the world and that challenges one to rethink what being human really means. Russell Martin, with *Out of Silence*, has written such a book, telling a story that is ultimately uplifting despite its sad and even tragic dimensions. . . . [It is] a book that should become a classic."
  —*Bloomsbury Review*

"The journey into language is a magical passage for any of us, and Russell Martin's brilliantly observed story of a boy struggling to speak takes us into the latest realms of how and why words come to us, and we to them. This is a provocative guidebook to our linguistic paths to humanness."
  —Ivan Doig

"A book of honesty, beauty, and lofty accomplishment . . . Martin uses Ian's affliction to consider the essential function of language in human development and the destiny of human civilization."
  —*Los Angeles Times*

"*Out of Silence* tells an amazing story of parental love and dedication."
  —*Pittsburgh Post Gazette*

"Juxtaposing the pain of childhood autism with theories of how language develops and function, Martin evokes the miracle of speech and the tragedy of its loss. A remarkable story. . . . Crucial reading for parents and professionals."
  —*Kirkus Reviews*

"*Out of Silence* is a stunning testimony to the grit and courage of a boy who longed for the gift of speech."
  —Richard Selzer, M.D., author of *Rasing the Dead*

"Russell Martin brings his best powers to bear in this book: luminous prose, fascinating research, deep insights, and true heart. . . . Read this book and you'll never take language for granted again."
  —Mary La Chapelle, author of *House of Heroes and Other Stories*

PENGUIN BOOKS

OUT OF SILENCE

Russell Martin is the author of five nonfiction books, including the widely praised *Matters Gray and White* (1986) and *A Story That Stands Like a Dam* (1989) which received the Caroline Bancroft History Prize and was a finalist for the Western Writers of America Spur Award for Nonfiction Book of the Year. His first novel, *Beautiful Islands*, was published in 1988, and he is the editor of *New Writers of the Purple Sage* (Penguin, 1992). Ian Martin Drummond, the child in *Out of Silence*, is his nephew.

RUSSELL MARTIN

OUT OF SILENCE

AN AUTISTIC
BOY'S JOURNEY INTO
LANGUAGE AND COMMUNICATION

PENGUIN BOOKS

PENGUIN BOOKS
Published by the Penguin Group
Penguin Books USA Inc., 375 Hudson Street,
New York, New York 10014, U.S.A.
Penguin Books Ltd, 27 Wrights Lane, London W8 5TZ, England
Penguin Books Australia Ltd, Ringwood, Victoria, Australia
Penguin Books Canada Ltd, 10 Alcorn Avenue,
Toronto, Ontario, Canada M4V 3B2
Penguin Books (N.Z.) Ltd, 182–190 Wairau Road, Auckland 10, New Zealand

Penguin Books Ltd, Registered Offices: Harmondsworth, Middlesex, England

First published in the United States of America
by Henry Holt and Company, Inc., 1994
Reprinted by arrangement with Henry Holt and Company, Inc.
Published in Penguin Books 1995

1 3 5 7 9 10 8 6 4 2

THE LIBRARY OF CONGRESS HAS CATALOGUED THE HARDCOVER AS FOLLOWS:
Martin, Russell.
Out of silence: a journey into language/Russell Martin.—1st ed.
p. cm.
ISBN 0-8050-1998-7 (hc.)
ISBN 0 14 02.4701 7 (pbk.)
1. Language and languages. I. Title.
P106.M3543 1994
401—dc20   93–28434

Printed in the United States of America
Set in Bodoni
Designed by Paula R. Szafranski

this is for the four of them:
Claudia, Boyce, Sarah,

and Ian

CONTENTS

. . . it was good to have all the world's words at the mind's disposal, so the mind could begin its task. All those things for which we have no words are lost. The mind—the culture—has two little tools, grammar and lexicon: a decorated sand bucket and a matching shovel. With these we bluster about the continents and do all the world's work. With these we try to save our very lives.

—*Annie Dillard*

OUT OF SILENCE

1
IN THE
BEGINNING

"Cow," he said, or tried to say, his bright eyes astonished by these creatures, the whole world still a wonderment for him at eighteen months, but now in need of names. Then "Cow," he tried again, and this time the word was unmistakable, nothing more than a quick, coarse noise that seemed somehow caught inside his excitement, yet what a feat it was, of course—all first words, as well as those that follow them for a lifetime, formed and uttered out of magic.

Late in the soggy, snowbound winter of 1985, Ian lived with his parents, his sister, and a collie with a chronically sunburned nose at a scientific research station surrounded by ponderosa woods and great granite outcroppings high in the Colorado Rockies, the laboratory, its outbuildings, and their nearby house carved out of a showcase cattle ranch. It wasn't particularly surprising therefore—in a world evidently populated far more by Angus-Hereford crosses than by people—that instead of *Mama* or *milk* or *more*, it was *cow* that first found its way out of this little boy's mouth. But what was very much out of the ordinary—what was curious at first, puzzling, then worrisome, gnawing, exploding at last into something catastrophic before finally it was simply the way things were—was that for the next five years, Ian didn't say "cow" again, nor did he utter another word.

—

Ian Martin Drummond, my nephew, my older sister's son, was born on August 2, 1983 in Normal, Illinois, to Claudia Martin and Boyce Drummond. Befitting that heartland birthplace, Ian was, it seemed wonderfully certain, a normal infant in every respect. He began to crawl at seven months, a bit earlier than average; he was walking confidently at eleven months, seven months sooner than some of his peers. His parents remember that he acquired other motor skills with equal ease, and generally he was more coordinated than his sister, Sarah, had been when she was his age. Despite an allergy to milk and chronic ear infections, the early, toddling Ian was a healthy, gregarious child who liked to be held. He quickly became fascinated by books, toys, and videotapes. He began to babble with great gusto. He liked to imitate Sarah as they played, and she and her parents remember with an enduring sense of sadness and of loss the day— at perhaps sixteen or seventeen months—when Ian employed a stick-toy to imitate his father, who was vacuuming the carpets; the day when Ian smiled broadly, seemingly on cue, as Sarah aimed a camera in his direction; the day when Ian proudly growled for Claudia to show her what the lion says.

But soon after he achieved one more milestone by announcing that first formidable word to the cows scattered in one of the ranch's roadside pastures, Ian received the fourth in a standard series of diphtheria-pertussis-tetanus immunizations, and as his physician cautioned he might, he fell soundly asleep as soon as he was home. He slept through the afternoon of March 6, 1985, and into the early evening; and without waking a single time—something quite unusual for him—he continued to sleep through the night. Although they were concerned by his reaction to the DPT shot, Claudia and Boyce had been assured that similar reactions were entirely normal, so they hadn't attempted to wake him as they periodically checked him for a fever, nor, of course, had they monitored him closely enough to know whether he might have suffered seizures during the night.

Ian, in fact, seemed fine on the second day, and soon his long slumber was out of mind; it was simply one more of the hundreds of odd or unexplained occurrences that cause all parents some fleeting concern before their resilient children bound back to vigorous life. They might have forgotten it entirely had it not been for the fact that not only did Ian suspend his efforts to learn to talk in the days and months and then years that followed that immunization, but also, and in almost every way imaginable, he became a different boy.

Boyce, now forty-seven, is a scientist and teacher; Claudia, forty-five, is a teacher too, one for whom that vocation truly seems to be a calling. And at twelve, Sarah is a writer already, one who seems to understand intuitively that a story's life is in its *telling*. She wrote this when she was seven:

> I aspeshly like Ian because he is my brother, he is very very cute he loves music, and he loves the song (I know an old laty) I am very foned of Ian, very foned Hes not very cute win he skreames, he's learning to talk, I beleve that Ian will someday talk as will as I can. . . . we all love Ian, and he loves us! some day I know Ian will talk.

For four full years, from the spring when an inoculation seemed to have assaulted his forming brain until the spring when Sarah first tried to describe her brother to a world she wasn't sure would understand him, Ian *was* very cute, but he wasn't cute when he screamed, and he screamed very much of the time.

No one could be certain why, but as his interest in speaking suddenly vanished, Ian became strangely terrorized by much of what he encountered: Neighbors whom he had known and liked now no longer could enter the house without inducing his awful shrieks; he would begin to cry uncontrollably when trips in the car deviated from precisely remembered routes; he would throw a terrible tantrum if, as part of his relentless daily routine, he could not go visit the cows. Ian abandoned the spoon with which he had become adept at feeding himself in favor of his fingers, and he would eat only a few specific foods—always round crackers, for instance, never square ones. He would wake in the night and laugh eerily, irrepressibly, for as much as an hour. In lieu of other kinds of play, he would position toys in long lines so straight that seemingly no child could have arranged them, or often in radial arcs that were equally perfect, surely equally impossible.

Ian didn't notice the new kitten Sarah was enthralled by; the dog he had befriended long before he now didn't seem to see. Indoors, he lived only in his room, his solitary life lived out to the constant, droning accompaniment of videotapes of children's cartoons— *Dumbo, Charlotte's Web, Winnie-the-Pooh*—each one played literally thousands of times, the proper movie at the proper time of day according to his inviolate internal schedule. Outside, Ian took great, obsessive pleasure in running fast alongside fences—picket fences, rail fences, barbed-wire fences, often as not—his eyes only an inch or two away from a serious injury, yet he virtually never stumbled, and not once was he cut or scraped. At night, following dinner (always in his room and accompanied by a movie; always six pieces of tofu, never seven) and an elaborate bath-and-bedtime ritual (the same dozen toys with him in the tub to stave off chaos), Ian at last would surrender to sleep, but only if his father was beside his bed, and only if an Emmylou Harris album was playing as his oddly essential lullaby—that music, like his immensely important movies, and like the daily rituals that seemed to run in a deranging and endless loop, the source of vital structure in his life, the source of some security, of precious peace, it often seemed.

Except for those few stimuli, and other than the times when he would welcome his parents' touch, their hugs and strong caresses, Ian lived in self-imposed, self-*demanded* isolation and in a perplexing kind of quietude, never attempting to speak, his babbling long since forgotten, a boy who once had been about to burst with language now silent except for his screams.

The diagnosis long since had been delivered, and autism was a disorder I had come to know firsthand by the time Barry Levinson's

Rain Man was released in 1988. Its Academy Awards notwithstanding, perhaps the film's most important achievement was its success
in bringing to so many people a basic awareness of this strange,
inexplicable, and enormously disabling disorder; and I know that for
those of us in Ian's family, the film came to serve as a kind of ready
explanation. "Have you seen *Rain Man*?" we would ask. "Yes, the
Dustin Hoffman character. Well, Ian's sort of Raymond Babbitt still
a child. He has the same need for sameness in his life, a similar
demand for ritual and for exacting detail. He's reminiscent of him
in lots of respects, except that Ian doesn't speak."

First reported in medical literature in 1799, autism (from the
Greek *autos*, or self) was considered a psychiatric disorder until only
recently. Generally characterized by a profound aloofness and need
for solitude; by odd, repetitive physical movements and gestures;
by variously heightened or diminished sensory abilities; and by pas-
sionate resistance to change—as well as by myriad disabilities with
language—autism tended to be called "childhood schizophrenia" or
"childhood psychosis," far more than the mere implication, of
course, that autistic children were demented, disturbed, deranged.
Renowned psychiatrists postulated that the condition was the result
of upbringing by severe, emotionally frigid mothers. Others were
equally certain that overly intellectual, rigid, humorless fathers were
to blame for the disorder's onset.

But as many forms of mental illness finally began to be perceived
as the results of abnormalities in the brain itself rather than as the
products of anguished, assaulted psyches, so autism too began to be
viewed as an organic, but still very mysterious, disorder whose
most compelling symptom seems to be multiple deficits related to
language: its reception via the senses, its processing and organization, its intimate role in cognition, its vocal expression. And only
just now, researchers in several parts of the world are growing convinced that it is fundamentally an expressive disorder. They maintain
that people with autism are neither psychotic nor somehow severely
retarded, but instead are the victims of a very deceptive syndrome
in which the brain, the cranial nerves, and the muscles of the mouth
and throat are unable to coordinate the almost unbelievably sophisti-

cated sequence of events that leads from a thought, an intention, to a successfully spoken word. Autism, some of them now persuasively contend, is not a cognitive disorder, and neither is it a personality disorder—not a sort of "selfism" chiefly characterized by an inability to interact with others. Instead, they point to a mounting—and even movingly symbolic—body of evidence that among autism's several critical deficits, the most profound is a lifelong problem with expressive language, proof, if we need it, that language is the one wondrous human achievement that weds the otherwise stranded self with the world.

Beginning at a time that now is a very long time ago—back when I was Ian's age—on each Wednesday morning I would rise before my sisters and my mother, and my father would drive me the few blocks to the early mass at Saint Barnabas's Church, where I would don the dark vestments that certified my importance in these mysterious, spiritual matters, then serve at Father Cole's side during the short, sparsely attended service. I still remember the somber, age-worn faces of the few women who almost always were in attendance, and in my mind I still can hear fragments of that lyrical liturgy drawn from the sixteenth-century *Book of Common Prayer*, as well as the psalms, Epistles, and Gospels that were read from the King James Bible, their lexicon so strange to me yet so melodious, the rhythms of those ancient phrases and their orchestral pace so mighty—mystical in the way they were meant to be—the sounds themselves somehow full of meaning.

"It is very meet, right, and our bounden duty," surely I heard Father Cole say a thousand times (or chant in his quaking yet courageous voice on certain feast days),

that we should at all times, and in all places, give thanks unto thee, O Lord, Holy Father, Almighty Everlasting God. Therefore with Angels and Archangels, and with all the company of heaven, we laud and magnify thy glorious Name; evermore praising thee and saying . . .

I remember that on Ash Wednesday morning every spring, as he rubbed sooty crosses onto our foreheads, in a hushed voice he would say to each one of us, "Remember O man that dust thou art, and unto dust shalt thou return," that admonishment a trifle grim, but its sounds so lovely in their whispered repetition. And I remember, of course, the Gospel from Saint John at midnight mass on Christmas Eve—we stalwart acolytes bearing torches at either side of the huge and heavy Bible, it too held by a boy like me who couldn't help but marvel at his special fortune—the words definitive and wonderful, yet still a little difficult to comprehend:

> In the beginning was the Word, and the Word was with God, and the Word was God. The same was in the beginning with God. All things were made by him; and without him was not any thing made that was made.

In the beginning was the Word. Imagine my fascination. The world—and we—began with just a *word*, with something spoken, I assumed. But if the word was *God*, then who would have spoken it? Or, if He was the speaker, on the other hand, then what incredible, catalytic word might it have been? I liked to think that perhaps the word actually was *Now*, or better, *Good*. The religious fundamentalists who filled my town would have assumed the word was *Don't*, but we Episcopalians were far more liberal than that, and although the question didn't really trouble me, it was one I liked to ponder. I knew about this bang the cosmologists lately had begun to speak of, and it seemed that perhaps that was the explanation: the big bang that came as time commenced must have been the sound of God, shuddering to speak, calling his own name, saying, Let's get started.

Speech came slowly for humankind, however. It arrived long past sunset on that metaphorical sixth day of creation, God's work all but accomplished, we hominids crashing wonderfully into consciousness with our first rituals, with rough symbols, and then at last with words. Cosmologists currently date the bang at perhaps twenty *bil-lion* years ago; the first animals, in contrast, began to crawl about on Earth some six hundred million years before our time. The earliest primates appeared seventy million years ago; the first fire-using, tool-making, *non-ape* people not emerging for another sixty-eight million years or so. We cannot know when the first meaningful words were uttered by the people now known as *Homo sapiens neanderthalensis*, but it is clear that our distant ancestors underwent a profound creative and cooperative florescence about thirty thousand years ago, at the time when *Homo sapiens sapiens* ("wise man") emerged—people taller, slimmer, more agile than the Neander-thals; a new kind of creature who produced the extraordinary paint-ings that survive in caves at Lascaux in southern France and Altamira across the border in Spain, who wore clothes and lived communally, hunting and perhaps waging small wars in concert with their kin, caring for those among them who were infirm; people who marked graves with stones and who sometimes buried their dead on beds of flowers; human beings remarkably similar to us, possessing the same brain, the same physique, the same larynx slid far enough down their throats that they could utter the full range of human sounds, down far enough as well that they could choke on food.

Strangely, the species *Homo sapiens* was and still remains the only mammal at much risk of choking. Horses, cats, and chimpan-zees, as well as you and I, have larynges that are located at the backs of our tongues—the two necessarily linked and interacting—yet we humans are anatomically distinct from all other mammals in one very critical respect. Because the tongues of nonhuman mammals are relatively short in relation to the size of their skulls—ending at the rear of their mouths—and because their larynges are therefore positioned high enough that they can shift them upward through their mouths to form a watertight seal with the entrance to their noses, they can—and do, of course—eat and breathe at the same time without any risk of food entering their airways. Efficiently and safely for all animals but us, air passes through the elevated larynx en route to the lungs while food and water are routed around it to the stomach.

In the curious human case, however, our tongues extend halfway down our throats, ending where our larynges are positioned behind the protruding thyroid cartilage commonly called the Adam's apple, resulting in what Charles Darwin noted in *The Origin of Species* as "the strange fact that every particle of food and drink which we swallow has to pass over the orifice of the trachea, with some risk of falling into the lungs," with a quick and panicked death the likely outcome. Normally, of course, the flap of tissue called the epiglottis covers the larynx as we swallow, then opens, allowing us to breathe again as food safely enters the esophagus, but the arrangement surely is flawed. And the thousands of deaths choking has caused each year for thousands of years would seem to defy the Darwinian principle of natural selection were it not for the subtle yet fundamental advantage it provides us: positioned at midpoint in our throats, our larynges allow us to make vocalizations that no other animals can match, sounds that Brown University linguist Philip Lieberman contends have been more important to the survival of our species than the certainty of safe and simple respiration.

Our species alone, for instance, can make *nonnasal* sounds by sealing off our nasal cavities and using our lips, tongues, and larynges to change the shape of our vocal tracts, producing a wide range of oral sounds that are easier for us to distinguish, one from the other, than are the less clearly definable nasal sounds. Also, our long, round tongues enable us to make *quantal* sounds—the vowels of the words *feet*, *shoe*, and *sock*, and the consonants in words like *go* and *kick*—sounds that further facilitate the encoding and decoding of our speech because they are less likely to be misinterpreted than are the tongue-tip-on-palate dental consonants employed in *to* and *do*, or the lip-closing labial consonants of *my* or *buy*. It is the range of distinct sounds that we can form, together with the rapidity with which we can form them, that make us much quicker at transmitting sound data than are other animals; Lieberman estimates that we are three to ten times faster than any other primate, an obvious advantage when it comes to communicating timely and complex information. "Consider the selective value of being able to communicate the encoded message 'There are two lions, one behind the rock and the other in the ravine,' " he writes in *Uniquely Human*, "in the same time as the unencoded 'lliiooonn rooockkk.' "

But what Lieberman posits for consideration far more fundamentally—in that recent book as well as in his earlier and highly regarded investigation *The Biology and Evolution of Language*—is his conviction that the development of the ability to utter that hard *e* that you hear in *feet* led to the florescence of language as surely as the development of the opposable thumb led to tools. And although that causal link between speech and language may at first seem simple enough, even obvious, it isn't necessarily so.

In fact, University of Hawaii linguist Derek Bickerton argues openly with Lieberman, contending that language did not develop as a means of facilitating communication but rather as a means of ordering and understanding the world. Bickerton's basic quarrel with a speech-based explanation of the origin of language can be reduced to what he calls the "continuity paradox"—the ticklish contradiction between the certainty, on the one hand, that language is the result of evolutionary adaptation and an equal certainty, on the other, that evolution, even via mutation, cannot produce something that is utterly new. Since human language is so very different from every other form of animal communication, Bickerton wants to know, how can it be the product of that communication? Where is the necessary evolutionary continuity? Finding it neither in the sliding of the larynx down the Neanderthal throat nor in the emerging ability to make uniquely human sounds—a range of sounds broad enough that communication could begin to grow complex—Bickerton instead lands on an evolutionary link that is rooted in the dense soil of symbol.

Language is not primarily communicative, he argues in *Language and Species*; it is representational. We did not develop language because we could make new sounds but because we had become *conscious*, ever more aware of new objects in our world, new conditions, and new possibilities, and we needed some sure and stable means of representing them—a way in which we could consider them, share them with others, relate them to our lives.

No creature perceives the world directly. The categories a creature can distinguish are determined not by the general nature of reality but by what that creature's nervous system is capable of representing. The capacities of that nervous system are, in part at least, determined by what the creature minimally needs in order to survive and reproduce. . . . The categories distinguished by frogs, it would seem, do not extend very far beyond bugs they can snap at, ponds they can jump into, and other frogs they can mate with. The categories distinguished by [monkeys] are more numerous, and those distinguished by our own species more numerous still, but the same principles apply.

As Bickerton examines the evolution of language, it seems to him that it was the emergence of syntax, the arrangement of representational symbols—signs, grunts, *words*—to create meanings that extend beyond those symbols themselves, that was the truly explosive catalyst for language. It was the evolution of the brain—some mysterious series of neuronal mutations—not of the supralaryngeal vocal tract, that made language possible. And had it not been convenient for early hominids to create languages out of sounds, he contends, they would have shaped them out of hand signs or perhaps simply from scratches in the earth.

Yet is it possible that both scholars are correct? Could simultaneous evolutionary adaptations have occurred that led to the rise of language—our throats and our cerebrums evolving separately but in symbiotic tandem? My linguistic credentials are more than merely suspect, yet that curious possibility seems so readily conceivable that I will risk it. Surely early symbol makers whose hands and arms were occupied with tools and children would have relished the sense they could make with sounds. Surely tentative, tongue-tied early speakers were made more eloquent by brains that could muster a simple lexicon and the rich variety of syntax.

And there are dozens more scenarios, of course, ripe for our imagining. Neurobiologist William Calvin, for example, entertains himself and his readers with speculations on whether language emerged simply because we couldn't resist the sounds that we—and we alone—could make with our mouths, akin to kids who learn to talk like Donald Duck, then do so for days on end solely for the special joy; whether intricate communicative gesturing, or even playing with shadow puppets on the fire-lit walls of caves, might have led to true sign languages that long preceded speech.

Or does Calvin's own, rather more elaborate, "throwing theory" make some serious sense? Among the cornucopia of things that intrigue Calvin—in his book of essays entitled *The Throwing Madonna*, as well as in the more recent *Cerebral Symphony*—are the likelihood that, very early on, certain brain functions were lateralized to a specific cerebral hemisphere and the further possibility that it was the development of the intricate technique of throwing rocks at escaping prey that prompted that lateralization. Neuroscientists have known for decades now that language function is lateralized to the left cerebral hemisphere in a huge majority of people: pick any dozen who pass you on the street, and perhaps one of them will possess right-sided language, but perhaps not even one. Yet what wasn't known until recently was that movement-sequencing skills—the linked abilities to pick up a rock or a football, for instance, to cock it behind your head, then to throw it forward—are also lateralized most often to the left side of the brain. Intriguingly, researchers have been able to demonstrate as well that oro-facial muscle sequencing—the ability, say, to purse your lips, then open them wide, then to stick your tongue out—is lateralized to areas just above and below the so-called Sylvian fissure in the left temporal lobe, an area of the left hemisphere that also controls a variety of language-producing and language-decoding functions. The question Calvin poses in that regard is this: Do activities as seemingly unrelated as speaking and throwing actually share much in common, and if so, is that commonality the ability to produce—precisely, reliably, and rapidly—muscle-movement sequences?

He believes the answer is yes. And what Calvin delights in imagining, in fact, is that as hominids began to heave stones at tiny targets—necessarily a one-handed, one-sided enterprise—their opposite cerebral hemisphere was correspondingly taxed (each cerebral hemisphere controls sensory and motor function for the *opposite* half of the body). In order for rock throwers to grow more and more proficient at the requisite and complicated series of movements involved in throwing, their brains, or at least a part of their brains opposite their throwing arms, had to become very good at orchestrating those movements, at sequencing. And as new skills slowly were acquired, skills that demanded equally complex muscle-movement sequencing—such as the movements of the mouth, lips, and tongue required in the pronunciation of *saber-toothed tiger* or its Cro-Magnon equivalent—it would have made obvious and efficient sense for the brain to control those skills with the sequencing computer it already had in place and in working order.

"So, did generalized human language evolve from specialized hunting 'computational' skills?" Calvin asks as he tidies up his argument. "Bootstrapping language through better throwing? If oro-facial sequencing built upon the throwing-sequencing machinery of the left brain, then it would be natural for the expanding repertoire of verbal expressions to also settle alongside in the left brain—and so to set the stage for more sophisticated language, hence culture, and science, and all the rest."

And all the rest. From beaning a rabbit with a well-aimed rock to linking the sounds that mean *You got him!* From the first paltry, faulty speech to *Peter Rabbit*.

No less a legendary linguist than Noam Chomsky is bothered by this kind of speculation about the origin of language. As far as he is concerned, early humans developed language because they possessed—and their descendants still do—what he calls a "language organ," an unspecified but nonetheless physiological piece of the brain, an organ not all that unlike the heart or the liver, and he views its origin as deserving no more sustained interest than theirs do. Chomsky's apathy toward matters paleontological plainly irks Lieberman and Calvin, and Bickerton is nettled enough by his colleague's disinterest to quip, "It would be strange indeed if physicists were to say, 'We will concern ourselves only with matter as it is now or as it has been in the recent past; the origins of the universe are of their nature unknowable and we shall not even try to explore them.' Why linguists have tacitly accepted just such a self-denying ordinance should be a topic of some interest to sociologists of science."

And surely Bickerton makes his point; surely the origin of this most *human* of characteristics—perhaps the only thing that truly separates us from our brother creatures—is an inquiry of real importance as well as fascination. The genetic makeup of *Homo sapiens* is ninety-nine percent identical to that of *Pan troglodytes*, the chimpanzee, yet we and chimps—even space-faring, sign-making, show biz chimps—bear faint resemblance to one another when it comes to the question of language. But what, if that's the curious case, *is* language?

Is it speech? Well, your parrot can speak, can mimic certain sounds you make, sounds you recognize as words, but your parrot surely doesn't possess language, does it? Then is language a system of representation—the sophisticated use of symbols? Consider in that regard the amazing messenger bees who "dance" against a honeycomb within their hive to indicate where they have found a food source, their intricate movements very specifically symbolic, capable of precisely communicating the supply's direction and distance from the hive. The process is little less than wondrous, but do bees then have language? Do whales? Do dolphins? Was a chimpanzee trained at Columbia University in the 1970s employing language when he signed *Tickle me* at times when he wanted to play, or even more intriguingly, *Me sorry hug me* after he had been scolded?

Distilling the essence of language is a bit like attempting to define love, and there is a simple reason why any number of scholarly and popular books on the larger subject of language steer well clear of actually *defining* it: you can far too readily land in a lexicographical corner when you attempt to do so. Yet near the end of the twentieth century, it is generally agreed that there are several components every true language must possess.

Early in the 1960s, anthropologist Charles Hockett, perturbed by the absence of a universal definition of language, bravely devised one of his own, one that contained thirteen different features. Thirty years later, Hockett's baker's-dozen definition has been whittled down to six components or so, and it may be that there is little left to whittle.

Every language, it seems safe enough to begin, must possess a lexicon, an alphabet, a code; simply, an agreed-upon set of symbols—sounds, graphics, hand positions—that singly or in combination represent its *morphemes*, its smallest decipherable elements. And every language also must possess syntax, a set of operating rules for manipulating its morphemes into meaning; and thirdly in that regard, a language must possess semanticity—it must be capable of eliciting meaning, something understandable.

On a kind of second tier of features, in every true language there is an arbitrary relationship between symbols and their meanings. It is only arbitrary, in other words, that in English the letters *c*, *a*, and *t*, in that order, represent the name for one kind of animal, while *d*, *o*, and *g* represent another; there is no direct relationship between the symbols and the animals in either case, no reason save centuries of convention why the names couldn't be interchanged. A language must be capable of productivity as well—it must generate and readily allow the incorporation of new or altered symbols. A language like ours, for instance, must be capable of creating meaningful new terminology as it is needed, words like *transmission*, *telecommunications*, and *Teenage Mutant Ninja Turtles*.

Lastly, and perhaps most importantly, every true language is capable of displacement, the ability to refer to things that are remote in time and space, the ability to discuss elephants without seeing one face-to-face, to refer to past events without somehow reenacting them. It is that feature of language, foremost among all the others, that makes most linguists willing to walk out on the limb where they assert that language is unique to humans. What is perhaps most improbable and most important about human language is our ability symbolically to bring both to mind and to dialogue people, places, and times that we haven't personally experienced, and even—when language sometimes soars and transcends—to very closely approximate them, to bring them to a kind of linguistic life.

Although we can marvel at messenger bees, we seem on solid ground in assuming that they, in turn, cannot marvel at some of our sharper stuff. Neither parrots nor the cleverest chimps can talk to you about school holidays or baseball scores. And while it does seem certain that many whales and porpoises are capable of intricate kinds of communication, employing their cries and sonar-sensing capabilities in ways we are just beginning to understand, it seems very unlikely—so far as we now know—that the most articulate of them can tell their offspring stories about the fine old days at sea.

It was Ian's apparent inability to hear his parents—the stories they spun at bedtime, the words with which they greeted him in the morning—rather than the fact that he wasn't speaking, that first led them to a physician's office soon after his second birthday to inquire about whether he might be deaf, or at least partially so.

Ian fought desperately to escape during the administration of a hearing test conducted by an ear, nose, and throat specialist in Colorado Springs in September 1985—his shrieks piercing the exam room, the doctor's outer office, the whole clinic, it seemed—and the procedure was deemed inconclusive. A subsequent and almost equally chaotic brain stem auditory evoked-response test, however, suggested that Ian had a moderate to severe neural hearing loss, so a second series of hearing tests was scheduled. Using Ian's bedtime music as a stimulus, this time the results seemed inarguable: his hearing was within the normal range, and the audiologist who confirmed it suggested instead that another explanation for Ian's strange behavior might be a disorder she called autism.

When Claudia and Boyce brought Ian to Denver's Children's Hospital in December of that year for a comprehensive evaluation, and to confront head-on their escalating concern that autism—about which they now knew only enough to be anxious, even frightened— might be at the root of their son's symptoms, they brought with them their own detailed summary of his developmental progress and regression, noting that, at twenty-six months of age now, Ian had lost his earlier interest in books and that he barely babbled anymore, that he insisted on precisely fixed routines and only played in strange and solitary ways, that he now was very fearful of once-familiar people and places, that he had become obsessively dependent on videotapes for solace and security, and perhaps most chillingly of all, Boyce wrote, "Ian seems to have lost all curiosity about the world."

No one was surprised, of course, when the huge and imposing hospital also seemed to terrify him on that cold, cloud-cast winter morning. He screamed and struggled ceaselessly over a period of several hours, attempting so desperately to get away that you might have assumed he was under attack; the several doctors who saw him could only examine him in cursory kinds of ways. Yet their impressions were uniform and, sadly, all too easy to come by: "Neurologic exam today was pretty impossible and could only be done by observation because Ian had a catastrophic response when approached," the pediatric neurologist wrote in his evaluation, yet "the impression is infantile autism with a possibility of expressive aphasia high. Dementia is also possible."

In her office later in the day, with Ian's trauma by now reduced to zombielike exhaustion, the developmental pediatrician similarly noted, "I observed all communication either to take place by crying or by touching and moving, usually a person, out of the way. . . . All his energy is directed toward maintaining sameness and control. He tunes out other people when he is successful; when he is not successful, then he becomes quite anxious." Her diagnosis: autism. Her kind and, it seemed, genuinely caring advice to Ian's parents: Do what you can to prepare your daughter and yourselves for this. You have some difficult years ahead.

Was it Ian's lack of language that induced his terror in those days? Could his absence of words, of the barest kind of substantial speech, have accounted for the tantrums? I remember being curious about

those possibilities as my sister called regularly with reports on Ian's
progress or, as more often was the case, as she confided via the
phone that his horrors seemed to be mounting. Would unknown
people, new places or situations, scare him less if he had words to
describe his special fears? we asked ourselves and each other. But
if the answer seemed to be yes, why wasn't every infant who still
lacked language similarly afraid? And if autism was a disorder that
largely undermined language, why wasn't Ian merely mute—silent
but untroubled? Why did so much of what he encountered in his
small and still-protected world somehow drive him mad?

Researchers estimate that autism occurs in approximately fifteen
of every ten thousand children, four times more often in males than
in females for reasons no one has yet explained, and although stories
of cures or miracle treatments always can find an audience, it is,
nonetheless, generally considered a lifelong disorder, one whose
symptoms change and may even disappear during its sufferers' six-,
seven-, sometimes eight-decade life spans. All people who have
autism exhibit some form of language deficit, ranging from odd or
seemingly immature vocal rhythms to the utter absence of speech,
and all abnormally process input from the senses—vision, smell,
touch, taste, and hearing. Some, for instance, cannot endure being
touched by other people or by particular kinds of clothing; some,
Ian among them, possess particularly keen peripheral vision; many
often appear to be deaf but, in fact, hear too well, with too much
sensitivity and too little of the kind of sound-filtering capability that
makes crowds, city streets, and construction sites bearable for the
rest of us. Imagine falling rain somehow sounding like machine gun
fire; imagine *hearing* the blood sluice through your veins; imagine
that your mother's calm and assuring voice instead comes at you like
a car horn.

There are three particular aspects of the decoding of sensory
information that tend to be abnormal among people with autism.
The registration of sensory information, controlled in part by the
brain stem, tucked at the base of the skull, is chronically, often
dramatically faulty; common visual stimuli such as bright lights or
moving objects often seem to go unnoticed, unobserved, while seem-

ingly trivial objects—a loose thread on a jacket, a crumb on a patterned carpet—receive rapt attention. The ability to modulate sensory input similarly appears to be flawed, leaving many people with autism unable to hear a focused conversation in a busy restaurant, for example, instead hearing each voice and *every* voice in a loud, confused, and congested jumble. In much the same manner, a hand placed on a shoulder or a forearm can seem like a stranglehold; a grape's slight acidity is little less than poison; an unfamiliar object—a chair, a doll, a ball—*invades* a bedroom, an otherwise safe environment, and holds it horridly captive. The ability to integrate information from the senses and to make that information meaningful similarly seems compromised, of course. The sight of a plate of spaghetti and its aroma can seem utterly unrelated, the brain registering one bit of sensory information as appealing perhaps, the other as repulsive; and the inability to use the senses to help locate one's body in space can impart something that you and I can only imagine as a kind of constant dizziness, making it difficult to plan and organize the series of muscle movements that lead a spoon to an open mouth, or that result in shoelaces successfully tied into bows—the senses getting in the way in those cases and in dozens more analogous to them—textures, shapes, sounds somehow overwhelming any number of intentional activities, interrupting their execution, leaving nothing certain except for constant chaos, allowing few responses other than terror.

Is it reaching too far to imagine, in that regard, that children with autism are slow to learn to speak—if indeed they ever learn—because, unlike normal children who begin to do so almost from birth, they cannot hear and then distinguish the special patterns of human speech; that unlike other children, often they cannot isolate and recognize the sounds *they* make with their own mid-throat larynges and long, round human tongues, initiating the kind of experimentation and playful practice that finally result in speech? No, it seems to me that those sensory deficits surely must be inhibiting factors.

And if language is about nothing so much as representation, as Professor Bickerton contends—a means of systematizing and making

sense of those things of which we're conscious, which we perceive
with our several senses—then surely too it is little surprise that
people whose senses offer them a barrage of screeching crosstalk,
seemingly blurred or sometimes microscopic sight, and the sense of
disorienting, imprisoning physical isolation are greatly compromised
as well with regard to language, lacking its essential raw materials,
absent the sharp percepts that give inevitable rise to symbols.

Likewise too, if language is anchored both in speaking *and* in
organizing, and if indeed we speak in ways akin to the way we
throw—planning, sequencing a dazzlingly sophisticated series of
muscle movements with each *yes*, each *go*, each wonderful *I think
so*—then is it any wonder that for a boy like Ian whose left cerebrum
simply couldn't assist him with his spoon at age two, nor at three or
even four—couldn't make his zippers or his awkward buttons be
obedient—saying "cow" again would have been an equally formidable task? Wouldn't it have been almost miraculous, even at age five,
for him somehow to shout, "I see lots of cows, and they are brown
and white and big"?

This is a story I seldom tell, the embarrassment still too strong I
suppose, its memory too prickly: We were dining that evening in an
oak-paneled ballroom in Denver's Westin Tabor Center Hotel, the
occasion sponsored by the Friends of the Denver Public Library
and honoring a group of Colorado authors—each of us "hosting" a
separate table, making small talk, eating steak, wearing the kinds
of clothes that writers seldom wear, feeling every solitary writer's
awkwardness in the face of such a fete. Accompanied by my friend
Barbara Walton, an acquisitions specialist for the library's Western
History Department, I was bluffing my way as best I could through
the evening's festive agenda when I calmly, yet very certainly, noted
that I couldn't breathe.

In the milliseconds that preceded that singular sort of realization,
I had felt a piece of steak begin to lodge in my esophagus, and as I
turned to ask to be excused from the table for a moment, somehow
I had sucked it into my trachea, where it firmly stuck, shutting off

the air flow, leaving me in a rather immediate spot of trouble. What happened next remains mercifully foggy in my memory, but I do know that I instinctively stood and that Barbara quickly moved behind me and attempted the Heimlich maneuver, but she is small and her efforts were unsuccessful. The next thing that I can be certain of is that the gentleman seated to my right decided that he would take a turn, grasping me around my waist, thrusting his entwined fists into my abdomen and up, as the manuals instruct, and perhaps four hundred people were able to witness as the culprit bit of beef arced out of my mouth and across the linen-covered table. You can understand that at that particular moment I was sure I would have preferred the sudden death.

Although I have come close to ending my life by choking only in that single instance, I do possess, I now know, an esophagus that is prone to spasms, blocking, when they occur, the passage to my stomach high enough, near enough to my epiglottis, that I'm far more likely to trap food in my trachea than you are—and your risk is bad enough. Nowadays, therefore, I carry a nitroglycerin spray in my pocket that I can use prophylactically prior to author banquets or therapeutically in the instant I sense something beginning to stick. As my mother long ago instructed, I endeavor to chew well and thoroughly; I attempt to pay attention; and I have a far clearer understanding than I did before that abashing evening in Denver of the gravity of the trade we have entered into in making speech a human staple.

Yet it is a trade we could not help but have made, even if the choice had been plainly put to us thirty thousand years ago or more. And if, in an equally fanciful sort of way, Ian could venture out of silence and begin to speak at some even greater risk, I would, nonetheless, quickly urge him to take it. Whether it commenced in our throats or in our budding, surely still-befuddled brains, speech propelled us beyond mere communication toward the possibility of a kind of interaction that perhaps we can only call communion—a means of sharing our very cerebrations, our darkest dreads, our dreams. Speech spawned the lush bouquet of language, or conversely, symbolic language lent speech its consequential substance—as you like it—but however it all unfolded once upon a time, the legacy is a kind of creature who can reach *outside* itself, audaciously imagining as much as the universe, inquiring too into things as secret as the soul.

And among the many things I learned early on from this wordless and much troubled boy in Colorado, for whom the world outside remained still distant, was that language isn't simply something we employ—an instrument, a vehicle, a tool—but instead perhaps it actually *is* our reaching, our attempt to truly see what lies in the broad field of our vision, to truly hear amidst all the clutter and the noise, to taste and touch and smell and even know.

2
THE URGENT TELLING
OF A TALE

"And then there was the bear," my maternal grandmother would remember, "but first you need to know about the dogs." In fact, we already knew about the dogs because we had heard this tale before— many times and each time to our delight—but we would beg to hear it again, of course, and so she would commence:

Our dog, Bill, and a dog called John Ross, the herder's dog, just fought continually. They couldn't see each other without a fight. I don't know what was the matter, but that was the way they were.

Anyway, one time we went up to sheep camp in the afternoon. Jim, the herder, was up the side of the mountain with the sheep, and Dad went on up. The sun was hot, so I went into Jim's tent because the flaps were up. I sat on his bed and started to read some old magazine he had lying around there. I didn't want to follow Dad up; the altitude always gave me a headache.

I didn't think of it until afterwards, but both dogs came in and lay down at my feet and never said a word to each other. They got just as close as they could get to me and put their heads at my feet, and I just went on reading. After an hour or so, I heard a little noise, and I looked up. There was old Jim with his eyes just bulging, his hands out like claws, coming right at me. He said, "My gun, my gun, my gun!" I didn't know what to think. I was so startled I couldn't think anything, but I'll never forget the look on his face. Then I thought maybe he was coming for me! I thought he might have gone mad.

Well, Dad was right behind him, as it turned out, and right behind them, six feet behind the tent, was a *bear*, sound asleep. He'd been there in the sun all afternoon. And the dogs knew it, and that's why they were so afraid and came in quietly for protection from *me*. Imagine!

When Jim rushed back out with his gun, that sleepy old bear got up and then just sauntered off across the meadow and up the rocks. I sure found out that day how much protection Bill and John Ross were, didn't I?

Yes, we invariably would agree, those dogs were fraidy-cats. But now—and since the subject was dogs—we wanted to hear once more about the mutt named Tip who loved to ride atop the high-stacked hay wagon, as proud as any king; and then too, there was the famous cat to be reminded of, the one she and her sister once had given fifteen names, the catalog of those names still clear as summer mornings in her memory.

The setting for these stories invariably was my grandmother's small sitting room inside the farmhouse where she had lived since her wedding day—pastures and lush hay fields spreading away from its windows toward the distant mountains. The tales she told from her rocking chair were her gifts to us, we knew, and each of her near two dozen grandchildren—then great-grandchildren whose numbers slowly but similarly grew large—understood that there was something wonderful in her words, some kind of magic in the soft and high-pitched melodies of her speech. Yet I think I realized only recently—several years now after her death—that it wasn't dogs or cats or bears that brought her stories to life; it wasn't how she had helped her father manage their tiny post office when she was a girl grown up beyond her years, or how my grandfather had loved to tease her when they were young and still childless and very much in love, that gave her stories substance. Rather, it was in the simple *telling* of her tales that those times and silly creatures and now-mythic events took on their meaning and assumed their special worth. We didn't long to live in those olden days she described; in fact, I think we tacitly understood that it was far richer, surely, just to hear her lilting recollections of how life once had been.

The creating and the witnessing of narratives are as essential to us as sleep. Stories in their many guises are as base and wonderful as sex, as delicious and irresistible as a cheeseburger ordered with everything. We tell our stories over countless cups of coffee in all the corners of the Earth; we unravel them on television in the minutes between commercials for detergent and disposable diapers. We call our stories the news; they commence as jokes or testimony offered under oath or this-crazy-thing-that-happened-yesterday, and sometimes we archly label them as literature. We project stories onto movie screens and we print them on the pages of books, and we simply cannot help but do so.

"What would we talk about, sitting around the fire at night, if we didn't have language?" Melvin Konner asks in *The Tangled Wing*, remembering the rhetorical way in which his Brooklyn College mentor Dorothy Hammond would respond to the issue of the origin of language. We had to create language in order to shoot the fireside breeze, she surmised, only a little facetiously, and Konner can't help but agree with her. Among language's many tasks, it is the vehicle with which we tell our tales, and they—those tales in their simplicity and all their wonder—occupy the very heart of what it means to be human. Every story, even every sentence, Konner writes, "creates in the mind of the speaker as well as the hearer not merely a picture but a realm of intricate mental events encompassing all five sense modalities. Say what you will about nonhuman creatures—their admirable capacities, their behavior, their consciousness—there is not a thing like it in the whole of the animal world." We are the storytelling species, *Homo once-upon-a-tempus*, our brains built for seeking out relationships among things, for creating cerebral sorts of order, and for sensing the rudiments of narrative structure: how it was in the beginning, the middle, and at the end.

Medical investigation into the brain's role in human speech and language has been under way for little more than a century, spurred initially by a bold but largely unsubstantiated paper presented by French physician Ernest Auburtin to the Society of Anthropology in Paris in 1861. In speaking before his skeptical colleagues, Auburtin explained that damage to the frontal lobe of the brain of a young man under his care had resulted in the impairment of the patient's speech, from which slender evidence Auburtin was willing to assert that language function must be localized there—an idea that ran sharply counter to the then-prevailing notion that the brain did little more than energize the other organs of the body, playing an important but far from central role in their many functions.

Among those who listened to Auburtin that day was Paul Broca, the secretary of the society and a surgeon with a special interest in the brain. Intrigued by what he had heard, Broca invited Auburtin to visit one of his own patients, a mature man who was speechless and whose right arm and leg were chronically weak. As it happened, the patient died the day after their visit, and at the autopsy Broca discovered a lesion on the left frontal lobe of the patient's brain. Soon thereafter, Broca's autopsy on a similar speechless patient showed damage to much the same area of the left frontal lobe. When he later published his findings from these and other cases, Broca pointed out that these lesions of what later would become known as "Broca's convolution" or "Broca's area" seemed to affect only the articulation of speech. The comprehension of speech, and sometimes even the ability to write, tended to remain intact. Most patients still could make sounds, and with much effort some could produce a few intelligible words.

During the decade that followed, interested scientists and physicians argued with some vehemence whether the total of eight cases

Broca had reported in which similar brain lesions resulted in similar aphasia (the loss or dysfunction of speech) were proof that there was a language "center" in the brain. Then, in 1874, a German medical student named Karl Wernicke complicated the question by demonstrating that damage to an area of the left temporal and parietal lobes of the cerebral cortex—damage that spared Broca's area, which lies above and farther forward—often resulted in a very different kind of speech loss. Unlike patients with Broca's area lesions, who could comprehend normally, patients with lesions in the region that now took on Wernicke's name tended to have great difficulty understanding what was said to them. And in contrast to the slow, frustrating efforts to speak that were common with Broca's aphasics, Wernicke's patients spoke smooth, rapid, even grammatical *nonsense*. Did these new findings mean that perhaps there were two language centers in the brain, one responsible for the production of speech, the other for the conveyance of meaning? Were these merely two of many centers? Or, in fact, was language so central—not only to speech but also to consciousness, cognition, and memory—that components of language function surely had to be located throughout the healthy brain?

In our time, these same questions—still unanswered satisfactorily—tend to be addressed in several, sometimes contradictory, ways, and the views of an American linguist by now have made as much impact on the debate as did those of the Europeans who began it. It was in 1957 that a young professor at the Massachusetts Institute of Technology published *Syntactic Structures*, a book that encompassed his life's work to that point, and an occasion of such import among the small and sometimes pettifogging fraternity of scientists of language that it became known simply as "The Event." Among the new and disputatious ideas espoused in that book by Noam Chomsky—perhaps the only linguist in the world whose name has become widely known outside his discipline's bounds—was the notion that all humans possess something he labeled a "language organ." Little interested in neuroanatomy, Chomsky made no attempt to specify this organ's location within the brain—there would be no Chomskian equivalent of Broca's or Wernicke's area. He was content simply to assert that there are "deep structures" within each human brain that are predisposed to the acquisition, even the invention, of language. In Chomsky's view, in fact, language's locus isn't in the throat or the left cerebral cortex so much as it is in the genes. And it is syntax, the set of "rules" that makes it possible to turn linguistic symbols into meaning, that our genes provide us. As Chomsky recently explained to documentary filmmaker Gene Searchinger,

> I'm enough of a materialist to think that language is in the brain. If you cut off someone's foot, he can still speak. In fact, it is useful to think of language as an organ of the mind. The brain is like every other system in the biological world: it has specialized structures with specialized functions, and language is one of these. But did we invent language because we were sentient? No more than we invented our circulatory system. What seems to be true about language is that its basic design is in the genes. The genes determine the structure and design of language.

In *Syntactic Structures*, Chomsky finds strong evidence for this genetic foundation: observing that every language's complex syntactic system can be reduced to a core group of rules and principles, which, curiously, it shares with *every other* language, he contends that languages aren't merely similar, one with any other; structurally, *syntactically*, they are identical—Japanese with Spanish, Navajo with Norwegian. And it seems most improbable to him that all languages might share their syntactic structures because they derive from a common ancestor—some protolanguage from some very long ago time. If that were the case, those earliest speakers of something that gave rise to language would have had to have created linguistic rules and patterns of astonishing sophistication for them to have survived unchanged till now. And that possibility, says Chomsky, is far less likely than what he instead sees as a certainty: our genes design us for language in the same way that they predispose us to walk.

But if Chomsky is correct—and an entire school of linguists

known as "behaviorists," "environmentalists," "empiricists," or simply as "anti-Chomskians," are convinced that he is not, arguing that
their colleague chooses to ignore ample and overwhelming evidence
that children who grow up in bizarre kinds of isolation *do not* acquire
language in the same way that they *do* discover how to walk—this
question remains: Where and precisely how does the brain initiate
and facilitate language? Put another way, what have our genes built
into our brains that predisposes them to the luster and the utility of
language?

A century and three decades after Auburtin, those queries still
irritate and challenge scholars in disciplines that range from literature and linguistics to neurophysiology and molecular biology, who
collectively are making important inroads into a basic understanding
of how our three-pound brains perform this most complex of feats.
Although their findings can't as yet, and indeed may never, prove
or disprove Chomsky's genetic structures theory, they do point to
the probability that the brain has *many* essential language centers—
Broca's and Wernicke's areas important among them but far from
the whole astonishing show.

Yet if language is located diffusely throughout the brain, contend
several scientists who champion the Chomskian perspective, then
surely the complex and capable brain should normally compensate
when language areas are damaged, effectively relocating and relearn-
ing lost functions, which in fact is not the case. If language is *not*
site-specific, they ask, why do minute brain lesions often wreak
such havoc? And conversely, why do some seriously damaged or
compromised brains remain adept at language?

Neil Smith, a linguist at University College, London, points to a
twenty-nine-year-old man named Christopher in that regard. So-
cially inept, the kind of person who once would have been called
"simple," Christopher cannot care for himself, cannot discuss abstract ideas or draw basic geometric shapes, his IQ having been
scored as low as 65; yet Christopher speaks sixteen languages and
can translate them effortlessly. His brain is abnormal, *sub*normal in
most respects, Smith says, but his language abilities are unaffected,
and indeed they are advanced beyond what most of us can imagine.

Doesn't Christopher's case strongly suggest the presence of a discrete language organ, a part of the brain where language resides independent of other brain systems and functions?

No, says University of Washington neurosurgeon George Ojemann, whose "mapping" of neural circuits with the use of electrodes in the brains of patients undergoing surgery convinces him that not only is language seated in many areas of the brain—often including the *right* hemisphere—but that its location is highly individualized, as unique to each of us, perhaps, as our fingerprints. Publishing his findings in the *Journal of Neuroscience*, Ojemann argues that, yes, Broca's and Wernicke's areas are important language-producing and -processing centers for most people, but so are several additional sites on the temporal and parietal lobes of the left cerebral hemisphere, each one comprised of a dense cluster of nerve cells about the size of a grape, each governing a different aspect of language function—from verb recall to reading—each interconnected with the others. Many people also have at least *some* aspect of language function located in their right hemispheres, he contends. Curiously, men tend to have more of the "essential language areas" located in their left parietal lobes than do women. Equally intriguing, native languages tend to be compactly sited and organized, while second and multiple languages often are scattered diffusely, seemingly as if nerve cells devoted to their various functions must seek out available space in mature, language-barraged brains—a convincing counterpoint to the notion of one or two language sites or a single language organ.

But could both contentions be, in part at least, correct? Do we actually possess an integrated "language organ" whose components are located in many individualized sites? At the University of Iowa, researchers Antonio and Hannah Damasio believe the answer is a qualified perhaps, and their complex "convergence zone" theory has won plaudits as well as serious interest from both the Chomskian and the anti-Chomskian camps. The Damasios agree with Dr. Ojemann that the brain does indeed possess multiple language-processing sites, but they disagree that the entirety of any single language function—comprehension of spoken words, for example—can be located in any single area. Rather, those areas whose importance Ojemann has demonstrated with electric probes are "zones" in which information from several disparate sites is coalesced, mediated, and made sense of—neural data converging there in language-encoding activities such as speaking, as well as in the decoding processes involved, say, in listening to a story about a sleeping bear. This is how Antonio Damasio explained the concept to the *New York Times*:

> When I ask you to think about a cup, you do not go into a filing cabinet in your brain and come up with a ready-made picture of a cup. Instead, you compose an internal image of a cup drawn from its features. The cup is part of a cone, white, crushable, three inches high and can be manipulated. In re-activating the concept of this cup, you draw on distant clusters of neurons that separately store knowledge of cones, the color white, crushable objects, and manipulated objects. Those clusters are activated simultaneously by feedback firing from a convergence zone. You can attend to the revival of those components in your mind's eye and from an internal image of the whole object.
>
> That same process is true of words. When I ask you to tell me what the object is, you do not go into a filing cabinet where the word "cup" is stored. Rather, you use a convergence zone for the word "cup" by activating distant clusters of neurons that store the phonemes c and u and p. You can perceive their momentary revival in your mind's ear or allow them to activate the motor system and vocalize the word "cup."

Yet if this convergence zone theory does indeed go some distance toward explaining the brain's basic language-processing system—and similar sorts of zones seem likely to be central to cognition and memory as well—how is it that widely distributed groups of neurons are able to fire simultaneously as required? Antonio Damasio believes that the convergence zones themselves are able to stimulate the disparate clusters, but he acknowledges that the actual initiating mechanism remains mysterious.

But however the process commences, it does seem probable
now that language convergence zones act as third-party mediators
between words and concepts, between concepts and words. And
from that perspective, it is the choate cerebral cortex, if not the
brain in its entirety, that acts as a language organ—its convergence
zones drawing data together, somehow sifting them, making momentary blends and blindingly quick interconnections, then issuing the
fresh impulses that result in comprehension, in symbols scribbled
onto paper or pecked onto a keyboard, in the uttering of a statement,
the urgent telling of a tale.

Like Ian, like Ian's long-suffering, caring, sometimes defiant mother,
I was young in empty country. I too grew up in a kind of careworn
pocket of Colorado that was scattered with cattle and sheep. Claudia
and I and Carol (the youngest of the three of us, a mother as well
now, and—doesn't it seem impossible?—escorting her older siblings
into middle age) were born at mid-century to parents whose parents
had seen a century turn, who long ago had ridden in horse-drawn
wagons out to high, dry government land that was bare but for
sagebrush, land they would "prove up" in time into pastures and
crop-striped fields. The Martins to whom I'm inextricably attached
long ago had emigrated from France across an ocean to Arkansas
before a few of their descendants similarly struck out at the beginning
of the twentieth century for far southwestern Colorado, where (it's
hard from my perspective to imagine) farming conditions were sto-
ried to be better. The Rutherfords, my mother's family, came to
Colorado nearly a hundred years ago as well, abandoning Red River
lowland country that lay across the Arkansas border in Texas.
    Like the Rutherfords, the Drummonds—Ian's father's clan—
once were Borders Scots, and like the Martins, they too eventually
wound their way to Arkansas. But unlike the others, the Drummonds
then were home, anchoring themselves to the South over subsequent generations, Boyce growing up beside the wide Ouachita
River in the grandly titled town of Arkadelphia in the years that
followed World War II, his soft and lilting accent still a strong

reminder of that sweltry southern place, those years when he was Ian's age.

My sister Claudia was named for my father, and of the three of us siblings, she is the one who most resembles him. She has his dark hair, his deep-set bright blue eyes, and in her face, like his, there is an ineffable sort of reference still to the villages and vegetable farms of Brittany despite his family's many generations on this continent. She shares my father's self-assurance and sometimes his stubborn resolve. Growing up in a dusty, backwater western town in the fifties and turbulent sixties, Claudia and her contemporaries in little Cortez missed much of the social and political turmoil that racked the nation in those days. She was a majorette in the marching band and salutatorian of her high school graduating class, and it wasn't until she spent two years in a remote corner of Costa Rica following college that she underwent the kind of sea change that marks—and makes—so many people whose formative years unfold in the midst of societal or cultural storm.

Claudia met Boyce in Gainesville, Florida, in the middle seventies. Both were married to other people, and among the illicit passions that bound them to each other was the promise of children; both were nurturers, it was obvious, and both were sure that it was within the context of parenthood that they wanted to spend their ensuing years. They married soon after the offer of a teaching position in the biology department at Illinois State University led Boyce to the Middle West, and before long Claudia was pregnant. Their first son, given the name Gareth in the first moments of a kind of anguish and overwhelming sorrow that I can only imagine, died as he was born.

Sarah, born healthy and vivacious and as blond as her father, followed in a year; and in only twenty-two more months, the similarly hearty, happy, likewise towheaded Ian Drummond came along, and the family seemed complete—years of tumult, pain, and disruption now behind them, it seemed. But when an offer arrived in 1984 for Boyce to direct a fledgling field station and research center on the rocky western shoulder of Pike's Peak, they could not help but give it serious consideration. It would be an opportunity for Claudia to return to Colorado, one that only the most callous native sons and daughters can turn away from; and the field station was in a setting rich with butterflies, which Boyce, a lepidopterist, found irresistible. So they uprooted themselves again, Sarah subsequently growing up amid deep snow and the drama of summer thunderstorms, many miles from schools and playmates, Ian gamely learning to walk on the ruddy pea-gravel that sufficed for soil beneath giant ponderosas.

Claudia was teaching part-time in the nearby town of Woodland Park—working with gifted children, which by now has become her ironic specialty—when Ian began to grow strange, when he went mute and terror overtook him. And surely that scholastic commitment, those other children for whom she was also responsible, kept her bafflement, her mounting grief, and her anger from completely consuming her as she tended to Ian's daily tantrums and did her best to protect the necessary precision of his schedule. She poured herself into her son with a thoroughly blended mix of motherly devotion and academic obsession; she vowed, despite the unique household in which her daughter lived, that Sarah would grow up feeling secure and entirely loved. Occasionally, she would recoil sharply against the well-meaning but less than sensitive people, like me, who tried to remind her that this was not the end of the world—because, dammit, it *was* the end of what the world might have offered Ian—and sometimes she simply would slump into a chair late in the evening after at last both children were asleep, pressing a cup of tea to her cheek and laughing or crying with some real release, wondering what else could come calamitously her way.

Sarah, a shy and delicate little girl who was quite verbal and clearly very bright—and who, I think, might have seemed achingly oversensitive in even the most ordinary household—had to contend now not merely with a younger brother who stole her parents' attention but with a sibling who virtually never acknowledged her, yet around whom every family activity and decision necessarily was centered, with a brother who seemed to be in incessant agony, and with parents who often must have seemed terribly distracted, if not utterly spent and unavailable. Instead of acting out in response to her plight, instead of deciding—as you can imagine she might have—to become as difficult as her brother was, Sarah retreated into fantasy. She listened voraciously to stories and her appetite for tales of elves and sprites and princesses seemed nearly boundless. She would become, quite completely, the characters in the stories she heard and saw, the characters in the stories she too began to tell—insisting that her bedroom was a forest or a fairyland or an enchanted castle, insisting that her name was Guinevere or Maid Marian or, more mundanely, Rainbow Brite—and her parents have reminded me that it was with the rich reality of narrative that Ian's sister Sarah somehow coped.

The relentless daily demands of the field station offered Boyce a commensurate if far less fictive avenue of escape. On de facto twenty-four-hour call, he had to play the roles of scientist and registrar, planner and proctor, counselor and plumber, and his own ongoing research also took him on occasion to Central or South America. The distractions that riddled his days kept him at a kind of emotional remove from his son's autistic chaos early on, although Ian specifically demanded Boyce by his side several times each morning and night. Boyce's ready sense of humor and soft-spoken southern countenance—as well as his work—seemed to buffer, for a time at least, the otherwise harsh reality; and it was Boyce who once funneled his amalgam of reactions to his family's complex circumstances into this rhyming verse:

> *Wordless now, a troubled mute*
> *It doesn't fit, he seems astute*
>
> *Across his face expressions spread*
> *But from his lips no word is said*
>
> *Bizarre behavior, ritualistic*
> *Yet loving, tactile—a rare statistic*
>
> *Just past two, a boy so strong*
> *But behind blue eyes, something's wrong*

Autistic-like, schizophrenic?
More exams, another clinic?

Parades of doctors, questionnaires
Endless questions, ours and theirs

Answers scarce and unconvincing
Understanding slow commencing

The future vague, a vast unknown
Uncertain growth for the seed we've sown

Although it must have seemed at times as if the chaotic visits to the clinics wouldn't end, they necessarily slowed, then stopped, before many months elapsed because there was little more that physicians could tell them, no medical treatment they could offer Ian except to recommend—a few of them—that he be admitted to an institutional behavior-modification program, the tough-minded, traditional sort that blithely utilize canvas straitjackets, Tabasco sauce in screaming mouths, and similar kinds of aversion therapy in an effort to inhibit unacceptable behavior.

In a follow-up to Ian's catastrophic initial visit to Denver's Children's Hospital, an EEG had been performed in those final frigid days of 1985—but this time with the otherwise terrified patient under sedation. The results of the electrical brain wave test were read as entirely normal, and neither had a subsequent CAT scan of his brain evidenced any abnormalities. An amino acid test was normal; a white blood cell screen was normal; tests of mucopolysaccharides, muscle tissue, organic acids, and chromosomes all were normal: very quickly, a variety of known and sometimes identifiable causes of autistic symptoms had been ruled out, and as the doctors explained to Ian's parents, those results were not surprising. Only ten percent of all reported cases of autism as yet can be linked to organic abnormalities. Neither Claudia nor Boyce had asked that January whether a DPT immunization nine months earlier might have set Ian's symptoms in insidious motion; despite their efforts to find *some* explanation for their son's dramatic transformation, that connection remained elusive, as unimaginable still as if his cutting teeth might have been the culprit.

Although she could offer little in the way of optimism, pediatrician Pamela McBogg had prescribed chloral hydrate to help Ian sleep. She had suggested that his parents experiment with his diet—to the degree that this finicky noneater would allow—to investigate whether food allergies might be exacerbating his symptoms; and although studies of vitamin therapies for the treatment of children with autism had shown inconclusive results, the doctor had averred that daily megadoses of the brain-stimulating B complex would be worth a trial. And instead of referring Claudia and Boyce to the kind of behavior-modification program that already was anathema to them, Dr. McBogg had suggested that Ian be evaluated by the staff at the University of Colorado's JFK Speech and Language Center, where, she assured them, they would encounter attitudes kindred to their own, and where they would receive relevant assistance in developing an intensive home intervention strategy, the kind of relentless, highly structured, and emotionally supportive socializing and schooling program that *might*—very slowly, surely laboriously—reacquaint and then reconnect Ian with the world.

Among the many health professionals who by now had met Ian, JFK Center director Sally Rogers and her staff were perhaps the first to express an immediate kind of attraction to him, declaring how handsome he was, exhibiting their fascination with his rituals and repetitions, and praising his several special skills, and they seemed not at all bothered by the fact that he shrieked in utter terror of them. They knew children with autistic behaviors well, to be sure, and they *liked* them, and Ian's parents understandably were drawn to these people who realized—as they did, of course—that there was much to like and to love in this little boy for whom almost all of living seemed so traumatic. "Ian is a 34-month tall, husky, attractive towhead with markedly deviant behavior," Sally Rogers straightforwardly began the lengthy write-up of the staff's assessment:

He demonstrated catastrophic reactions, with crying, screaming, and agitated motor outbursts, to new situations and new

people, which did not diminish over the three days of his
evaluation. . . . Ian appears to demonstrate developmental
delays in all areas. There is no evidence of symbolic play or
symbolic thought processes occurring either in his play or in
the descriptions of his behavior that his parents provided. He
does appear to have mastered some sensorimotor skills, but
there is no evidence yet of pre-operational thought. Thus, his
cognitive development appears to be in the 12–24 month
range, with object permanence skills at the upper end of it
and symbolic, social, and language development at the lower
end of that range. . . . Prognosis for children with autism is
never optimistic, but autistic children vary considerably in
the level of functioning which they ultimately achieve. Ian's
responses to the intensive interventions which his parents
provide in the next year or so will provide some indication of
where in the range of abilities of autistic children Ian will fall.

And with the center staff's periodic support, as well as the help
of others with some insight or expertise in autism who were scattered
around the region—and with the daily devotion of Carla Crittendon,
a recent college graduate in special education whom Boyce and
Claudia had hired and housed at the research station for ten months,
taking on Ian as a kind of gritty, postgraduate introduction to her
difficult field—they did intensively intervene, spurred by the fear,
as they did so, of what might befall him if they did not. They demanded much of Ian every day for the next thousand days, challenging his intellect and ever expanding his repertoire, encouraging
him—carefully, cautiously—to reach outside himself, yet deferring
as well to his singular wants, his ritual needs, his horrible fears, his
parents each day desperately seeking meaning in his behavior, trying
to understand who he was and why he acted as he did.

One good day often was followed by three days thick with chaos;
a mood that had seemed fine in the busy morning might well explode
in the otherwise languid afternoon. Without any means of understanding why, one stranger would be welcome—even in Ian's bedroom—while another, perhaps even someone he had known,

couldn't enter the house without his awful objection. Overseeing Ian's daily schedule often seemed like one part parenthood to two parts rescue mission, a task for tightrope walkers as much as puzzled teachers—the meticulous journals Boyce, Claudia, and Carla kept during that time reflecting each day's uncertainties, the giddy gains, the losses. This is Carla's entry for June 11, 1987:

Bad day.

Claudia left early, just as Ian wanted to go out & he tantrumed until I took him out for a ride to Panoramas. He still fussed a lot though, & when we got back home he would not stop screaming until we went on another ride. One ride to Evergreen Station & a third to Panoramas later, he was still very fussy. Pooh Bear & tofu helped. Boyce put him down; he slept for 2 hrs. & wanted to go for another car ride about 5 min. after waking up. I tried to get him to play in the yard twice— both did not work. We came back inside screaming & thrashing. He finally calmed down with Pooh Bear (4th time today!) & I tried a worktime with just a few of his favorite books. He screamed & got furious all over again & almost ripped Busy Bear in half. He calmed back down with chips, then Cl. & B came home & Cl. was able to get him to play in the yard after 10–15 minutes of crying.

Lots of teeth grinding today.

But on a Sunday three days later, Claudia reported much success:

AM: I forgot to move the car out of sight, but just one ride to Panoramas was OK. He got out & ran happily.

WORKTIME: 30 min. Very good.

Books: A Sleepy Story, I Am A Bunny, Bialosky Goes Out, Ian's Birthday, My Horse, Busy Bear, Colors

Games: all ×4—wiggled his own thumb. Too excited about "open/shut" to clap on his own

Toys: wood animals puzzle ×2—excellent! circus puzzle ×1—excellent.—flying flags;—button can;—button & chip can together, just 2 prompts;—block tower of 6, 2×, no prompts

PM: 2× going out to yard, swinging & playing on glider & slide (w/ my prompting)

Bedtime: Ian went to get his pajamas for Boyce. No crying but laughing all night long.

By the autumn of 1987, there were days that seemed little less than stellar breakthroughs, proof of Ian's progression toward some kind of normalcy. This is Boyce writing on November 9:

When I got home (6 pm) Ian "asked" for 1-2-3 game, removing and lining up the 3 couch cushions himself. After supper, I played with him in his room from 7:30 until 8:45—a new variant on the "stand behind seated Boyce, flap his hair, and get flipped over in a somersault" game. Variation was the addition of a billed cap, which Ian put on my head (I secured it, saying "put hat on"), then he would knock it off before flapping my hair and being flipped by me. He obviously loved it, keeping it up for over an hour.

Ian does a lot of imitative behavior with his movies now. Examples: In Free to Be, runs when Atalanta runs (has been doing this one for weeks). In Secret of NIMH, asks for bath water to be trickling when Nicodemus, Justin, and Mrs. Brisby are in the boat under the old mill and there is water dripping down. In Goldilocks, Ian opens our front door when, early in the movie, the bears open their door to go outside. Ian also turns off the lights in his room early in the movie when the poor quality of our print makes the scene dark. He "falls down" when Goldilocks sits in Baby Bear's chair and it collapses.

Only one week later, however, Ian was refusing to watch *any* of his videos except for a cartoon version of *Robin Hood*, demanding that it be started again the moment that it ended, watching it ten, even twenty times in succession, flapping his fingers or other objects in front of his eyes as the television droned nearby. On November 19, Claudia made this entry in the journal, her scrawled handwriting reflecting her mounting stress:

> Ian is in <u>bad shape</u>. He sat in front of the TV w/ only snowy picture and flicked toy cars in front of his face for 30 min. after the movie ended. Then on his ride he fussed & would not run even though I carried him down into the trees. I even tried driving the car over to the fence & he still would not get out of the car. He stayed in the car for 30 min. alone w/ door open after the last ride & finally came in on his own. Pointed to movie—<u>Robin Hood</u> again. Awoke from his nap—watched <u>Robin Hood</u>, then sat on floor and flapped cars in front of his face for 2 ½ hours!! This breaks my heart. What regression!

Better days finally followed, days when Ian didn't need—what was it?—the stimulation or the security of his particular types of perseveration, the flapping of objects inches from his eyes, the same movie played time after time after time; days when he would smile at his sister and, for the briefest moment, would seem to pay attention to the ways in which she played; days when he actually didn't scream. There were wonderful, if only occasional, times when books truly could capture his attention; and there were others, equally encouraging, when his movies seemed to offer him something more than utter sameness, hour on maddening hour, times when they were bright and fascinating stories and Ian simply was a receptive, wide-eyed child.

There have been occasions when people whom I care about have commented to me with some concern, "Isn't it a shame that Ian is so fixated by television?" They've tended to be, it is true, the sorts of people from my own generation who see the cathode-ray tube as the flickering mesmerizer of the masses, the source of most everything that's wrong with the world—from rampant illiteracy to the hoary rise of Ronald Reagan—and who claim that the only TV they ever have watched has been "Masterpiece Theatre," on the rarest of occasions and on someone else's set.

I don't share their sentiments in general, and in Ian's context, I'm sure I've responded to them querulously, feigning uncertainty about just what they mean, then telling them, in effect, that I don't think they understand. You see, it isn't as though Ian were a classic kind of couch potato, and he *does* have some taste, after all; he doesn't watch Sally Jessy Raphael or "Rescue 911." In fact, he is entirely *un*interested in anything that is broadcast—not Bert and Ernie or Bryant Gumbel on a daily basis, not the Super Bowl once a year. Instead, Ian is a movie buff—he keeps his own collection— and people who've seen *Casablanca* or *The Rocky Horror Picture Show* twenty or thirty times can't hold a candle to him. He has seen the animated *Charlotte's Web*, I would wager, fifteen *hundred* times; and his parents regularly have had to make new copies of it and other favorites because he literally wears them out.

Boyce and Claudia shudder to think, I know, what their lives would have been like if Ian had come their way prior to the dawning of the age of the videocassette. While other families curse their VCRs for being so nearly unprogrammable, Boyce instead has added VCR repair to his household repertoire, and he and Claudia have always hoarded hand-me-downs and closeout specials against the nearby day when Ian's current machine surely would die. In his early days of trauma and throughout his life, Ian seldom has been far from a videotape player and its companion television and their uncanny capacity to calm him—but what I mean, of course, is a given *movie's* ability to quell a raging tantrum, its knack for a time, at least, for setting things right by telling him a tale.

I've often wondered whether he as readily might have relied on, let's say, toasters—the ritual, dependable dropping of the bread into tandem slots, the building, rising heat, the coils glowing orange, the bread transformed at last and popping up with some completion—to anchor him throughout his day, to provide him with some solace. Could building forts from plastic blocks, or making mountains out of mattresses, or banging his head relentlessly against a bedroom wall, God forbid, have served him as successfully as his movies?

I'm convinced the answer is no. From an uncle's necessarily patchy perspective, it seems sure to me that Ian's movies have made all the difference, that they've given him far more than repetition, that they have *meant* much more than sameness. Even at ages two and three, it was clear that Ian truly watched and listened to what unraveled on his bedroom television. He would carefully, meticulously line toy cars across the carpet, his eyes never seeming interested in the screen; sometimes he would demand that favorite music play simultaneously with a movie, their combined sound tracks creating a cacophony he somehow seemed to need; yet he would scream in sudden anguish if *Dumbo* didn't begin at the beginning, and with his frightened cries he would plead with his parents for them to speed the tape through the portions of *The Return of the Black Stallion* and *Lady and the Tramp* that he found terrifying. He began early on, as Boyce noted, to mimic scenes from some of them, and dolls and toy representations of cartoon characters—the ensemble cast of *Winnie-the-Pooh* in particular—became his bedroom buddies, his fastest friends, vital allies against what lay beyond his bedroom door.

What Ian's movies offered him—it seems to me, most importantly—was the organizing, ordering, delineating aspect of narrative. With their bright colors, festive music, and busy animated action, they were, nonetheless, a comforting, *quiet* counterpoint to the sensory bombardment that otherwise beset his brain. They offered him, even couched inside cartoons, realities—limited, controlled, mercifully measured—that he couldn't manage, that he couldn't distill on his own. And every narrative, each one of even the simplest stories, is its own reality, of course, a realm unto itself, a world comfortably contained.

"To classify consciousness as the action of organic machinery," sociobiologist Edward O. Wilson wrote in *On Human Nature*, is in no way to underestimate its power. In Sir Charles Sherrington's splendid metaphor, the brain is an "enchanted loom where millions of flashing shuttles weave a dissolving pattern." Since the mind recreates reality from the abstractions of the sense impressions, it can equally well simulate reality by recall and fantasy. The brain invents stories and runs imagined and remembered events back and forth through time.

Millions of flashing shuttles, their pattern ever dissolving: it is a fine metaphor and it's reminiscent of the necessarily more prosaic notion of the convergence zone—the momentary interweaving of disparate threads of neural data into a fabric that becomes the word *cup*, the word *cow*, in the milliseconds before another word is woven and a story is under way. In a normal brain, notes Wilson, the senses supply the raw material out of which consciousness is shaped, and "reality" is merely the ordered collection of those myriad bits of information.

What happened in Ian's case, I conceive—and surely what happens still—is that those convergence zones for language, as well as for certain kinds of cognition perhaps, chronically retrieve too much of one type of sensory information, too little of another, integrating them poorly or perhaps not at all—the intricate, momentary synchronizing demanded by the linking of words into sounds and concepts rendered haywire, neural data converging, to be sure, but only in a kind of utter disarray. If that indeed is this little boy's predicament, if neural information tends to run rampant in his cerebrum instead of blending, fusing, harmonizing toward some successful end, then is it any surprise that stories—tales he knows so well that they effectively become his own—matter enormously to him? Doesn't it make some simple sense that he finds musical melodies and rhyming verse equally attractive—essential, *ordered* counterpoints as well to the tumult inside his skull?

It's true, of course, that some of his obsession with his movies can be accounted for by his demand for daily ritual—the desperate need for today to commence with *Pooh* because yesterday did, as did the day before—yet that need for sameness in his schedule is obviously also a desire for structure and a kind of order he otherwise can't impose. Stories on videotape simply offer him that much more—a world in which the toys of a boy named Christopher Robin come to life again every day, in which a bashful bear named Pooh is always hungrily obsessed with honey; or a similarly secure, dependable place where a young elephant turns his ridiculed ears into wings, where he soars *absolutely* each time the tape begins to turn and the story once again is told.

What narrative offers each of us is exegesis, a commentary on what we encounter in our lives, yet it may well be that the *process* of describing and explaining is far more important than any specific thing described, explained, or interpreted. It may be that narrative is a kind of mimicking of the way our brains successfully order and make sense of information. It may be that for Ian, narrative offers him the only order he knows.

There is a fundamental and, to my mind, fascinating question, one I can't begin to answer, a question even the cleverest scholars tend to shy away from or amble carefully around, and it is this: Is abstract thought possible without language? Put another way: Is language the sole medium through which we think?

It may be some years since you've done so, but think for a moment, for example, about Winnie-the-Pooh. Are you doing so with words? Or is it with wordless *images* that you bring him back to mind? Now name his playmates and re-create, as best you can, the place they inhabit. The names, of course, are linguistic symbols, but are you otherwise employing language? If your melon is much like mine, the truth is that you can't be sure. You simply begin to think about a bear—or your troubled bank account, or the brain-taxing business of Stephen Hawking's black hole evaporation theory—and the process is so sudden and encompassing that you can't describe or decipher it.

Albert Einstein reportedly was convinced that he thought in images absent words. Near the opposite end of the thinking spectrum, I suspect that my cognition is mostly word-based, and among my slim evidence is the fact that although I seldom can tell you the color of someone's eyes, I often can recall that person's peculiar turns of phrase, and song lyrics and advertising jingles stick with me for decades, to my discouragement and regret, perhaps because the "thinking" I've done about them has tended to focus on their words. Those two examples may say as much about my memory processes as my meager stabs at what neuroscientists call "higher cortical thinking," yet nonetheless, those are my suspicions. I believe I rely more readily on language than on pictures or far more ephemeral *concepts* to contain and organize my thinking.

Derek Bickerton, who envisions language as arising from our need to represent reality—a view that locates him in the vicinity of Chomsky's camp on the language organ question—believes that language and thinking are inextricably intertwined, and his argument in support of that perspective is simple and straightforward: The kind of cognition of which humans are capable clearly involves symbolic representation, and if thinking and language are *not* interrelated, then the brain necessarily has evolved two (or even more) distinct and separate representational systems, and that possibility would seem so uneconomical and impractical as to make it most unlikely. Bickerton does imagine, however, that a single and perhaps innate representational system could logically be as adept with images as it is with words. "It is quite conceivable," he writes,

that thought processes conducted entirely in linguistic terms could, before arriving at conscious levels, be translated into imagery. Alternatively, images could simply take the place of words, but they would still have to be organized by syntactic mechanisms. In either case, if the elements of thought, whatever they might be, were not arranged in some type of formal structure in which their relations to one another were lawful and predictable, but instead they were just allowed to swirl around as they pleased, then no serious thought process could be carried through. Thus, either some mysterious additional way of structuring thought is available, or syntax discharges that function.

Syntax again. Rules and regulations. Bickerton's contention, over-simplified, is that we employ rules, some sort of structure, to mediate and control thinking, much as language demands and is built from rules. And surely the complex cerebral symbol-making that evolved as human language began to flourish bears much in common, if indeed it doesn't share everything, with the symbolic processes at the core of abstract thought. It is a notion that answers the question of whether we can think without language by eclipsing it, by positing the possibility that one does not depend on the other. Rather, per-haps, language and thought are separate channels of the same repre-sentational river, its banks and its gradient shaped by syntax, its course unconstrained and limitless.

Considering that argument for a moment, Hannah and Antonio Damasio's theory of cerebral convergence zones comes back to mind. The Damasios argue—persuasively, it seems to me—that the cere-bral cortex contains physical, identifiable, exceedingly sophisticated, and surely fragile zones that mediate the many components of thought in precisely the same way they coalesce and control lan-guage. Might syntax—whether it is genetically coded or the product of cultural imitation and experiment—have its neural locus in these zones? Is it possible, at least to some degree, to account for the wide range of intellectual and linguistic capabilities among our species by anatomical and neurochemical dissimilarities within convergence zones? I have said that Ian's cerebral disarray may be explainable, perhaps even in large part, by damage to one or more of them, but is it therefore syntax that Ian so seriously lacks?

"About the age of three," observes critic Peter Brooks in his book *Reading for the Plot*,

> a child begins to show the ability to put together a narrative
> in a coherent fashion and especially the capacity to recognize
> narratives, to judge their well-formedness. Children quickly
> become virtual Aristotelians, insisting upon any storyteller's
> observation of the "rules," upon proper beginnings, middles,

and particularly ends. Narrative may be a special ability or competence that we learn, a certain subset of the general language code which, when mastered, allows us to summarize and retransmit narratives in other words and other languages, to transfer them into other media, while remaining recognizably faithful to the original narrative structure and message.

Every weary parent understands firsthand that early explosion of interest in stories to which Brooks refers—every child's need for an endless sequence of simple stories that explain when that time called tomorrow will at last commence, where Daddy is always going, or how and why he bakes a cake. Every enchanted parent knows how stories read at evening bedsides and shared cozily on sofas introduce wonder and worlds of possibility into their youngsters' lives. Even people like me who aren't parents can begin to apprehend children's desire and their utter demand for narrative rules. Stories must have characters—they must be *about* mothers or kids or cats or scary monsters. They must be located in time—once upon a time or perhaps that time we still remember—as well as place, and they must describe or attempt to re-create transitions, shifts, passages from one place to the next, from one condition to another—dogs must shy away from bears or a bear must get his head stuck in a hive—but something has to *happen*, a story has to have a plot.

In a file of family memorabilia that is actually just an overflowing cardboard box, my parents keep the first formal story I wrote, one I titled "Green Valley League," its short manuscript typed for me late in the 1950s by my father, the only copy still extant on long-since-yellowed onionskin. I probably was eight or nine when I wrote it, and I suppose I offer that as something of a mild defense; you'd think that after thirty years or so, you might grow a bit more sanguine about your work, but this case simply doesn't seem to warrant it:

There was going to be a little league in Green Valley, the town Bob lived in. Bob's team was called the Cubs. The coach was Mr. Dell. Bob wanted to play shortstop, but a boy twelve was going out for shortstop too. His name was Dan. He was very good. Bob thought he would have to work really hard to beat him. Bob saw that Dan's glove was new but his was getting old and worn out. Dan began making fun of it. "Look at your glove, Bob, where did you get it, in the trash can?" "No, my dad gave it to me two years ago," said Bob. "I don't think that there is anything wrong with it." Then the coach said, "Get out in the field and we will work our way up to bat." The first boy struck out, then Dan hit a fly ball, but another boy caught it. Bob was up next. He hit a ball out of the park. "That was a good hit, Bob," said the coach. The next day he told the boys where they would play. Bob just made it for shortstop. Dan played right field. "Thanks, Coach," said the boys. "We think we will have the <u>very best team</u>."

I underlined those last words for an effect that's now lost on me, and I can't help but cringe at the story's leaden tone, among other things, at its blatant moralizing, and a kind of hale and brave-hearted attitude that would have befitted Horatio Alger. It's curious to me from my present vantage point that the story seems more readily reflective of the kinds of boys' sports books we read in the 1950s than it is of anything I truly knew or was concerned with in my life—it's a story about baseball stories—yet it is a passingly adequate narrative nonetheless. Its main character—its protagonist, in the lingo of the English department—is Bob, of course; the setting is summer in Green Valley, and the thing that happens is that with pluck and a level swing Bob does indeed make the team. Its attendant subplot, if you will—and the thing that makes its author seem far too prissy for comfort—is that despite the talent of the boy named Dan, surely it's his little taunt that results in the ridicule of right field.

Now, compare that narrative to a story called "To the Moon," written only the other day by my sister Carol's nine-year-old daughter, Laurel, its text composed in her still-awkward hand and accompanied by an illustration, bound with staples into a little book on sheets of orange paper:

Once not long ago, a young man told himself that he had to do something in his life so it would not be wasted on junk food. So he went to the moon, where he met a moon girl. They got married that very day. And they had a moon kid and lived happily ever after, trying to understand each other.

Laurel's drawing shows a "moon girl" saying "Ooo hhhh do" in a bubble over her head, and the young man responding "What?" I laughed heartily when I first read it, and Laurel *is* a comic, yet even at age nine she surely understands the delightful double entendre of her story's final words. They describe the very literal problem of translation, yet they also represent a universal kind of conundrum—the fact that often you can't seem to figure out the very people to whom you're closest, or even more specifically, that happily-ever-after is a condition filled with pitfalls. Laurel has written a symbolic story—a tale about more than it seems to be on its surface; she too has obeyed narrative's rules, and never mind the fact that she's also subjected her poor uncle to fiction-writing shame.

My grandmother, Roxie Elizabeth Lewis Rutherford—"Dandy" to Laurel and me and almost everyone else—didn't consider herself a storyteller. She wasn't the sort of person who takes up folktales in lieu of arts and crafts, and *she* would have told you that it was her husband who had been the raconteur. For her, telling stories was simply a natural and congenial means of communicating, a lifelong entertainment, a languorous, word-lit way of connecting with the people whom she cared about until the winter day she died. "Well, sir," Dandy would say colloquially, and that was the certain cue that she was remembering a story. "Well, sir," she would add minutes later to signal the tale's turning point, its subtle epiphany, occasionally its crisis. Her stories weren't meant to moralize or to be blatantly instructive, and she seldom offered a commentary other than to exclaim, "Can you imagine?" *Can you imagine?* she would ask us as her stories closed, and it was as though she were asking, "Isn't life the most amazing thing you've heard of?" It was as though she were inquiring whether the story itself had come alive.

Stories had shaped and delighted Dandy's eighty-eight years, and although she seldom, if ever, wrote one down or gave any conscious, calculating thought to a story's telling, she too knew the rules. She, like you and me, understood them intuitively, and it seems sure as I mention her that narrative must be, in Brooks's terminology, "a certain subset of the general language code." The fundamental elements of syntactic structure, common to every language, are subject and predicate—noun and verb. Each language's basal components for conveying meaning are simply and identically those two—a person, a concept, a *thing*, coupled with the action it undergoes or a statement of its condition—and they bear far more than a basic relationship to the fundamental elements of narrative: character and plot.

The bare structure of a story duplicates and surely is closely kindred to the simplest process of sentence structure—sensory, cognitive, syntactic, and lexicographic data momentarily merge in our cortices, and it is their sudden and inscrutable convergence that allows us to give breath to stories in very much the same way that it permits us, seemingly effortlessly, to link nouns with verbs. The rules are simple, and they are inescapably shared. The sentence *Ian cannot speak* is constructed of the same neural materials as is a tale about two mongrel dogs who can't muster much in the way of courage. The fanciful sentence *Ian speaks beautifully* is built in much the same manner as a story about a resolute, romantic man who ventures to the moon. Both sentences and stories are utterly constricted and contained by their consonant structures, yet those same structures allow *limitless* combinations of subject and predicate, of character and action. Our brains—those of almost all of us—are marvelously adept indeed at blending morphemes into meaning, at performing the kind of neurochemical alchemy that turns symbols into substantial sentences, then sentences into an infinite trove of tales.

Ian was three years old when Dandy died. She lived long enough to know and to grieve in her own internalized way about the torment and the isolation he suffered. He was old enough at her end to have been able to visit her country house on a few occasions and to have run with real and visible relief beside the weathered fence surrounding it. She would remain wonderfully calm, almost beatific, as Ian screamed near the chair where she spent her days, and she always would mention to my sister what a beautiful boy he was.

In the weeks before Dandy died, my mother had discussed with her whether some of the money that she would derive from Dandy's small estate might go toward buying Ian a computer, and Dandy had responded with a kind of quiet pleasure. My grandmother had been born the year before the century turned—almost a decade before Orville and Wilbur Wright convinced the world that they had found a way to fly—and she had been fascinated seventy years later when some young men actually made it to the moon. She had never seen a personal computer, but despite her advanced years and her own isolation, she was intrigued by what she had read and heard about these small, surely magical machines that could store and retrieve and readily manipulate language. It seemed to her that, yes, one day a computer just might give Ian a surrogate sort of speech. It seemed to both of them that perhaps it could enable him to shape words into sentences in time, that it just might allow him to tell his stories in a way his brain alone could not. "Can you imagine?" she asked my mother in her small and soon silent voice.

3
IAN CAUGHT
IN INFANCY

Infancy, a word we tend to associate only with the first few weeks and months of a child's life—life's brief beginning, a time, almost solely it seems, of suckling and untroubled sleep—comes to us from Anglo-French by way of Middle English, and it is most distantly rooted in the Latin word *infantia*, which means "without speech." Curiously, whether we are eight months or eighty years old—too young to have taken up words or old enough that stroke and disease insidiously have begun to take them from us—those of us who cannot speak are caught in the clutch of infancy. At ages two and three and then at four, the growing boy named Ian Drummond remained a troubled infant—absent speech, bereft of the kinds of language skills other children take command of in those years, Ian somehow lacking the cerebral apparatus with which this most *human* of his talents otherwise would have emerged.

Only three weeks following conception, the human embryo, three millimeters in length, has formed two paired structures at one end of its simple neural tube—bulging, symmetrical pieces of tissue that soon will become a brain. By the twelfth week of gestation, the brain's cerebrum and cerebellum have taken shape; at four months, the several forebrain structures are intact and the cerebrum has begun to form the lateral fissures that distinguish its temporal lobes; and at eight months, the fully developed brain is tightly packed inside the bony box of the cranium. By birth, an infant's head is almost half its body length; its brain weighs a quarter of its adult weight, and every one of its *billions* of neurons already is intact. Except for the intricate coating of long nerve fibers with insulating myelin and what in two years' time will be a doubling in its weight, the brain at birth is entirely ready to function, to begin to form the dazzling interconnections between its neurons that will allow it to engage with the world, to recognize, remember, and learn, someday even to speak.

Whether the phenomenon can be accounted for by the presence in the brain of a Chomskian language organ or whether it is simply the product of decidedly less mysterious natural selection, every human newborn with normal hearing quickly begins to focus on the sounds of speech. Tests performed in experimental settings have shown that six-month-olds can distinguish between "ah" and "ee" sounds made by their mothers and that they likewise can discern the differences in those sounds when made by voices they have never heard. And just as infants spend the first six months of life listening to the sounds of speech, they devote the subsequent half year to trying them out for themselves. Babies begin to babble four to six months before their first word emerges, making speechlike sounds in a manner that is unmistakably playful, pleasurable; and intriguingly, they tend to begin to make the same sounds at roughly the same times and in the same sequences regardless of the language they have become accustomed to and are about to learn to speak— Arabic, English, or Chinese.

First words, the first fledgling elements of speech, are little more than labels, a means of identifying those people and objects the youngster considers most important—*cow, cookie, Mama, me*—the child's initial sense of self taking shape in the simple context of naming names. Then, subject-only utterances give way to subject and verb: an eager "me, me!" is soon supplanted by the more communicative "me juice," and not long later the phrase "give juice me" introduces a grammatical object well before a child gains command of the particularities of syntax and grammar. Finally, and now from a certified speaker—language alive in his or her brain—a sentence like "please give me some apple juice" emerges as if by some sleight of mind, a true linguistic accomplishment. And perhaps even more remarkably, toddlers at fourteen months and even tykes of four or five years are capable of learning two very different languages simultaneously, as effortlessly as one alone is acquired, and although their limits seldom are truly tested, they likely are capable of learning many more. Those first few years of a child's life appear, in point of fact, to be *for* learning language, for discovering ten thousand things through imitation and endless hours of play, for playing foremost with language.

Although Ian's first forms of autistic play were limited to his silent and solitary imitations of action in his movies, by the time he was three he did begin to entertain himself—to explore and exercise and even have a bit of irrefutable fun—in several other ways, normally alone but occasionally even in the company of others. He loved, for instance, to tug and push his mother, father, and sister Sarah into precise positions in their long, sunlit living room, where they could serve as sentient sorts of fence posts whom he could run beside; and it seemed sure that it would have become one of his favorite recreations—combining the joys of running, repetition, and a real if rather peculiar way of interacting with his family—had it not become quickly obvious to the other three that they simply could not allow themselves to become prisoners to that particular pastime, stuck in place perhaps for hours as Ian brushed beside them, racing back and forth across the carpet.

But his other entertainments tended to be far easier to sanction—less disruptive of some semblance of regular family life, if often equally unusual: It was during the year he was three that Ian seemed to discover trees—the ponderosas, Douglas firs, and aspens that he lived among—and he would spend long stretches of time outdoors licking trees as if to determine what their taste could teach him, similarly pressing his cheeks against their trunks, craning his neck to peer into their upper branches, running past them in lieu of posts or people. And then he discovered water to similar delight, splashing in puddles and fearlessly jumping into shallow pools. Bathtime too became an occasion he eagerly sought out, several times a day if his parents would acquiesce—the tub's warm and soapy water a realm he comfortably could enter with his prized plastic figurines, Pooh and Tigger and ten others joining him for his nightly soak, an environment where you could watch him subtly unwind, physically and somehow even emotionally, where the water seemed to hug him or caress him, or at least to offer some support, where he was free simply to splash and kick and play. Ian also became an intrepid climber, as fearless clinging to the upper rungs of the ladder that led to a loft in his bedroom as he was in the water, regularly scrambling up the metal slide outside the house with what appeared to be a kind of cool disinterest, scrambling too to the tops of the granite knobs as big as barns that lay scattered across the rolling steppe.

In his isolation—his bedroom door often shut to shield out some noise, some simple commotion he couldn't stand—Ian would spend hours burrowed under blankets pulled from his bed and mounded on the floor, sleeping bags and clothes dumped from drawers offering similar subterranean pleasures, the boy becoming a mole. And on those days when it seemed safe to venture into the larger world of the living room, he would pull the cushions from the couch and try as well to bury himself beneath them, or angle them to the floor to turn them into a makeshift, spongy slide.

But for the longest time, Ian didn't play with vocal sounds in any way. Unlike other children, he didn't babble as if engaged in some splendid experiment, he didn't try to imitate words he heard. He seemed instead to be deaf, hearing nothing—neither his mother's patient and tender pledges nor the songs his father sang, neither his sister's carefully scripted fantasies nor his own continuing shrieks. He seemed as mute as those rocks and trees were, incapable of speaking polished words, incapable of their practice, unable to make himself understood, as other children could, with nascent sounds that sprang from his mouth.

Theoretical explanations of how normal children somehow utter their first words and then rapidly acquire language tend to be composed of opposing and contradictory perspectives. It isn't surprising, nor is it news, that one of them is championed—quite persuasively, for many people—by Noam Chomsky. Yet it is curious that many of Chomsky's ideas about the specific ways in which language comes to life in almost all children first emerged not in the context of his own primary writing but rather in his 1959 review of Harvard psychologist B. F. Skinner's 1957 book *Verbal Behavior*, a widely influential account of how language is acquired, then used throughout a lifetime.

Skinner's ideas dominated psychology back in that era, particularly his contention that all of human behavior is best explained by what he called operant conditioning. In the context of the theory that has become known as behaviorism, an "operant" is any action that achieves a specific outcome. If the outcome is favorable, the probability increases that the action will occur again, and the action is "reinforced"—positively reinforced if it produces some sort of pleasant or attractive outcome, negatively reinforced if the operant is followed by the end or removal of something painful or unpleasant. If, on the other hand, the outcome of an operant is unfavorable, the probability *decreases* that it will occur again, and rather than being reinforced, that operant is "punished."

In terms of the acquisition of language, Skinner theorized, all linguistic stimuli are external—morphemes, words, sentences—and an individual child develops the ability to respond to those stimuli via the principles of operant conditioning, the spoken word "juice" tending to result in the offering of juice, for instance, while "juice please" is even more likely to produce the desired result. But a specific operant can be generalized to apply to a variety of related behaviors as well, and can also be associated with a wide range of unrelated behaviors. "Cookie please" is readily "learned" by general-ization, in other words, and "teddy bear please" is acquired with similar ease by means of association. In Skinner's view, a child learns to talk, just as he or she learns to walk, because talking tends to produce so many favorable outcomes.

But Chomsky was unpersuaded by a theory based entirely on response to external stimuli. Although he could imagine, for in-stance, that the rules of operant conditioning might comprehensively account for the way in which an infant shakes a rattle, then shakes it again repeatedly because he or she delights in the sounds it makes—or the way in which a child learns to walk because certain operants, certain physical actions, result in the positive reinforce-ment of reaching a parent's outstretched arms—Chomsky simply dismissed Skinner's attempt to treat language analogously. Neither Skinner nor anyone else could make the case, he argued, that lan-guage acquisition was solely the product of external conditions, in part because its "stimuli" inherently were so difficult, if not impossi-ble, to identify and quantify. And how could Skinner account for one of language's most elemental attributes, its creativity? If lan-guage was acquired solely from external sources, were the concepts of generalization and association enough to explain the ways in which children begin to link words they have never heard linked before?

In Chomsky's opposing view, language acquisition cannot be imagined to be set in motion by external forces, by stimuli that lead to specific linguistic responses. Instead, he proposed the existence of a "language organ" in every child that receives external input in the form of so-called primary linguistic data—parents' words, phrases, pauses, and inflections. The acquisition device then some-how cooks that data down into the stew of syntax—the linguistic rules and regulations that the parents' words adhere to—finally allowing the output of a grammatically acceptable version of the very language from which the original data have been drawn. What emerges is a facility with that language that is capable of enormous creativity, of course, because it is not mimicry, nor is it a specific operant response. Rather, it is language built on an innate apprehen-sion of those rules and on a similar ability to employ them, on what

Chomsky labeled a "universal grammar," which he has defined more recently as "a characterization of the genetically determined language faculty. One may think of this faculty as a 'language acquisition device,' an innate component of the human mind that yields a particular language through interaction with presented experience." The average six-year-old, in other words, becomes expert at speech production and comprehension because he or she is born with its rules already in hand, or, if you will, somewhere within the neural walls of that acquisition device.

Chomsky's assessment of the way in which children acquire language seems clearly wrongheaded to a linguist like Philip Lieberman, who remains far more charitable toward the ideas of Skinner and his fellow behaviorists than does Chomsky and who argues for the primacy of evolution, rather than syntax, when it comes to the question of language's rules and regulations. The fundamental flaw in the universal grammar theory, as far as Lieberman is concerned, is that it assumes that all humans are born with an identical "plan," a genetically coded set of interlocked principles, components, and conventions that allows a child to turn the aural data of spoken speech into creative language—a system in which every component plays a specific and crucial role, and in which every component therefore is always present in everyone who learns to talk. But that assumption, he argues, flies in the face of the formidable verity of genetic variation: No two individuals (save identical twins) are genetically alike, and those genes at the specific chromosomal locations that account for each particular aspect of who we are vary between us and our parents about ten percent of the time. It is an evolutionary certainty, Lieberman contends, that if a universal grammar were genetically transmitted, all its components could not always be present in every individual. If a genetically coded "language faculty" is absolutely necessary to acquire language, he writes in *Uniquely Human*,

[t]hen it would follow that some children would lack one or more of the genetically coded components of the language faculty. Some "general principle" or some component of the "markedness system" would necessarily be absent in some

children because it is genetically transmitted. This is the case for all genetically coded aspects of the morphology of human beings or any other living organisms. . . . A biologically plausible universal grammar cannot have rules and parameters that are so tightly interlocked that the absence of any single bit of putative innate knowledge makes it impossible for the child to acquire a particular language. In other words, we cannot claim that a single set of innate principles concerning language exists that is (a) absolutely necessary for the acquisition of language and (b) uniform for all human beings.

Yes, Lieberman acknowledges—anticipating the responses of Chomsky and fellow "nativists" who view language as genetically innate—all people do have lungs, hearts, brains, and it may be that all of us also possess universal grammars, but if so, and as is the case with those other organs, they necessarily would vary from person to person, and in some people, they necessarily would be faulty— faulty far more often than could be accounted for by children like Ian who do not learn to speak. Instead, suggests Lieberman, children learn how to speak simply because they know how to play.

Lieberman does not argue with the notion that the input of parents' (particularly mothers') spoken speech is a crucial and catalytic component of language acquisition; without it, the acquiring process could not get under way. But as far as he is concerned, "there is nothing very mysterious about syntax," particularly with regard to its supposed innate role in turning complex, sometimes contradictory, often garbled input into grammatical output. What happens instead, he posits rather more concretely, is that children begin to respond to the language sounds they hear simply by imitating them. Studies have shown that newborns at just a day or two of age are capable of imitating adult facial expressions, and by age six months children can imitate the sounds their mothers make; by nine months, they are able to imitate expressions, sounds, and activities they discerned the day before; by fourteen months, they can replay by imitation what they saw or heard a week ago. Are these children dutifully and determinedly going about the business of learning language as they do so? No, says Lieberman, they are *playing*, a highly evolved form of behavior that allows us to learn a multitude of things, languages among them, without having to knuckle down or even to sit still—learning by association, generalization, analogy, and the kinds of trial and error that are the nuts-and-bolts business of Skinner's behaviorism.

There is no argument among these linguistic partisans that children learning language are confronted with what would seem to be a daunting task. Although it takes them years of schooling to master geometry or algebra, they quickly come to grips—in the most casual of look-Ma-no-hands fashions—with a system of communication and representation that scientists cannot completely or even adequately describe. It isn't surprising therefore that one attractive explanation for children's cheery facility with language's complexity is that knowledge of its rules, or perhaps the rules themselves, are innate, somehow built into every baby. But that perspective digs too deeply and with far too blunt a shovel, Lieberman believes, when a much more plausible possibility can be observed readily in almost every household. Children learn language so effortlessly, he contends, because they inherently are so playful, so curious, because they can pay rapt attention without knowing they do so, and because their brains are utterly impelled to learn.

Children—and former children as well—daily employ a diverse and varied number of so-called cognitive strategies in order to learn, one of the most important and fundamental of which is known as "concept formation," or rule learning. And in the context of learning the rules of language, children make use of concept formation to acquire the foundations of syntactic structure; syntax isn't so complex that it must be innate, Lieberman says, but rather it is so simple that it's discernible just from listening.

All humans are adept at generalizing—forming categories, patterns, and rules from separate cases or incidents—and children begin to generalize very early on. Their interest in naming objects, for instance, is part of an obsession with creating categories—all four-legged animals likely included in a category called "dog" at first, then soon divided into subcategories called "dog" and "horse" and "cat." Similarly, and surely unaware, children generalize from the language that they hear, noting—among many other things—that utterances tend to come in bursts separated by breaths, that key words receive intonational stress, that those words are made up of specific sounds, and that words, once recognized, tend to be grouped in repeated and dependable patterns. As children then begin to imitate what they hear, their first words, not surprisingly, tend to be those key words, words their parents have spoken a thousand times and each time have given a vocal stress. Later, as they begin to link words grammatically, their grammars simply reflect those orderings, those rule-governed arrangements that they have heard most often. If they hear "I goed to town" more often than "I went to town," then *I goed* becomes grammatical; if "I went to town" is commonplace and "Town went I to" is odd, then the latter is discarded. Rather than depending on an innate rule-dispensing system, they depend instead on their abilities to generalize from observation—learning by listening, and then by imitating those curious articulations that they most often hear.

In making this behavioral kind of case, however, Lieberman does not quarrel with the proposition that the acquisition of language involves specialized brain mechanisms or some set of highly evolved neural capabilities. The brain's adaptability and its task-specific prowess, in fact, have allowed us to achieve all manner of miracles in the millennia since we lumbered to our feet. But there simply is no need, he argues by analogy,

to postulate a special-purpose innate fork-using mechanism to account for the way that children learn to use forks, or universal clothes or cars grammars to account for the way that people rush to outfit themselves in the latest style in clothes or cars. Imitation and a desire to "be like the others" clearly can account for most of the short-term changes in human culture, and perhaps for many of its major achievements.

Of all our human acquisitions and accomplishments, only language is utterly dependent on being acquired at an early age, during the "critical period," from twelve months of age to six or seven years, perhaps to the onset of puberty, during which time language proficiency must be won, if it ever will be. By the time we become adolescents our language-acquisition device seems somehow to have atrophied, or perhaps to have moved on to another neural occupation. Have the folds and creases of our cortices by then become so definitively formed that we cannot reshape them and effectively teach ourselves new tricks? Do we forget after only a short expanse of years how to pay wide-eyed attention and to play?

From the cows he first was fascinated by to the elephants and monkeys in his movies, from the squirrels and rabbits he encountered in the nearby forests to a wily character called Tigger he certainly seemed to cherish, Ian, like most children, took great interest in animals, particularly if they were at an imaginary or spatial remove from him. He would utterly ignore long-suffering Sheila, the collie who had come west with the family from Illinois, when she would wander into his room, and the cat Sarah lived for during that time surely seemed invisible to him. Yet books like *The Smiley Lion* and *Franny Bunny* at last began to intrigue him—*books!* to his parents' pure pleasure and excitement—Ian sitting still and seeming briefly comfortable beside them as they read, Ian sometimes pointing with the help of their wrist prompts to the colorful drawings of these creatures, sometimes even pointing to the words his parents read. He still loved to—still demanded to—make the daily drive to call on the cows, and despite his fears and anxieties about most exotic settings, he once responded with his own sort of enthusiasm to an experimental trip to the zoo. In subsequent visits to zoos both in Denver and in Colorado Springs, Ian would demonstrate—by means of those places where he chose to run ritually back and forth—the animals he liked best: snakes of all shapes and sizes, as well as the apes, who would stare inscrutably back at him.

They did then and still do intrigue me—these two choices he made without anyone's direction or influence. Wasn't it curious that a boy who was terribly afraid of so much that seemed innocuous was,

nonetheless, drawn to those slithering reptiles that so many of the
rest of us are innately fearful of? And what did he see in the faces
of the gorillas, orangutans, and chimpanzees that made him tarry
near their cages? Did their silence make them seem kindred to him?
Did the cages themselves seem to be something he knew well by
analogy?

Much experimentation has been done during the second half of
the twentieth century in an effort to determine whether our close
cousins the apes are capable of acquiring true language, and several
impressive results indeed have been obtained—from the young go-
rilla named Koko in California who built a working vocabulary of four
hundred signed words to the sardonically named Nim Chimpsky, a
chimpanzee in New York City who once spontaneously produced a
string of sixteen words in American Sign Language (ASL): *Give
orange me give eat orange me eat orange give me eat orange give
me you*; a lot of words for a rather simple request.

This series of separate studies began in the 1960s with a chimpanzee named Vicki who was trained literally to speak, but her vocabulary was limited to four words—*mama, papa, cup,* and *up*—each
produced only with real effort and pronounced in a kind of whisper.
Then early in the 1970s, a chimp named Sarah made news when
she mastered rudimentary elements of a visual-symbol language,
reaching a level at which she could begin to communicate creatively,
generalizing from a phrase like *Randy give apple Sarah* to *Randy
give banana Sarah*, a very subtle but nonetheless significant step.
Subsequently, two chimps called Sherman and Austin, who were
trained simultaneously to use a similar visual language called Yerk-
ish, were sometimes observed using it to communicate privately
with each other after class sessions had ended and trainers had gone
away for the day.

But surely the star of these whiz chimps was Washoe, a chimpanzee who was brought at eleven months of age to live with Allen and
Beatrix Gardner and their family in Nevada, each of whom had
learned ASL prior to her arrival. In Washoe's presence, the Gard-
ners communicated only in ASL, and soon she began to sign herself.
By the time she was five, her vocabulary included at least 132 signs.

Her exaggerated, expansive style of signing was similar to that of human children learning ASL, and she could employ the signing equivalent of intonation to give her words emphasis; but she seldom offered more than a two-word utterance, and she was far more repetitive than human children normally are, whether signing or speaking. Yet Washoe had become quite creative: After she had acquired the sign for *flower*, she began to use it in the context of a variety of smells, but as soon as she learned the actual sign for *smell*, her use of *flower* reverted solely to its proper usage. Impressively, a nightcap she had never seen before she called a *hat*; a Brazil nut seemed to her to be a *rock berry*; and the first time she saw a duck, she labeled it a *water bird*.

In the intervening years, no other pongid has significantly surpassed the achievements of Washoe and her fellow captives. The most precocious of them have been capable of reaching a language level roughly comparable to that of a two-and-a-half-year-old child, and they have learned—normally, and perhaps significantly, only with the aid of the rigorously controlled techniques of operant conditioning—how to use complex symbolic systems to communicate. Yet they have been unable to progress beyond those plateaus they reached, and that, as well as the virtual absence of a grasp of syntax, combine to make most researchers unwilling to call their communication "language." But if these chimps and gorillas aren't employing language, then what is this marvel of which they've become capable? If Nim Chimpsky isn't using language when he signs *Me sorry hug me*, what else can we possibly call it?

Derek Bickerton, the University of Hawaii linguist who, like Chomsky, views an inherent sense of syntax as key to language's emergence in our species as well as to its acquisition by each of us individually, posits intriguing answers to those questions in *Language and Species*. There are at least two allied but fundamentally distinct *types* of language, Bickerton contends—both having come to us evolutionarily in ways Philip Lieberman wouldn't argue with—what Bickerton calls "language" and "protolanguage," and the case he makes for them depends as much on rare examples of so-called wild children who have grown up in worlds without language as it does on eloquent and pioneering pongids like precocious Nim and Washoe.

It was in the autumn of 1970 that a tiny thirteen-year-old girl—just four feet six inches tall and weighing fifty-nine pounds—appeared with her cataract-blinded mother at a social services office in suburban Los Angeles, the two of them seeking help, seeking asylum from the father and husband who long had made their lives nightmarish beyond belief. Inside the father's autocratic and horrific household, the girl—who became known by the pseudonym "Genie"—had been harnessed naked to a potty chair since infancy, able to move only her fingers and hands, her feet and toes, the room where she was kept empty except for the potty chair and a wire-covered crib where she sometimes was placed at night, her only glimpse of the world two slivers of sky she could see above the curtains that covered the windows.

Genie was incontinent when she first was examined by doctors. She could not chew solid food, her vision was very poor, she could not stand erect or fully extend her limbs, and she virtually was mute. She understood the words *red, blue, green, brown, Mother, walk*, and *go*; she could utter only what sounded like "stop it" and "no more." Genie was admitted to Children's Hospital of Los Angeles for initial treatment of severe malnutrition, and as she slowly began to gain strength and then quickly to acquire new skills, she also became the subject of an enormous amount of curiosity on the part of social scientists from several disciplines. By the time a battery of tests determined that Genie was not retarded—although, as hospital psychologist James Kent put it, she was "the most profoundly damaged child I've ever seen . . . [her] life was a wasteland"—a number of researchers in linguistics had become fascinated by her, by what, in particular, she might now be able to acquire in the way of speech and language skills. Yet although Genie did make enormous progress, although she could say "I want Curtiss play piano," "Think about Mama love Genie," and could utter hundreds of similar simple

phrases by 1977, seven years after her liberation, her language skills
seemed stuck at that rather primitive level.

 According to Susan Curtiss, the UCLA linguist who had worked
most intensively with Genie during those years and whose doctoral
dissertation had been published under the title *Genie: A Psycholin-
guistic Study of a Modern-Day "Wild Child,"* Genie quickly had
developed an impressive vocabulary, but, in large part because she
had aged beyond the critical acquiring period by the time she began
to learn language,

> she never mastered the rules of grammar, never could use the
> little pieces—the word endings, for instance. She had a clear
> semantic ability but could not learn syntax. There was a tre-
> mendous unevenness, or scatter, in what she was able to
> do. . . . One of the interesting findings is that Genie's linguis-
> tic system did not develop all of a piece. So grammar could be
> seen as distinct from the non-grammatical aspects of language,
> and also from other mental faculties. . . . She demonstrated
> that after puberty one could not learn language simply by
> being exposed to it.

Yet as Russ Rymer would note in his *New Yorker* series based
on Genie's story and the research she engendered, her linguistic
development also posed a substantial theoretical conundrum:

> Though it appeared to affirm Chomsky, it could also be read
> as refuting him. If some parts of language were innate and
> others were provided by the environment, why would Genie's
> childhood hell have deprived her of only the innate parts?
> How could a child who lacked language because she had been
> shut away from her mother be proof that our mothers don't
> teach us language? Why should she be unable to gain precisely
> the syntax that Chomsky said she was born with? . . . [I]f
> syntax is "innate" why must it be "acquired" at all?

Derek Bickerton's sharply drawn distinction between language and protolanguage considers those questions by forging a linguistic—actually, a *proto*linguistic—link between adolescents and adults like Genie, who have been deprived of language, normal children who are acquiring their initial speech, and the speaking apes, connections that at first perhaps appear implausible. Bickerton is convinced that the kinds of language the three groups produce have much in common: they are comprised solely of lexical (vocabulary) items and they lack discernible grammatical structure—the same observation Susan Curtiss makes regarding Genie's speech—and Bickerton goes to some length in making his case for their commonality.

Yet if all are virtually the same sort of speech, why does only one of the three transform itself into fully flowered language? Bickerton's response is that no satisfactory or even passable explanation is possible so long as it depends on the assumption that mature language evolves or derives from its primitive counterpart, so long as language acquisition is seen as a single continuous process. But on the other hand, he writes,

> [i]f we assume that there exists some primitive type of language—some protolanguage, as we might call it, that is just as much a part of our biological endowment as language is, but that lacks most of the distinguishing formal properties of language—then all three . . . can be readily explained. Genie acquired protolanguage because protolanguage is more robust than language (having formed part of the hominid endowment for much longer) and it does not have a critical period. . . . Genie's acquisition ceased because the faculties of protolanguage and of language are disjoint, and acquisition of the one in no way entails acquisition of the other.

This is the core of Bickerton's contention: Hominids and pongids alike can pick up protolanguage, whether at thirteen months or thirteen years or thirty. And it is this rough and spotty kind of speech that is acquired through the application of normal cognitive processes to the input of experience, in much the same way that Philip Lieberman describes. Yet the other sort of language—the one almost all of us acquire when we are small as if by some strange metaphysical frolic, the one that depends on syntax for its clarity and nuance and a kind of fluid grace—clearly must be latched onto very early in our lives; and we alone among the primates, among *all* animals so far as we know now, are capable of achieving it. It is a curious thought to consider: It isn't our ability to communicate that makes us unique; neither is it our register of words that we can count into the many thousands. What sets us truly apart, it seems, is that while we are young—and somehow *only* then—we discover how wonderfully to weave those words.

But Rymer's queries still echo here: If Chomsky is correct in claiming that this stuff called syntax with which we create true language is genetically handed down to us, then why does it disappear? Or if, in contrast, Lieberman's outlook is the clearer one, then why is it that we can acquire words at any age, but grammar only in the years soon after we are infants?

There came a time during Ian's early and utterly speechless years when, from his parents' perspective, the reality of his autism inevitably lost the kind of desperate immediacy it had assumed since his diagnosis. The terrible calamity that had beset them as the eighteen-month-old Ian became so strange was transformed, as surely it had to be, into a chronic but curiously integral component of their lives. Ian—and they—plainly were faced with something that was not going to go away, something that could not be cured in a doctor's office nor enticed to vanish with cheery attitudes or pop psychology or prayer. *This* was who their son was—a boy tormented by the slightest inconsistencies in his daily schedule, a boy who could not communicate in any way—and those two conditions seemed certain to persist for a very long time to come. What Ian faced so fundamentally, and what his sister and his parents had to confront in ways that sometimes seemed commensurate, were days and years ahead that would be limited severely by his bizarre rigidity and that would be filled with the terrible frustrations of his involuntary silence, of all that he necessarily would have to leave unsaid.

Late in the evenings during that time when Ian still was wordless, Claudia and Boyce would sit at their dining room table, spiral notebooks and sheets of paper spread between them, making that day's entry into Ian's developmental logbook and outlining new worktime exercises they might try tomorrow, but sometimes also peering bravely into future days—categorizing the pros and cons of the places they might live once Ian came of school age, setting immediate goals that seemed attainable for him, goals as well for themselves. It was obvious, for instance, that Ian needed to learn to help himself in several ways—how to start and change his movies, how to find his toys and then dependably put them away so he could find them the next time, how to dress himself and to don boots and jackets as the weather warranted, and approaching four now, he really *had* to be potty trained, or at least urged toward that end. Some strides needed to be made toward improving his fragile health, and in concert with Denver doctors they planned to experiment with vitamin therapies and to test for a variety of potential allergens, from foods and liquids to cleaning compounds. And, of course, they had to try every trick they could coin to entice Ian to eat a more balanced and complete diet than solely the tofu, muffins, and pancakes to which he otherwise seemed very willing to limit himself, shape and texture evidently more compelling culinary attributes for him than were smell and taste.

In an effort to enlarge Ian's experience—to draw him out of his room and multiply the stimuli he encountered day to day, to ease his fears of the unfamiliar—Claudia and Boyce pledged to acquaint him with new kinds of entertainment and with novel ways to play. Already he was attracted to many kinds of music, and the piano his father and sister played seemed at times to intrigue him; perhaps Boyce could teach him some simple melodies. His large-motor skills, particularly those involving his hands and arms, remained poorly developed, and as a means of improving them, it seemed possible that he could learn to play with balls or to pull a weathered wagon, to propel himself in a swing or on the tricycle his sister by now had abandoned, to jump on a tiny trampoline or even to dance: water play had proven to be a vital physical outlet for Ian, and perhaps with patient encouragement he could develop an interest in those others. And *perhaps*—but surely for some time to come this just remained a dream—they could come up with activities the whole family could take part in: perhaps one distant day they could go for a hike or even on a picnic; in some distant summer they could go camping overnight, all four of them perhaps, Ian away—unimaginably—from the security of his room and the reassurance of his movies.

There wasn't much extra money to make the possibility seem tenable, but Boyce and Claudia also spent many evenings and more than a few anguished conversations discussing how desperately they needed some sort of dependable daily help—ideally someone who could assist with Ian, but at the least someone to assume several of the household chores that now seemed to consume the little leisure time they had—bathrooms often cleaned when Claudia was sleepless late at night, Boyce ritually rising early to attend to yesterday's dishes. Carla Crittendon, who had arrived at the research station in January 1987 and quickly had befriended Ian and helped him make substantial progress, would be leaving in November. Sandy Oldham—who lived with her husband and a daughter Ian's age a couple of miles away, and who was therefore their nearest neighbor—had developed a similar rapport with Ian early on; she could baby-sit for him without his objection, take him on walks, and make sure his schedule unfolded as it had to, and she often arrived at the research station with breads and pastries in her arms in addition to her warm and loving support. But Sandy had become pregnant with her second child and no longer would be able to work for them, and Boyce and Claudia dreaded that looming prospect. Lately they had advertised in local papers and in the *Christian Science Monitor*, the *Special Education Journal*, and even the Sierra Club's monthly magazine, offering their spectacular setting and a commensurate challenge with a special little boy, but so far no one had responded.

In the long run they knew—night after night rubbing their eyes and reminding each other how late it was as still they sat and talked—

that the isolated setting they liked so much in so many ways might, nonetheless, become an added burden. Sarah was attending kindergarten now, but to get to school she had to spend an hour on a bus each morning and another hour en route home in the afternoon; and it had to be assumed that in the coming years bus rides of any length would not work for Ian. Neighbors and friends like the Oldhams were few in number among the ponderosas; doctors, supermarkets, and shops were at least forty-five minutes away on rutted roads; financial considerations such as salaries, equity in a home, and retirement had to be contended with as well, and so, once again they had begun to consider another move.

But more than anything else surely, a more pressing objective than all the others spread before them nightly on the table, was their need—their profound obligation as his parents—to try anything and everything that might give Ian a voice, a way to express himself, a means for him to connect first with them, then one day with the world around him. That goal was elementary in itself, of course—it seemed as fundamental as freedom; it *was* freedom, after all, but everything they had ever read warned them that if autistic children were to learn to talk, they had to be well under way by five or six. If Ian were to gain only partial speech, it seemed that even that achievement would bring those other goals closer to his reach and to theirs. If Ian could express his needs in only the most simple ways, surely it would follow that his tantrums would subside to some degree. If he could tell his family how he felt and what he longed for, wouldn't that in itself draw him out of his isolation, out of solitary silence toward something akin to the harmonies of music? Wouldn't travel and experimentation, even the lacing of shoes or simple toilet training, all come far easier for him if he had some words, if only he could question, if ever he could answer?

I don't remember receiving a call to alert me to some miracle, but I do know that Claudia and Boyce were absolutely delighted when Ian began again to babble. As he had when he was still an infant, back before the insidious onset of his symptoms, during the summer of 1987 he quite simply began to utter some sounds that had nothing to do with his becoming agitated or distraught, that were far from fussing or crying, and he seemed rather interested in what he now could achieve, not proud so much as clearly curious that finally he too could make them with his mouth.

Claudia, Boyce, and Carla by now had documented many words and phrases that they were sure Ian understood: his name and the names of family members, for instance; the words that signified certain foods and movies; questions like *Do you want a bath?* and statements such as *Time to go for a ride.* He understood *horse* and *monkey* and *bear*—plus *cow*, of course—*mittens* and *tooth-brush* and *blanket.* Like a child of eighteen months or so, like the child he once had been, he could claim dozens of words in his receptive vocabulary now while still unable to pronounce one. Yet this new babbling *was* speechlike; it was segmented into phrases and it varied in intonation; often it was simply the repetition of a single consonant, but sometimes the consonants were those that were parts of appropriate words: "Tttt," he sometimes would respond as his mother touched a tree and pronounced its name; "Gggg," he fairly shouted when he was eager to go for a ride.

For nearly two years by now, Ian had been able to request assistance by taking his mother's or father's sleeve and pulling one of them toward the coatrack or the closed front door, the refrigerator or his VCR, and lately he had acquired the interesting ability to select a movie he wanted to see by choosing among the single large words taped to the spine of each videocassette: PIG, BEAR, PONY, DUMBO. He couldn't be *reading*, could he, this boy who still couldn't speak? But however it was that he invariably made the correct association—the movie he wanted with the word—now he sometimes emphasized those selections, as well as requests of every kind, with a bit of babbled speech.

But babbling was only one of Ian's expressive accomplishments these days. At four he still could not pronounce a recognizable word, yet he *was* communicating in meaningful ways, and the means at his disposal now were several in addition to his screams. Early on, Kathy Reis at the JFK Center in Denver had recommended a home program for augmenting Ian's communicative skills; essentially, it was composed of two parts. First, Claudia and Boyce (Sarah and Carla too were enlisted toward this end) had attempted to plainly, simply, but ubiquitously label verbally Ian's activities and interests along with each of the objects he encountered during his day. "Ian eat," one of them carefully would pronounce with every bite of food he took; "Ian watch Pooh Bear," he would hear each time that movie commenced; "Brush teeth," "Put on boots," "Go for ride; see cows," they said to him throughout every day—not baby talk but a kind of truncated talk, absent articles or adjectives or prepositions, something akin—I now note—to what Bickerton calls protolanguage.

Second, they introduced Ian to American Sign Language, or rather to a few specific signs in ASL—*eat, shoes, bear, book, more, open*, and some others; signs for *mother* and *father*; the closed fist that represents the letter *S* for *Sarah*; the same fist with the small finger extending upward, which is *I*, for *Ian*. As constantly and consistently as they could, they attempted to make eye contact with Ian and to sign the appropriate word to him in dozens of contexts, physically assisting him as well with his own versions of the simplest signs—a clump of fingers pressed to his mouth for *eat*; the fingers of both his hands held similarly and their tips touched together for *more*. And finally, following dozens of days—hundreds of them—of maddening effort that showed precious little reward, Ian did begin to equate a few specific signs with his needs. Although it was awkward for him, although his hands and arms were far less dexterous than his feet, he began to sign *eat* sometimes when he was hungry, and then he generalized that sign—in precisely the same way that Lieberman outlines the process—to mean "want" in several unrelated situations: signing *eat* when he wanted his Tigger figurine, for instance, signing *eat* when asked if he would like to go outside. Similarly, *open* meant "open"—a toy box or a closet—but it also came creatively to mean "I need to communicate" or, sometimes more insistently, "Hey, I'm trying to tell you something"; and his sign for *movie* sometimes surely meant "Oh, boy, this is fun."

But despite their slavish consistency with signing, and despite Ian's minimal successes in acquiring signs himself, his parents intuited after a time that he was unlikely to become truly proficient, that ASL probably would never be his principal language, in large part because of the chronic difficulty he had in coordinating the movements of his hands, but also because he already was so clearly oriented to pictures—to video, of course, but increasingly as well to illustrations in books. He spent considerable time those days flapping the pages of a favorite book—one page at a time and the pages of the book front to back—an inch or two in front of his eyes. Photographs too had begun to attract his interest: he liked to select individual family members and friends from a group of photographs; he liked to find photographs of himself among the stack; and not long before he had expressed himself rather unambiguously by angrily throwing a photograph of his father to the floor while Boyce was away on business.

Sensing that, at least for the short run, Ian could communicate best via the vivid presence of pictures, Boyce and Claudia recently had initiated—in concert with speech and language professionals at the Capron Institute for Rehabilitation in Colorado Springs—a "total communication" program that sought to capitalize on Ian's visual strengths and to offer him still more avenues for expression. Following his initial evaluation in October, Pamela Anderson, director of the institute's augmentative communication program, had made these assessments of his capabilities:

1. Ian demonstrates potential for sustained visual attention when motivated and in a familiar activity. Visual perception and tracking skills seem grossly intact. He is able to pair a picture to an object and can discriminate between two pictures.

2. Ian demonstrates the ability to activate battery-operated toys with a switch. Cause and effect skills are basically intact. He is also able to activate cause/effect software on the computer, although attention span for this activity is reduced at this time. Ian's performance on the computer is highest when his efforts are rewarded by immediate visual and auditory

stimuli. Ian could eventually access a regular computer keyboard.

3. Ian demonstrates potential to utilize communication systems both electronic and nonelectronic to manipulate his environment. At this time Ian requires a photograph of the communication he is attempting to select. It is anticipated that eventually Ian will be able to move to a more abstract symbol system.

Although neither Ian nor his parents abandoned their basic efforts with ASL, under the umbrella of the new program signing would begin to lose its precedence to a less abstract means of communication: first a simple series of photographs laminated in plastic, a hole punched into a corner of each one and the small bundle bound together on a key ring—a readily portable collection that included images of the family car and Ian's television, of course, as well as specific foods and articles of clothing, the bathtub and his books, the tape recorder that he depended on to play his essential music, and photographs too of the canine, feline, and human members of the household. Although Ian usually didn't initiate the use of his specialized photo album, he did sometimes seek it out—bringing it on occasion to his mother or father and finding the picture that referred to his desire. Far more often, however—in the midst of an agonizing tantrum or in the moments when one seemed certain to commence—Claudia or Boyce would grab the ring and, flipping frantically among photographs, try to intuit what he needed, what seemed essential at that moment, Ian ultimately reaching out, their hands supporting his flailing arm, to touch the photo that was proffered correctly even when he was terribly distraught.

Whether it was employed on his impetus or his parents', Ian soon was proficient with the ring of photographs, and by December of that year he had graduated to true picture boards that allowed him to choose among several options. His parents prepared for him cardboard picture boards for foods, one for movies and one for books, a board whose images represented a variety of possible outdoor activities, a board that showed several places the car might go (the picture of cows soon smudged by his fingers), even a board that gave him the opportunity to choose whom he wanted to be with, who might help him with his bath or ready him for bed.

Although Ian's perplexing need for a kind of definitude in his daily schedule remained unchanged, and although he still had to spend big blocks of time in sheltered privacy if he was to maintain a fragile peace, you can imagine what a breakthrough the boards were, how the days inside that isolated mountain house now were very different, filled with promise, occupied by a boy who—even if only in fragmentary ways—finally could be understood. Ian no longer had no option but to scream, and neither were his parents limited anymore to intuition and guesswork, however well-honed it long since had become. At last all the members of the family could *communicate*—very normally, it even occasionally seemed—Ian's ability to understand what was said to him growing in big bounds by now, his ability to express himself still sharply limited, of course, but seemingly limited at the moment only by the numbers of pictures to which he could press his small and awkward hands.

Because Ian had begun to show such visual promise, because of his long and successful relationship with video screens, and because staff members at Capron now were convinced that he could readily adapt to a keyboard, the computer my mother and grandmother had discussed and made possible arrived at Christmastime—an Apple outfitted with developmental games and learning aids, a machine that rewarded Ian's attentions with bright colors and bells and whistles, and although his attention span was short—as it had been and still remained with all his endeavors save the movies—Claudia and Boyce now appended computer time to his daily regimen.

Carla had left the research station and their small family circle only recently, and, like the other three, Ian missed her very much—he missed *her* surely, but he also suffered from the sudden absence of the role she had played for almost a year in his mornings, the locus she had assumed for him each afternoon. The computer could not take her place, of course, but the timing of its arrival was opportune, and it wasn't long before you could sense an interesting sort

of symbiosis between Ian and the Apple. Like other kids his age, he
noticed nothing whatsoever about it that engendered intimidation,
and perhaps it was the ease with which he did take to the keyboard,
his hands and fingers steadied with his parents' help, as well as his
quick mastery of several simple word and symbol games, that made
the boy and the machine seem so jointly suited—the wonderful
photograph his father took of Ian at his desk silently contemplating
the colored screen, his chin resting on his fist, soon finding its way
onto my mother's refrigerator, where it long since has remained.

It was not the same refrigerator—and there may have been a couple of them in the interim—but there was a time too when my
picture was on display in that kitchen at the northern end of Market Street, back when I still lived at home yet was absent for a
year. The year was 1968, that reach of days racked by tragedy and
tumult throughout the United States, and I was away in Spain,
where the fascist Franco still kept an ersatz and shameful peace, and
the photograph my parents kept showed me in jacket and tie and
counterfeit European Levi's standing at the base of the Colón monu-
ment there where the *Ramblas* spilled into Barcelona's harbor—a
kid from the world claimed by Columbus come east with innocent
and dazzled eyes.

I had gone to Barcelona as part of a school-year-abroad program
sponsored by Andover and Exeter, the New England prep schools,
and I was the third emancipated preppie in as many years taken
in and made to feel marvelously at home by Domingo and Maria
Pérez and their four children in a small fifth-floor apartment in the
seaward-sloping Grácia district, situated between Gaudí's surreal
Sagrada Familia and the enchanting psychedelic mosaics of his hillside Parque Guell—or Parc Güell in the region's proud, poetic
indigenous language, Catalan. But Spain's aging autocrat had out-
lawed Catalan back at the end of the civil war, made it a crime to
speak it in public places. Even in homes like the Pérezes', Catalan—
or correctly, *català*—was still spoken in a kind of whispered confidence and, it seemed unmistakable, a certain familial defiance.

Like Franco himself, Domingo Pérez had been born and raised in Galicia (its own regional language, Gallego, more akin to Portuguese than Castilian Spanish), but he had come to Barcelona as a young, determined teacher soon after the war, and in part because he subsequently had met and married the dark and beautiful *catalana* Maria Ballonga, his Catalan by now sounded nearly native. So we were a trilingual clan when we gathered in the evenings in the apartment's tiny sitting room, its space all but consumed by the broad dining table—Domingo dutifully speaking Spanish because, after all, that was the language I had come to Spain to try to learn; his eldest sons, Antoni and Josep Maria, unable to resist the smattering of English they had gleaned from my predecessors, from brief sojourns spent in England, and from their studied devotion to Pete Seeger; Maria and the two younger children (as well as Maria's widowed mother, who was with us each Sunday afternoon for the ritual roasted-rabbit dinner) speaking Catalan, forgetting despite their best efforts that it was as foreign to me as Finnish. The always-black-clad *Senyora* Ballonga, unlike the others, spoke only passable Spanish, and I remember that her solution to the dilemma posed by my presence often was to stop in midsentence and fairly shout at me in Spanish, "*¿Me entiendes?* [Do you understand me?]"

The honest answer would have oftentimes been no, but I seldom betrayed that truth, and the kid they called "Martín"—serviceable and simple in Catalan or Spanish, my first name a nightmare—spent a school year at their table far more richly rewarded than I was baffled, and my Spanish had improved enough by the time I bid them a sad and awkward good-bye in the early summer of 1969 that it approached a facile-tongued sort of fluency. My spoken Catalan, in contrast, remained nonexistent except for the lyrics of a song or two the older boys had taught me, as well as some practiced phrases I could entertain the table with, yet my *receptive* Catalan by then was capable of letting me in on lots of stuff—a few intriguing secrets and several conversations surely not intended for my ears.

As I think back after a quarter of a century on that splendid, life-shaping year, it's difficult to remember in much detail the rudiments of acquiring a second language or a few words of a third. I do know

that as the equivalent of a junior in high school, I was well past the
critical language-acquiring period, but there is no question nonetheless that Spanish somehow flooded into me and my fellow schoolboys
abroad despite our teenage inattention to the process. Our academic
coursework was conducted in Spanish, and a yearlong grammar class
(whose daily arrival none of us ever was eager for) successfully taught
us the intricacies of past and future indicative and subjective cases,
plus much more in the way of Spanish's syntactic particularities.
Those formal kinds of language-learning enterprises, together with
the way we acquired it rather more organically from our foster families and on sidewalks that teemed with citizens till well past midnight, on neighborhood *futbol* fields and in the cafés and clubs that
seemed to me to be such casual fonts of culture, combined to bring
that new language vibrantly to life.

I was *trying* to learn Spanish, and I succeeded ably enough, and
I even possessed sufficient Catalan by the time I returned to Colorado that perhaps I could have claimed it as a protolanguage, yet
there was a fundamental difference between the adolescent acquisitions I made at the rim of the Mediterranean and those that Ian
struggled to attain at a much earlier age high on the shoulder of Pike's
Peak. And surely there is an overwhelming distinction between my,
or anyone's, efforts to learn secondary languages and the attempts
of the California girl called Genie to make herself something of a life
at last by acquiring her first.

Although every infant is capable of acquiring two or more languages
concurrently, and although people in possession of one language
obviously can succeed very well in learning others—a grasp of one
language's syntactic structure somehow generalizing to an accessibil-
ity to another's—cases like Genie's make it appear irrefutable that
unless one particular tongue is mastered early on, whether it's English or ASL or Tagalog, then it becomes almost impossible for *any*
language ever to burgeon into a kind of formal and creative fullness.
And that issue, of course, remained a fundamental concern with
regard to Ian during the long, snow-smothered winter of 1988. Still

mute, he nonetheless was making significant linguistic progress. But was it enough, and had it initiated soon enough for it someday to generalize to speech? Was the spoken English he now could understand, at least to some degree, enough to teach him syntax? Was communication now expressed through signs and pictures enough to generalize someday to the rich abstraction of words?

At four and a half, Ian remained an infant, yet he was not retarded in the normal sense, and, in fact, he could demonstrate his intelligence in a widening number of ways. Over the course of the year just past, he had begun to learn how to communicate despite his silence, to use visual symbols to represent a variety of conditions and desires, and in so doing he wonderfully had been able to present his parents with hope. But their nascent hope had not eased their anxieties, nor had it answered the nagging question that still lingered like the snow: What *was* it in the brain of this beautiful little boy that kept him speechless?

Tests that linguist Susan Curtiss had performed on Genie in the middle 1970s had demonstrated that although her right cerebral hemisphere functioned normally, her left hemisphere clearly and quite abnormally did not. Dichotic hearing tests had shown that the *right* side of Genie's brain was processing the input of spoken words, and was doing so exclusively. Brain wave monitoring correspondingly had shown that, when hearing spoken sentences, Genie's left cerebral hemisphere remained as inactive as if it had been removed—and it was effectively *dead* to far more than language function. But why was it that, unlike almost everyone else in whom most language functions are localized to the left hemisphere, Genie's minimal language skills had seated themselves on the right?

Writing in 1981, Curtiss speculated that "Genie's case suggests that normal cerebral organization may depend on language development occurring at the appropriate time," and she buttressed her commentary with a 1978 study by Helen Neville, a Salk Institute neuroscientist, who had determined that deaf children who learn American Sign Language in early childhood localize language functions on the left, while those who are deprived of sign language early on, then learn it later in life, *do not* use their left hemispheres for language *or* for other complex cortical functions. "Relating Neville's data to Genie's case suggests that language development may be the crucial factor in hemispheric specialization," Curtiss continued. "When [language] develops, it determines what else the language hemisphere will be specialized for. In its absence, it prevents the language hemisphere from specializing for any higher cortical functions."

Neuroscientists have known for some time that fetal brains are asymmetrical, their left-sided speech areas growing observably larger than the right even before birth. Newborns lying on their backs keep their heads turned to the right nearly ninety percent of the time, paying scant attention to the world that lies to the left; they respond more quickly to food stimuli offered from the right than from the left, and the hearing in their right ear is demonstrably superior just a few weeks following birth—all correlative to genetically coded left hemispheric dominance as well as an anatomical predisposition for receiving language. And consider this: sophisticated electrical response tests of infants as young as twenty-four hours reliably record right-sided electrical activity in response to nonspeech sounds—bells, whistles, the barking of a dog—but *left-sided* activity in response to spoken words.

Built on these and related findings, Curtiss's bold contention becomes a fascinating and even frightening possibility. If correct, its implications are commensurately enormous. If it *is* language that effectively patterns our left cerebral hemispheres for its own purposes and for many others, if it *is* the dawning of language itself that physically *creates* neural networks and convergence zones, and that somehow transfers language's complex representational processes to every sort of abstract thought, then language is even more profoundly important than we heretofore have known.

And if Curtiss is correct, it seems to me, then Chomsky's "language acquisition device" has to be considered nothing more than the nascent left cerebral hemisphere, the geography of its sulci and gyri largely still unshaped. If she is correct, his "universal grammar" surely, and quite simply, is the physical organization that that hemi-sphere subsequently assumes via the primary catalyst of linguistic input—a process not mysteriously or inexplicably innate but rather one passed to us straightforwardly by evolution.

The essential and overwhelming difference between us and the apes may well be reducible at the end of the day to the fact that, very long ago indeed, our brains became capable of being organized and set into specialization by external symbolic stimuli—by sounds that came to *mean* something—while the pongids' brains similarly did not. And the tragic difference between Genie and you and me may simply be that we were exposed and introduced to language at precisely the time when our brains became dependent on it for their further and much fuller development—language in that context a kind of current that energizes our cortices' abstract circuitry, a jolt, a spark that Genie never received.

There are, of course, critical differences between the adolescent Genie and Ian caught in infancy till four: While Genie appeared to have a normal brain, Ian's brain clearly had been beset by a very complex disorder. Genie was horrifically, unimaginably abused al-most from birth, while Ian had been constantly and attentively cared for and enormously loved. In her cell-like room, Genie was deprived of almost every kind of stimulation; Ian, in contrast, always had been bombarded by external stimuli—movies and books and music and speech and endless opportunities to play—often despite his protesta-tions.

Yet the possibility remained during that long, languorous winter, as Ian quickly began to outgrow his clothes, that, like Genie, he might not *experience* enough of language at this critical period for him ever to become truly proficient at its use. Among the many things his parents couldn't help but consider late into each night—their thoughts and conversations diverging in every direction—was whether, in the midst of its constant turmoil, Ian's precious cortex had been and was being set alight with language.

4
A Deficit of Symbols

Living far from towns or cities, living almost totally inside himself, Ian Drummond nonetheless was known by many people now. It was true that a few longtime friends of his parents and even some family members had distanced themselves so far from him and from them in these recent years that they effectively had left their lives: Ian's anguish and his parents' daunting predicament somehow were more than those people could contend with, and Boyce and Claudia's own sense of isolation and aloneness inevitably had mounted as people with whom they once had been quite close awkwardly but steadily had slipped away. Yet others—new acquaintances as well as intimates with whom they otherwise might have lost touch, strangers, and friends of friends or family—had been drawn to them in contrast. Parents themselves, most of them, they had been captivated by the shuddering realization that something similar might have befallen *their* beloved children; others had been fascinated by Ian's curious, startling uniqueness, and they had seemed to need to know as much about him as they could know; still others were not drawn to him so much as simply propelled by their kindness and compassion.

Doctors at Children's Hospital in Denver who had stayed in occasional contact with Ian and his parents remained intrigued by how much emotion this little boy could express in comparison with other children with autism with whom they had worked—how he seemed, quite atypically, to thrive on his parents' attention and ready comfort. In a similar but less optimistic vein, JFK Center staff members couldn't help but be astounded by the degree to which Ian demanded exactitude and daily sameness; he was far more ritualized than *any* child they ever had encountered. Ian's Denver allergist almost never saw him in person—visits to his office or to any other simply remained too catastrophic—yet he stayed in regular touch by telephone and had become quite engaged by the possibilities that food allergies and Ian's recurrent yeast infections might be exacerbating his autistic symptoms. And it did seem sure by now that the massive daily dosage of vitamin B_6 the allergist had prescribed—as well as the drug Nystatin to help keep the yeast in check—had shown real results: Ian's sleep patterns improved, his chronic teeth grinding abated, his attention span lengthened, and his demeanor seemed decidedly more at ease.

In Colorado Springs, speech and language professionals at the Capron Institute, some of whom had been skeptical initially about how successful Ian's home-based augmentative communication program could be, now were delighted by his bounding progress, and they lauded Boyce and Claudia's work in that regard in wonderfully supportive ways. When the Pike's Peak Board of Cooperative Educational Services—the legal entity that was charged with meeting his special-education needs—began to consider how Ian best would be served when his school career commenced in less than a year, Capron director Pamela Anderson wrote them explaining that Ian's current home program was "an unusual one because most parents, and, in fact, many professionals, are unable to implement the programs that we suggest as we suggest them." But in this case, she continued,

Ian has progressed much more quickly than almost any child does when they first begin using an augmentative system, let alone a child with autism. When we began working with Ian, we were skeptical as to his abilities even to use an augmenta-

tive system. And the point here is that Claudia Martin has
been able to fulfill two different roles for Ian. Of course, she
is his mother, but secondly, she has shown an unbelievable
potential and skill in teaching Ian the skills he needs to be a
successful user of an augmentative communication system. . . . I can count the number of times on one hand where
I have felt that a parent was best to facilitate the learning
process, but in this case, I honestly feel that Claudia Martin
is the best person for the job of educating Ian.

Neither Claudia nor Boyce had ever considered a perpetual
home-schooling program for Ian. Both were convinced, in fact, that
what public school would offer him in the way of socialization and
something akin to the life of a regular kid would be enormously
important. But special-education administrators at the Board of Cooperative Educational Services already had broached the possibility
of Ian attending a day program for severely developmentally disabled
children in Colorado Springs the next year instead of the local kindergarten, and his parents' opposition to that idea had been immediate
and total. They had taken the resounding support of the people at
Capron not only as proof that they, his parents, were the best arbiters
of Ian's needs and progress, but as proof also that he was an impressively capable and increasingly communicative child.

Ian had advanced so quickly, in fact—from simple picture cards
to boards that allowed him to point to his choice among several
options, and on to a kind of undaunted and interactive ease with his
Apple's keyboard—that Claudia and Boyce and the Capron folks
were taking a subsequent step. On a long-term trial, its costs covered
by Capron, Ian now was being introduced to a portable speech
synthesizer that effectively would speak for him when he pressed
one of several picture-coded, pressure-sensitive keys. Called a VOÌS
(the phonetic spelling of *voice*), it was a remarkable little device only
lately brought to the market by a company called Phonic Ear. It was
roughly the size of a notebook computer and it could be programmed
phonetically to say virtually *anything* in flat and uninflected tones
that reminded me, at least, of the way the Jetsons' robots spoke—

statements like "I want a cookie" sounding far less like they came from one of the phone company's canned voices than from some curious human/computer verbal cross.

Its memory capable of storing four "levels" or "vocabularies" of words and phrases comprised of sundry combinations of the forty-five phonemes (speech sounds) that occur in spoken English, the VŎIS was adaptable to various settings and situations by switching from one level to another and by placing a corresponding plastic overlay on its keyboard—Ian utilizing a worktime vocabulary, for instance; one for domestic situations that included meals, bath, and bedtime; a third programmed for activities and play. Although skeptical at first, leery because anything new ran counter to the strict control he constantly strived for, Ian nonetheless was fascinated by a picture board that *spoke* when, with his mother's or father's help, his finger pressed a drawing of a television, a box of French fries, or a cow—and, as had happened with his picture cards, it wasn't long before that poor picture of the cow was smudged from repeated pressings. Ian *liked* initiating speech, it was obvious—his unmistakable, strained sort of grin quickly spreading across his face—and it didn't seem to matter that the voice he now could muster was manufactured by this machine. "I want to watch a movie," he at last could announce in a funny robotic voice; "I feel sick," he finally could explain. "Yes," the VŎIS allowed him to respond, a word that opened up a world for him; "I want to go see the cows," he now could say with this surrogate, and before long, he was saying so every day.

I have written often here about Ian's constant tantrums—the sudden, terrible screaming that would commence as the slightest change occurred—a single, small plastic figurine absent from his bath tonight; a left turn made at the intersection of two county roads in the midst of some simple errand rather than the usual right; one cracker too few on his tray, two chicken nuggets too many. And on those inevitable occasions when videotapes would break, or three feet of snow would fall in the night, making the roads impassable for almost all of the subsequent day, or when, perhaps worst of all, the power would fail and the house would go dark and neither movies nor music would issue from Ian's machines for minutes or for hours, he would writhe in what you had to assume was physical pain, shrieking until his voice was gone, his terror seeming total, screaming for two hours without cease, sometimes for three or four before utterly exhausting himself, before he finally could surrender to a kind of drained and defeated daze.

But in making regular reference to his anguish, to the daily constancy of his screaming, I wonder whether I've also diminished a necessary sense you should have of its dreadful presence, and of the totality it assumed in his life and in the lives of his sister and parents. Am I inadvertently crying a kind of wolf as I describe still one more tantrum? Am I misleading you by making it seem that the screaming eventually became commonplace, as acceptable as Ian's absence of speech? What I hope to convey in counterpoint is that Ian's outbursts of terror—the sudden, screaming certainty that his whole world was coming unstuck, his internal trauma exploding in only one or two terrible episodes on the best of days, enduring hour after hour on the worst—wore him and his family down, day after similar day, in what seemed to be nothing short of barbarous ways as I observed them from some distance.

Moments of peace in their household were as fragile as the butterfly wings that Boyce painstakingly spread open on his mounting boards, as fleeting as the fairies who would descend to Sarah's room, then disappear as someone opened her door. They lived each day, each hour—all four of them—on a precarious and tensioned tightrope, aware always that they would fall from it just as soon as the tiniest detail went awry—Sarah responding to the piercing onset of each new round of screaming by retreating into her room and her fantasies; Claudia and Boyce exchanging quick, unspoken glances as the shrieking commenced in order to determine which one of them in the current context might best be able to settle their son, or simply to decide in half a second whose turn this one was, Claudia's eyes, her whole face, exhibiting a terrible resignation each time, as though she had been trusting that the tantrum twenty minutes ago might have been Ian's very last.

I need too, it seems to me, to try to express as clearly as I can that as Ian began to communicate—first with a few fumbling signs in ASL, then with pictures and with painted cardboard sheets that offered him a smorgasbord of choices, and now with his marvelous speaking VÒÌS—his life and his family members' lives indeed were made much easier, more *normal* in a most important way. Ian was proud that he could communicate, even if only selectively, and he was ever eager to "say" more. Yet this new ability to express himself did not diffuse or end his tantrums in ways all of us long had hoped it might. Their numbers were lessened, it was true—an outburst blessedly avoided at those times when he could explain what he needed, when he quickly could alert his parents to the thing that wildly was going wrong—and fewer tantrums, four instead of five on a given day, three instead of four, were something very substantial, much to be thankful for. But the difficult reality that Ian and everyone else had to face was that even with the voice that the VÒÌS now offered him, he remained a captive of this bizarre and aggregate disorder called autism—nascent communication not enough to quell it, budding language, sadly, far from enough to tear apart its huge hold on his brain.

In a journal article published in 1919, American psychologist Lightner Witmer described a patient he called Don whose behavior seemed strange and singular, and which was difficult to explain in the context of the then-current understanding of disorders of the psyche. His was the first modern mention of what now has become known as autism, that label first applied a quarter-century later by child psychiatrist Leo Kanner, who similarly described eleven patients under his care at the Johns Hopkins Children's Psychiatric Clinic in Baltimore whom he believed suffered from a mental illness characterized by "inborn autistic disturbances of affective contact."

In documenting his patients' syndrome, Kanner noted these children's "inability to relate themselves in the ordinary way to people and situations from the beginning of life," as well as their "ego weakness," which he saw manifest in their unwillingness to look others in the eye, to answer questions or carry on conversations, or, among those who would speak, to use their names or the personal pronoun *I*. Additionally, Kanner's patients exhibited inappropriate and sometimes extreme fear of ordinary objects and situations— dogs, loud noises, flashing lights, darkness, and even an utterly innocuous spot on a wall or rug—and he noted that their faces constantly tended to express "an anxious tenseness, probably because of the uneasy anticipation of possible interference."

Despite his own observation that many of his patients displayed one or more autistic symptoms "from the beginning of life," Kanner postulated in 1944 that the disorder was, in fact, caused postnatally by their parents, in particular by "refrigerator mothers" whose "emotional refrigeration which the children experience . . . cannot [help] but be a highly pathogenic element in the patients' early personality development." It made strong sense to Kanner that the "prolonged affective deprivation" these children had suffered accounted for their bizarre behavior, and the fact that four or five times more cases of autism now were being reported among boys than girls seemed to support his theory: Emotionally frigid women who adequately could relate to their daughters nonetheless tended to be cold, aloof, and uncaring in relation to their sons.

Yet by the early 1950s, Kanner himself was puzzled by some inconsistencies: Why did children with autism almost always have normal brothers and sisters if parenting styles were the disorder's unhappy genesis? And why did it also affect some children whose mothers clearly were warm, loving, and caring? Noting that about ten percent of parents of children with autism did not fit the frigid stereotype, Kanner publicly wondered whether a biological abnormality might, in fact, play a role in the disorder's etiology. But by now other psychologists and psychiatrists were pointing fingers at parents as well, and some of them, like Cornell University Medical College psychiatrist J. Louise Despert, were willing even to attack them:

The fact that parents can be sick emotionally without being aware of it and can have their pathological symptoms brought to light in the setting of parenthood with such tragic effects on the child is shocking and challenging . . . the negative mother does not truly want her child. She has little capacity to devote herself to him, and this fact comes to light very clearly in the way she handles the infant. . . . It seems to me that the mother of the child who develops autistic behavior is an extreme case of this negative woman, and unfortunately the infant is the first to sense her unconscious hostility.

Despite Kanner's growing skepticism about whether parents unwittingly inflicted autism on their children, and notwithstanding the thorough refutation of that notion in the 1964 book *Infantile Autism* by Bernard Rimland, a San Diego psychologist who worked for the United States Navy and who was the father of a son with autism, the focus on psychological trauma as autism's ultimate catalyst continued into the 1970s. Bruno Bettelheim, a University of Chicago psychologist and author of *The Empty Fortress*, a widely reviewed and strangely influential assessment of autism that was published in 1967, contended that this disorder, like all childhood psychoses, should be examined with the understanding that "the patient is always right," and by extension therefore, his or her parents were always wrong. As far as Bettelheim was concerned, a child with autism behaved bizarrely and unacceptably in order to seek revenge on inattentive, uncaring parents. If a boy with autism incessantly beat a chair with a stick, he explained, "he's symbolically punishing his mother for rejecting him."

Nobel laureate Nikolaas Tinbergen, a professor of animal behavior at Oxford, similarly used his 1973 Prize Lecture—a rather unlikely platform—to propound his conviction that autism was "an anxiety neurosis which prevents or retards normal affiliation and subsequent socialization." It was *not*, he bristled, due to "genetic abnormalities or to gross brain damage, but to early environmental influences. The majority of autistics, as well as their parents, seem to be genuine victims of environmental stress."

Three decades after Kanner's seminal article had appeared, eminent psychiatrists and psychologists on two continents still could not surrender the notion that if these children behaved abnormally, then surely their parents were to blame. And there was no small irony in the fact that it was Rimland, the parent of a son with autism, who finally and forcefully challenged that view and opened the door to investigations into a neurological basis for the disorder's onset. Referring to those who implicitly had accused him and others like him of causing their children's trauma, Rimland wrote:

> The damage and torment [they have] wrought upon parents whose lives and hopes have already been shattered by their child's illness is not easy to imagine nor pleasant to contemplate. To add a heavy burden of shame and guilt to the distress of people whose hopes, social life, finances, well-being, and feelings of worth have been all but destroyed seems heartless and inconsiderate in the extreme.

From my vantage in the 1990s, and knowing one boy with autism as I do, it is frankly difficult for me to fathom how practitioners of psychiatry and clinical psychology could have so thoroughly misunderstood this disorder for so long. What on earth could have kept them blind, decade after decade, to autism's many *physical* manifestations, other than a kind of addled adherence to the limited vision of Sigmund Freud? Why did parents seem to them to be likelier culprits than did damaged brains? I can as readily imagine these men and women concluding that grand mal seizures were psychogenic— patients slipping into unconscious, convulsive states because of their inabilities to confront reality, or some such prattled explanation. Yet despite their collective wrongheadedness, the psychological establishment's claims finally were refuted by Rimland and then by many more researchers committed to the tools of science; and seizure disorders, in fact, actually played an important role in at last bringing their attention to bear on the brain.

What had been waiting in vain for observation since Kanner described his first eleven patients was that children with autism tended to suffer as well from several other disorders—principal among them epilepsy, mental retardation, cerebral palsy, and peripheral nerve deficits. Those disorders clearly were caused by brain abnormalities rather than cold or cruel parents, and the links between them finally began to be investigated. Separate studies soon indicated that half to three-quarters of children with autism were mentally retarded, although that designation tended to be as fuzzily defined as autism itself, and although accurate assessments were difficult to make with children who didn't speak. More concretely, however, a 1963 Yale Medical School study determined that among a group of fifty children with autism, twenty-one suffered from some type of epilepsy—ranging from classic convulsive attacks to the strange staring spells that are known as "absence seizures." And equally intriguing, children with autism also tended to suffer from a highly disproportionate number of movement disorders—paralyses, asymmetrical muscle weaknesses, spasticity, muscular dystrophy, or cerebral palsy appearing often among their numbers, a more benign kind of reluctance to use hands and arms or a generalized sort of physical awkwardness also often seen. Kanner himself had noted that "several of the children were somewhat clumsy in gait and gross motor performances," but by the middle 1970s, new studies had shown quite clearly that among children with autism, too much or too little muscle tone was very commonplace. Those findings in turn led to subsequent investigations of whether the odd alienation that was a hallmark of so many people with autism—and which for so long had seemed to be psychological—might also, in fact, be rooted in neurological abnormalities.

Neurologists and neuroscientists who had taken an interest in autism were well aware by the 1970s that children affected by the disorder often acted as though they were deaf, that they tended to avoid looking directly at objects or other people, that their faces seldom showed emotion, and, of course, that most of them were mute or had significant difficulty speaking. Given their professional focus on the observable, palpable brain and nervous system rather than this far less substantive thing called the psyche, it wasn't surprising therefore that instead of finding some traumatic psychological disturbance as the nexus of these several symptoms, they noted what seemed to be the symptoms' clear and common *neurological* link—

the twelve pairs of cranial nerves that control all input to the brain
from the body's sensory organs.

Identified, named, and numbered nearly two thousand years ago
by the Greek physician Galen, the cranial nerves are comprised of
three pairs of nerves that separately transmit sensory information
from the nose, ears, and tongue; four pairs that control input from
and movement of the eyes; two pairs that link the brain with facial
sensation and expression; the paired accessory nerve that facilitates
movement of the neck and shoulders; the vagus nerve, which regulates the seemingly automatic actions of the heart, lungs, stomach,
kidneys, and intestines; as well as the glossopharyngeal nerve, which
transmits taste sensations to the brain and controls the movement
of the throat and its several speech organs. It was a fascinating
possibility. Could autism, at least in part, be accounted for by some
mysterious malfunction of multiple cranial nerves? The answer, of
course, seemed obvious. And it obviously was yes.

If that correlation seems less than stunningly conspicuous, however, let me remind you of Ian Drummond—a boy whose symptoms
began with something much like deafness, and who to this day seems
literally to be attacked by loud and piercing noises. Let me remind
you too that Ian loved to smell everything he encountered and to
lick much of what he paid attention to, similarly pressing his cheeks
against big boulders as well as the bark of trees, his figurines as well
as his food. Ian seldom seemed to look directly at anything, but his
peripheral vision was acutely focused and quite sensitive; and surely
his flapping of book pages and running past fixed objects, his head
cocked at a curious angle, provided him with particular visual pleasures. His infrequent smile seemed strained, somehow forced, as I
have said, and otherwise he gave face to few expressions; he slept
poorly when he slept at all, and he severely ground his teeth whether
sleeping or awake. Ian had gone silent as his several symptoms
commenced, of course—his first word disappearing, even his babbling suddenly stopping before slowly, haltingly returning. Like
many people with autism, he suffered regular stomachaches and
diarrhea, and some of his senses—hearing, smelling too it seemed—
were heightened rather than diminished. So much of who this boy

was and how he behaved surely had to be tied inextricably to the functions of his cranial nerves, and once I had noted that, a dense layer of mystery at last began to fade for me—Ian's singular actions and many unusual demands finally assuming some context, explainable now purely in pathological terms, a dozen or more of his critical nerve pathways somehow seriously impeded.

But wasn't autism *more* than a sensory disorder? If only damaged cranial nerves were responsible for Ian's and others' deficits, how could their need for exacting ritual be explained? And what might any of us make of Ian's overwhelming need for the structure and the sense he took from stories? Did he lack spoken language solely because his glossopharyngeal nerves didn't serve him as they should, or was there something more?

The two optic nerves, which transmit neural signals to the brain when images appear on the retina at the back of the eye, are actual extensions of the brain itself—tied to forebrain structures located beneath the large and wrinkled gray cerebrum. The olfactory nerves, true nerves, similarly connect the mucous membranes high in each nostril to two forebrain "olfactory lobes," but the ten remaining pairs of cranial nerves terminate in the brain stem. Very old in evolutionary terms, the brain's root and its core, the brain stem juts up from the spinal cord at the base of the skull and is positioned below and behind the cerebrum, where it serves as a sort of relay station both for sensory signals traveling to the cerebrum and for motor signals flowing out from the cerebrum to the body's peripheral nerves and muscles. The brain stem too acts as an initiator of many "higher cortical functions"; it separately controls consciousness and regulates essential life processes. And it *may*, in fact, be within the adjacent cerebellum, its functions intimately linked with the brain stem, that the cranial nerves are impeded or somehow otherwise interfered with in people who have autism.

In two separate 1980s studies, researchers at Massachusetts General Hospital in Boston and the University of California at Los Angeles found, at autopsy, significant atrophy in the cerebella of nonretarded adults who had suffered from autism, noting in particular that the patients' cerebella contained far fewer Purkinje cells than are present in normal adults. Bundles of long-axoned, many-branched neurons (nerve cells) that are presumed to release a neurochemical that depresses the too-frequent firing of other neurons, Purkinje cells have been assumed for some time to play a major role in the smooth and orderly processing of sensory information. But the autopsy studies also revealed more intriguing information: according to Massachusetts General neurologist Margaret Bauman, coauthor of one of the studies, neurons in normal brains begin to push away from each other soon after birth as their cell bodies sprout more and longer branches, and glial (glue) cells that support and nourish the neurons begin to proliferate in the spaces between them. In the autistic brains Bauman examined, however, this maturing process had been sharply arrested. And a "clear zone" between cell layers in the entorhinal cortex, which normally fills with glial cells by about fifteen months of age, remained unfilled into one patient's adulthood. "We're very surprised at how devastated the cerebellum is in the two autistic brains we've studied," Bauman commented, "but a heck of a lot more than Purkinje cells are involved," and she noted her suspicion that damage to the cerebellum probably occurred prior to birth.

Brain stem and cerebellar studies of living patients with autism conducted with magnetic resonance imaging (MRI) by radiologist Eric Courchesne at San Diego's Children's Hospital Research Center in 1987 and 1988—and which found corresponding losses of Purkinje cells among the eighteen subjects studied—similarly pointed to the possibility of prenatal cerebellar damage. But, "our data suggests that it is also possible that, in some cases, the abnormality may begin somewhere in the first or second year of life," Courchesne said in an interview following the publication of his findings in the *New England Journal of Medicine*. "The cerebella of these autistic people are much smaller than normal. That is a fact. . . . But the real question is, 'How many people or what proportion of the autistic population show these phenomena?' "

Could smaller cerebella, containing too few critical Purkinje cells and therefore too little of some fundamental neurochemical, actually be the cause of the apparent cranial nerve abnormalities in Ian and others with autism? Or was autism's etiology likely far more complex than that, the result, perhaps, of damage to a variety of structures throughout the brain and nervous system? And might the disorder ultimately include as culprits as well damage to language and thinking centers and their convergence zones in the cerebral cortex?

"At this point, we don't know if we have the dog or tail," explained Edward Ritvo, head of UCLA's brain stem study, his perspective coincident with those of most neuroscientists. Ritvo earlier had labeled those "decades of psychotoxic theorizing [about the cause of autism] . . . a black mark in the history of medicine," and now in the late 1980s, in contrast, he was quite willing to confess that he and his colleagues still truly knew little more.

I got to know one neurologist very well in the 1980s because I had gone to watch him work. And although this neurologist's frantic and stress-charged medical life was utterly new to me as I began to trail a step or two behind him, racing through his days, I actually had known him for decades by then as my dearest friend. The book that was spawned by my experience is *Matters Gray and White*, and it was written during the reach of time when Ian's symptoms first flared into an all-consuming crisis, when the demands of Boyce's work and his family were pulling him in frustrating and discordant directions, when Claudia and I actually were estranged for some months—her future, her family's future, seeming destroyed by what they had begun to face, her anger venting like steam at times when she was challenged.

Certain of the value of *my* perspective, I had tried to convince Claudia that despite the constant demands imposed by Ian, and, of course, because of them, she should seek counseling for herself. And callously, I had tried to tell her that her circumstances were not so bad. Accompanying my friend the neurologist on his rounds, lately I had seen people in desperate predicaments, I wanted to explain to her—young people whose peripheral nerves had gone haywire, their arms and legs and even their eyes abandoning them because of an autoimmune disease, a man in middle age who remained conscious following a brain stem stroke yet who was unable to move *anything* except his eyes—and I had tried to assure her that, by comparison, Ian's future might be very bright. That I could presume to try to make those comparisons now seems shamefully unfeeling to me, but nonetheless I had tried to do so, and in response, Claudia had dismissed me, much as she had done with others who simply didn't understand.

I didn't understand many things as I began to observe the physician I call John Ferrier in the book, whose real, curiously bicultural name is Patrick Sternberg, and who then practiced neurology in Boulder, Colorado. I didn't know, for instance, how nascent and still only spottily successful therapeutic medicine actually is; I didn't appreciate the awesome complexity and artistry of the brain's hundred billion cells, or the number of ways in which those cells and their connective circuitry can go awry. I didn't understand that disease can ennoble people as readily as it can cripple their lives, and neither did I know much at all about the miraculous way in which life's fragility lends it much of its meaning.

During the year and some months I spent sitting adjacent to Patrick's desk and standing at his flank near patients' hospital beds, I had watched him examine and treat children with mild forms of epilepsy they likely would grow out of, as well as elderly people whose lives had been ended well before the end of their days by the cruel atrophy of Alzheimer's disease, and for whom he could do nothing. I had observed his fine-tuning kind of management of the medications of patients with Parkinson's disease, Tourette's syndrome, and multiple sclerosis, with migraine headaches and other kinds of chronic pain; I had been present as Patrick referred for surgery patients with benign or mushrooming malignant tumors, as well as others with ominous occluded arteries, and I'd watched with fascination as he struggled to help aphasic patients regain the speech that strokes and viruses had taken from them.

There had been the sweet, round-faced college student from Japan whom I called Yoshi, who had suffered an arterial thrombosis while swimming—portions of his left temporal lobe disastrously deprived of blood and its oxygen, leaving him in the days following the

accident with no receptive understanding of English *or* Japanese,
unable to speak either language, the right side of his body similarly
stilled. There had been the truly tragic patient whose pseudonym
was Salvador Maldonado, a man in his early fifties who had suffered
a massive brain stem stroke and who, as I've mentioned, could
move only his eyes—a man hauntingly, frighteningly, trapped by his
brain's massive destruction, conscious enough for months by the
time I met him that he could move his eyes up or down in yes-no
responses to questions, conscious enough too, you had to presume,
that he understood his awful dilemma, able to hear and comprehend
what was said to him but never again able to speak. And I vividly
recall the drama student I called James, whose brain suddenly had
been infected one winter day by the herpes virus, a potentially
catastrophic viral culprit that curiously tends to lodge in the cerebrum's frontal and temporal lobes when it steals its way into the
brain, death resulting almost certainly absent medication, permanent language loss very likely unless the medication is administered
quite quickly:

> I had never seen the anxiety in Ferrier, the fear that he might
> be as helpless as his patient was, as I saw on the day that
> James's brain became infected, his right side and his speech
> slipping away from him in the midst of his fevered struggle.
> Some of Ferrier's anguish certainly had to do with the ominous
> possibility that James's virus quickly would kill him, but the
> death of a patient was not new, and Ferrier had even remarked
> during a black moment in the middle of that long afternoon
> that a sudden death from encephalitis would not be such a bad
> way to go. Instead, I am sure that it was the possibility that
> James would recover from his virus with only part of a brain,
> a part that could not speak, that so vividly frightened Ferrier.
> In many ways, it is speaking and being spoken to that most
> directly define who we are and how we relate to others around
> us. The Latin root of the verb "to converse"—*conversari*—
> means to live with, to keep company with; we converse in
> order to live with those we encounter. Without speech, each

of us would be isolated, terribly alone—and we are not an animal who chooses to live in isolation.

Ian as well as James was on my mind as I wrote those words, I remember—both of them young men with much ahead of them. One, at only nineteen, was in desperate danger of losing his speech, even his comprehension of language; the other was a boy of four who might never claim them. But James fully recovered: with the quick and critical help of an antiviral drug called acyclovir, his encephalitic drama had had a happy ending. Ian's condition, on the other hand, likely would remain static for the long term, and his brain probably would not—could not—be set entirely right by any drug. Yet I wasn't troubled by questions of fairness or the absence of some celestial justice as I considered and compared them; I had seen enough of disease and its miseries by then to know that no one is rewarded by robust health and no one is punished with the onset of a racking sickness, that trouble visits one of us instead of another in ways that aren't mysterious but, merely, plainly random.

As I watched Patrick at work for those many fascinating months, observing his sudden, flaring self-doubt as well as a subsequent and commensurate resolve in the face of small and large emergencies, I realized that this glimpse of mine into neurological medicine not only was wonderfully fortunate but also was something singular. I was not the anxious patient in gown and stocking feet whose brain now was suspect, and neither was I the physician who was charged with *doing* something efficacious. I simply, raptly watched and listened, awkwardly at those moments when I couldn't be sure whether I really ought to be so privy to someone's sad or brutal physical secrets, but always in a kind of awe at what it meant for a person to confess with clear fright in his or her voice that something was much amiss, at what it meant as well for another person to pledge to try to help.

And there was something similar, I knew, in my relationship with Ian and his family. I cared about my sister and those closest to her, of course, and I thought I knew myself well enough to understand that my concern and love for Ian was magnified by his disability. My wife, Karen Holmgren, and I did not have children, didn't long for them, and at those times when I considered the question, I couldn't help but wonder how *I* would have responded as a parent to Ian's incessant demands or to the constancy of his screaming. Yet that was an issue I would not have to resolve. From an uncle's easy vantage point, Ian was a boy who captivated my intellect and who stirred my too-latent emotions, a nephew I learned from as well as loved, but I knew too with a kind of recurrent guilt that I never would share my sister's parental circumstances, her anguish or her responsibility, and there would always be those several ineffable things that I could not know and would not feel as entirely as she would.

Claudia read *Matters Gray and White* almost immediately after the copy I sent her arrived at the research station in January 1987, the book's publication coinciding with our grandmother's death. We had been awkwardly out of touch, Claudia and I, since the previous spring, but her telephone call was very welcome and our estrangement seemed to wash readily away as we discussed Dandy's valiant final days and the radiance of her life, and although we never directly discussed those words and issues that had set us at odds, we nonetheless attended to them. We talked at length about the book and her impressions of it, about Patrick and the brave patients I had been privileged to meet, and although our words were tangential with regard to those clumsier subjects, it seemed that they nonetheless met their mark.

As neuroscientists began to delve deeper into the organic causes of autism late in this century, they hoped to discover something substantive with regard to the disorder's drastic impairment of language. Half of all people with autism remain mute throughout their lives, and virtually all of the other fifty percent are severely language deprived—their vocabularies never larger than those of normal three-year-olds in many cases; their speech remaining primitive and echolalic, absent the creativity lent by syntax, many forever incapable of correctly using words like *yes*, or *I*, or their given names.

There seemed to be several possibilities that might explain autis-

tic aphasia: The speech organs themselves might be minutely damaged, although they are readily observable and tend to appear
entirely normal in children and adults with autism. The paired glossopharyngeal nerve that innervates the larynx, tongue, and vocal
cords, and the muscles surrounding them—the electrical impulses
it carries causing them to move in concert—might well be impaired.
Or the way station that is the brain stem, where the glossopharyngeal
nerve terminates, where its sensory information is delivered and its
motor impulses are conversely sent their way, might also be
flawed—and those several studies by now had shown dramatic abnormalities indeed in the brain stems of adults with autism. But was
that likely the entire picture? Was the etiology of autism's language
malfunction likely limited to the brain stem and a single pair of
cranial nerves?

Neurologist Margaret Bauman, for one, was convinced by the
1980s that much more was involved, and some of her investigative
focus now had widened to include the adjacent, wishbone-shaped
limbic system, responsible in part for emotion and memory functions. Psychologist Bernard Rimland, who back in 1967 had established the Institute for Child Behavior Research to encourage
scientific investigation into autism's causes, also was intrigued by
whether memory impairment, rooted in damage to the limbic system, might play a significant role in the inability of people with
autism to organize and pattern language, as well as other abstract,
cognitive functions that take place in the cerebral cortex. But others
had strong suspicions now—and some had had them for some time—
that much of the problem might lie in the cerebrum itself, and might
result very directly in those same kinds of patterning, sequence-
creating, and symbol-making deficits.

With what has to be considered an impressive prescience, psychiatrist Leon Eisenberg, a colleague of Kanner's, noted as early as
1956, during autism's otherwise dark "refrigerator" days, that "severely autistic children exhibit a preoccupation with the sensory
impressions stemming from the world about them, but seem unable
to organize perceptions into functional patterns." Fifteen years later,
Michael Rutter, a child psychiatrist at London's Institute of Psychia-

try, spoke less of sensory "preoccupation" than sensory impairment, but he too recognized the possibility that a higher cortical problem might well severely limit the ability to make sense of symbols, therefore robbing language of its raw materials. "A central deficit in processing of symbolic or sequence information is likely to prove the basic defect . . . in infantile autism," Rutter concluded in a paper published in 1971. And in recent years, Harris L. Coulter, a medical historian who has written extensively on encephalitic reactions to childhood vaccination, has described the central autistic deficit as an inability to "create and manipulate the *symbols* which normal people use to represent and act upon external reality . . . ," stranding children with autism in a world without abstraction, leaving them even "unable to 'play,' since play, like speech, is a largely symbolic activity."

But *how* might symbol manipulation be impaired in the cerebral cortex? How can we account for the tendencies of people with autism toward prodigious mathematical and musical skills, which are exclusively abstract and symbolic enterprises? If Ian lacks language because he cannot make sense of symbols, then is he so attached to the figurines of characters in his movies because he believes they actually *are* those characters? How did he acquire those signs, those few symbols in ASL? And how could he have made the necessarily symbolic connection between a picture on a board and his own need or desire? How could Ian now condone and clearly appreciate the words his VÖIS could say?

One possible answer to those questions, an answer for which only I can be held accountable, relates to linguist Susan Curtiss's impression that "normal cerebral organization may depend on language development occurring at the appropriate time," and it's rooted as well in my ready acceptance of her subsequent contention: "When [language] develops, it determines what else the language hemisphere will be specialized for. In its absence, it prevents the language hemisphere from specializing for any higher cortical functions." Neuroscientists have known for some time that one of the brain stem's several functions is to initiate neural activity—thinking, remembering, the understanding or speaking of a word—in the cerebral cortex, to set those processes in motion. Isn't it analogously possible that during childhood's critical language-acquisition period, it is the ancient and primitive brain stem that stutters to life with sensory input from the ears' acoustic nerves—with the sounds of speech, in other words—the brain stem in turn setting in nearly magical motion the process by which the left cerebral hemisphere begins to make sense of those sounds, those neural signals ultimately organizing the left hemisphere in ways that allow it to replicate them as speech, the result the dazzlingly complex patterns of neural circuitry that give shape to language's full florescence?

If that scenario seems plausible—and I think perhaps it does—then isn't it equally credible that brain stem impairment in a child with autism makes it difficult if not impossible to transform the sounds of human speech into cortical linguistic symbols? Isn't it possible that early damage to the brain stem renders it unable to relay to the left hemisphere those catalytic electrical impulses that at last result in language?

Soon after Leo Kanner's landmark introduction of autism into the medical literature in 1943, he and other psychiatrists and psychologists began to scour archival case histories to try to determine whether, in fact, the disorder had existed undetected or misdiagnosed till then, yet they could find only a handful of cases of young patients whose symptoms had seemed similarly "autistic." By 1958, however, Kanner's own files included nearly 150 cases, and by the early 1960s, pediatricians, child psychologists, and child psychiatrists around the country were reporting a comparative explosion of cases. "Childhood autism had been a rare entity in the pediatric clinic before 1964," wrote New York pediatricians Mary and Campbell Goodwin. "We had seen six autistic children during the preceding twelve years. They had prepared us for complexities in management and uncertain prognosis. They had not prepared us for the events that followed, as sixty-five children came, in turn, to the center."

In an attempt to understand that surge, the investigative tools of epidemiologists began to be applied to the question, and for compelling reasons: One of the first possibilities that crossed anyone's mind was whether an infectious agent, heretofore rare, was becoming ubiquitous, or whether some change in the general environment might loom as a still-undetected culprit. Statistically, at least, there seemed to be a few certainties in the beginning: the disorder affected far more boys than girls; the kids caught in its conundrum of behaviors tended to live in cities or suburbs; they came from well-educated families; and quite curiously, they seemed, as a group, to be unusually good-looking.

Although Kanner never pushed the notion that parents in general might have grown strangely cold and uncaring in the years after the war, he did openly wonder whether parents who came from the professional class might be more aloof or less attached to their children than were their contemporaries whose lives were not as driven by their work. And there was an intriguing medical connection in those earliest cases: of Kanner's initial hundred patients with autism, eleven parents were physicians, three were nurses, two were psychologists, one was a physiotherapist, three were Ph.D.s in the sciences, and one was a laboratory technician. Additionally, many parents who did not work in the medical field themselves reported family members and friends who did. In taking histories of those same hundred children, Kanner found that seventy-four of the fathers and forty-nine of the mothers had graduated from college—extremely high percentages in the 1930s and 1940s.

No one knew quite what to make of these several findings early on, and neither could anyone explain why they did not remain consistent as reported cases of autism multiplied exponentially in the ensuing decades. The four-to-one boy-to-girl ratio remained unchanged, and health-care providers continued to note handsome facial features in many children with autism, but those earlier familial findings had no bearing by the 1970s: data showed that autism now was distributed evenly across the population—geographically, ethnically, socioeconomically, the disorder affecting fifteen of every ten thousand children, more than forty-five hundred children each year, numbers that remain unchanged today. Around the world, autism currently is encountered far more often in developed than undeveloped countries, but in Japan and the United Kingdom, to look at two modern societies, the disorder's incidence is only about five in every ten thousand births—lower than that of the United States yet statistically comparable.

Although Kanner initially had written that the disorder, which might well have become known as "Kanner's syndrome," differed "markedly and uniquely from anything reported so far," there were, in fact, many people born prior to 1940 who suffered similar symptoms: they were children and adults, many of whom now lived in asylums, who had been diagnosed as suffering from "post-encephalitic syndrome," attributable to permanent neurological damage caused by fever-induced swelling in the brain during early childhood and characterized by a wide variety of sensory and motor deficits, retardation, and strange, solitary, antisocial behaviors. Perhaps the most insidious of several causes of early childhood encephalitis were common infectious diseases such as mumps, measles, chicken pox, and pertussis (whooping cough), the latter, in particular, capable of inducing catastrophic fevers. In describing in 1942 the massive disabilities pertussis-caused brain damage could induce, Columbia University neurologist Josephine B. Neal noted the "very crippling residuals with motor as well as personality handicaps [caused by] small hemorrhages in the brain [as well as by] inflammatory processes. . . . It is, therefore, possible to get almost every possible motor, intellectual, epileptoid, and personality deviation and combinations of them." Subsequently, a major Swedish study of the effects of whooping cough concluded that "pertussis may be associated with the most varying kinds of cerebral complications and that they do not appear to be confined to any particular region but may be cortical, subcortical, or peripheral."

Although vaccines to protect children against measles, rubella, and mumps weren't formulated and made available until the 1960s, the first vaccine against pertussis was produced as early as 1925. A "whole cell" vaccine, one made from the same bacterium that causes whooping cough—a bug widely agreed to be among the most virulent that humans commonly encounter in terms of its ability to wreak widespread havoc—the vaccine wasn't widely available until early in World War II, when federal health officials and growing numbers within the general medical community began to press for its use. Pertussis was a horrific disease, and parents who were cognizant of that, and who knew that now a new vaccine could protect against it, eagerly brought their infant children to be immunized, a series of whole-cell inoculations beginning as early as age two months.

There were reports of adverse reactions to the vaccine, ranging from deep sleeps to high fevers, from long periods of high-pitched screaming to difficulty breathing and tonic-clonic convulsions, but most people in the medical community were convinced that those side effects were temporary and that they were far outweighed by the risk of contracting pertussis itself. By 1960 or shortly thereafter, in fact, the pertussis vaccine had been combined with vaccines against diphtheria and tetanus, and the so-called DPT vaccine was legally required in most states before children could enter elementary school.

What seems astonishing in retrospect—and what seems utterly unconscionable if you are a parent like Claudia or Boyce who dutifully made certain that your child was inoculated against bacterial harm—is that despite decades of mounting data on severe reactions to pertussis and DPT vaccinations, despite the coincident and crescendoing incidence of "mild" neurological disorders such as dyslexia, hyperactivity, and learning disability (among more than seventy different syndromes commonly grouped together as "minimal brain dysfunction") and a similar explosion in the far more damaging but equally multifarious disorder called autism, no one had noted openly, publicly, *cautiously*, the possible correlation between them until 1985—the same year that Ian received his final DPT inoculation.

It is true that by the mid-1980s, Connaught Laboratories, one of several makers of the DPT vaccine, included in the small print of its package insert a warning of possible side effects that ranged from rashes and respiratory difficulties to high fevers and prolonged high-pitched screaming. Additionally, the insert noted, "more severe neurological complications, such as a prolonged convulsion or an encephalopathy, occasionally fatal, have been reported. . . . Rarely, an anaphylactic reaction (i.e., hives, swelling of the mouth, difficulty breathing, hypotension, or shock) has been reported. . . . Sudden infant death syndrome (SIDS) has occurred in infants following administration of DPT."

Yet it fell to Harris Coulter, director of the Center for Empirical Medicine in Washington, D.C., and a historian whose many books have chronicled the evolution of medical orthodoxy in the United States, to make the initial charge—*forty years* after Josephine Neal's initial inquiry into the tragic disabilities that pertussis-caused brain damage could induce—that much of autism was caused by the administration in very early childhood of the whole-cell pertussis vaccine. In two recent books (*DPT: A Shot in the Dark*, coauthored with Barbara Fisher, founder of the organization Dissatisfied Parents Together, published by Harcourt Brace Jovanovich in 1985; and *Vaccination, Social Violence, and Criminality*, published in 1990 by North Atlantic Books), Coulter has amassed weighty and overwhelming if circumstantial evidence against the pertussis vaccine and has called for studies to test its causal link to encephalitis-induced autism, minimal brain damage, and the death by apnea (breathing cessation) that is commonly called SIDS. Shunned by drug companies and large segments of the medical community as alarmist and blatantly antipharmaceutical in his bias, Coulter nonetheless has persuasively captured the attention of autism specialists such as Bernard Rimland, and in addition to raising a critical kind of alert to unwitting parents, he has laid many latent puzzlements to rest.

At last, of course, there is a clear explanation for the initial prevalence of autism among the children of well-educated parents, many of whom had heard from colleagues or friends in medical circles the great good news that a vaccine now could guard against pertussis; and there is also an explanation for autism's subsequent expansion into the general population as vaccination programs grew widespread, then became mandatory. It seems possible as well that boys contract the disorder far more often than girls because they tend to be slower developmentally, their brains therefore more vulnerable at ages when the inoculations normally commence; and the lesser rates of autism's incidence in nations such as Japan and the United Kingdom similarly might be explained by the fact that vaccination series in those countries normally are not initiated until children approach two years of age (compared with two months in the United States), and in England pertussis vaccination, although common, remains entirely elective. And as the link between the pertussis vaccine and autism begins to grow apparent, is it too farfetched to wonder whether the curious handsomeness that children with autism tend to evidence can be explained, in part at least, by minor malfunctions of the facial nerves, causing facial muscles to be chronically flexed in ways we tend to find appealing?

In its most basic presentation, Coulter's argument is comprised of three related statements of fact: The pertussis bacterium is known to cause swelling in the brain, which often results in indiscriminate, diffuse, and permanent damage; vaccinations against many types of bacteria are known to cause reactive encephalitic swelling; and until early 1992, when a putatively safer half-cell vaccine was introduced, the pertussis vaccine in the United States had been composed of the whole cell of the bacterium that causes pertussis itself. It isn't an incautious leap, therefore—buttressed with the mountain of epidemiological data Coulter has amassed—to conclude that for fifty years the pertussis vaccine has been the cause of much brain distress and permanent dysfunction. Neither a rabble-rouser nor someone fearfully decrying demon medicine, Coulter convinces people like me that while "the vaccination program is, of course, not responsible for every instance of [these] disabilities and social woes, it nonetheless makes a substantial contribution to them. . . . [And] it is the only possible cause of a mass epidemic of clinical and sub-clinical encephalitis," one he sees clearly manifest in SIDS and in myriad kinds of developmental delays and learning disabilities, as well as in the sensory, symbolic, and linguistic deficit called autism.

—

Boyce breathlessly had told the sheriff's department's radio dispatcher that "a retarded boy" was missing because the word *autism* was one with which few people were familiar.

Claudia and Sarah both were at school that early December morning, and Ian and Boyce had gone for their ritual morning walk. An inch of new snow covered the ground that until last night had been hard and bare; Ian was bundled in his parka and snow boots, and he had spent nearly half an hour in obvious delight running close beside a barbed-wire fence that separated two pastures. When that daily enterprise was done—an activity he depended on as much as seeing the cows or watching his several movies—he willingly led Boyce back to the house. Then, as also was his habit, he ran for a bit along the outside perimeter of the fence that surrounded their home. While he did so, and as his father waited and watched him, Pete Glasser, the foreman of the large ranch on which they lived, drove up to fetch the cake pan that his wife, Donna, had dropped off— complete with cake—some days before. The two men chatted for a moment, then Boyce went inside the house to retrieve the pan, noting Ian as he walked back out. But in the few seconds that ensued—time enough only for Pete to start his truck and drive away—Ian vanished, disappearing somewhere among the fat-trunked trees.

It was not uncommon for Ian momentarily to slip out of his parents' fields of vision: he ran with great relish and always with his own unspoken agenda, and walking with him was akin to trailing a curious pup—or a normally frantic four-year-old, for that matter. Yet every other time that Ian suddenly was out of sight, Claudia's and Boyce's instincts had led them to him in only seconds. But on this winter day, Ian had *not* gone back to the barbed-wire fence; he had not gone into the lab building or the dining hall or any of the station's other buildings; he hadn't gone into the house, nor was he in the car, and Boyce's worry quickly mounted as he searched in widening circles through the trees. Ian's small bootprints in the snow might have offered Boyce some assistance, allowing him simply to track his son, but by then the two of them already had walked in a wide area, and the myriad tracks that Boyce now surveyed were too many and too random to offer clues.

There had been enough traffic on the nearby county road, its snow packed hard, that footprints would have been similarly difficult to discern if Ian had headed down the road, but that nonetheless seemed to be the most likely possibility now, and, puffing hard for breath, Boyce ran in the direction he guessed Ian would have wanted to go, cognizant as he went that if Ian had done what *he* was doing, he readily could have run headlong into a car rounding one of a succession of blind curves. Thirty minutes into his chase, still without a sign of his son, Boyce knew he needed help, and although he felt sure somehow that he was heading in Ian's general direction and was tempted to run on, hoping he'd encounter him around just one more turn, he made himself stop and return, racing, to the house.

The sheriff's dispatcher wanted a description of the boy, wanted to know how long he'd been missing, and when Boyce pinpointed their location for her, she told him that by chance an officer in a four-wheel-drive vehicle was only a few miles away, and said she would notify others as well. Boyce explained that the boy couldn't speak, and that he might seem terrified of anyone who approached him, and then, this time in his pickup, he headed back down the county road, scouring its shoulders for footprints as he drove.

At last, farther down the road than he had run the first time, Boyce discovered what appeared to be prints veering away from the road toward a fence that ran parallel to it, and he stopped the truck to take a closer look at them. But *if* they were Ian's tracks—and the snow had begun to melt enough by now so that he couldn't be sure they were—they seemed only to lead back to the road, and Boyce was about to continue in the truck as a sheriff's vehicle rounded the corner and approached him. The officer had seen nothing yet, he said, so he and Boyce made the quick agreement to drive the road in opposite directions, Boyce increasingly panicked as he drove— afraid he might not find Ian around the next bend, afraid he *would* be there, his run halted by some unsuspecting car. But Boyce didn't know what to assume as very soon the sheriff's vehicle raced up

behind him, lights flashing to catch his attention—perhaps with Ian
in tow, perhaps with some terrible news. What the officer now knew,
instead of either of those two polar possibilities, was that a small,
blond boy had been dropped off minutes ago at the nearby country
store at Evergreen Station by a middle-aged woman who had continued on her way. The boy was crying, the officer knew, but the report
he'd received on his radio had said he otherwise seemed fine.

Boyce still can feel the fright, the numbing fear that swept over
him that morning, when he infrequently recounts this story, and he
remembers too a kind of sudden and profoundly emotional melting
that accompanied the officer's good news. The two men drove to
Evergreen Station together and found Ian inside the store, seated
beside a hot potbellied stove, crying still but not screaming, the
storekeepers doing what they could to calm him, trying to settle him
with animal crackers because this surely was the unusual little boy
who occasionally visited the store with one of his parents on that
specific errand.

The woman who had brought Ian to them, they said, had found
him on the road that connected the towns of Florissant and Cripple
Creek. He had been running at the roadside, heading north in a
direction he seldom traveled in his family's car; he was crying softly
as she stopped and he had readily climbed inside her car. Boyce
asked whether the woman had told him she would take him to
Evergreen Station—a place-name Ian knew very well—but the
storekeepers said that hadn't been clear.

It was hard to believe: the distance from Ian's house to the place
on the Florissant road where the woman picked him up was more
than four miles; he had run that far—down one winding road then
turning left where it intersected with another—on slippery, snow-
covered surfaces in just an hour. His sense of direction was remarkable, his father knew—and as I have mentioned, he always would
object to the slightest deviation in one of the intricate routes he daily
drove with his parents—so Boyce had to assume that Ian knew
where he was running. But what would have been his destination?
Or was he headed nowhere, running solely in a kind of frenzied
getaway, and was this some new behavior they would have to be

very wary of henceforth? Ian had been happy and quite calm in the
minutes before he vanished; he had been outside for much of the
morning and had met his several ritual needs. What had happened
to him? Why had he seemed to be running away? And just as mysteriously, why had he been so willing to surrender his short journey?

Boyce had broken down as at last he saw Ian sitting beside the
wood stove, and they had cried together for some minutes before
the much-relieved storekeepers asked the father why the boy
couldn't speak. Boyce was grateful for their kind attention to Ian,
and at any other time he willingly would have explained to them in
some detail about a rare disorder known as autism. But the only
answer he could give them at that moment was, "I just don't know."

The DPT inoculation that likely had played a causal role in Ian's run
that day, and which surely had set the course of his life, was the
fourth in the standard infant series; that dose, commonly administered at eighteen months, is the one that most often provokes severe
reaction. But in Ian's case, it had not been followed by an obvious
encephalitic response: he had not developed a high fever, had not
suffered a seizure; nor did vomiting, breathing difficulty, or inconsol-
able crying commence in the hours after he received the shot. He
had, however, fallen into a deep and unusual sleep, one of several
signs of "mild" reaction, the sort of response Ian's doctor had cautioned his parents to expect.

What that physician had not told them, and what he probably
had not known, was that even as early as 1985 the several makers of
the DPT vaccine already were warning of its possibly serious allergic
side effects and its inadvisability, therefore, in children with ongoing
milk or wheat allergies—allergies Ian and his parents had had to
contend with since his birth. "Allergic hypersensitivity" was "an
absolute contraindication" against the use of its vaccine, Connaught
Laboratories had noted in liability-protecting language printed in
tiny type in its package insert, but Ian nonetheless had been inoculated, his poorly informed doctor and his trusting and acquiescent
parents at his side.

The notion that the fundamental reactive process to the pertussis vaccine might be an allergic one was not new in 1985, however. A 1954 study on neurological problems that commonly resulted from vaccinations of all types had found that most were induced by encephalitis related to "anaphylactic hypersensitivity." A 1976 study conducted by Washington, D.C., physician Mary Coleman had found that eight of seventy-eight patients with autism also suffered from celiac disease—severe allergy to wheat, and sometimes to milk as well—*eight hundred times* the incidence of celiac disease in the general population. And a 1983 Stanford University School of Medicine animal study clearly had indicated that children with allergies of several types were likely to overreact to the pertussis vaccine—all of which information Ian's parents had not discovered until their son had been profoundly disabled for some years.

Their reactions to the news that Ian likely could have been spared autism if he had been kept clear of the pertussis component of the DPT vaccine had been mixed and were surprisingly contained, it seemed to me. They were angered, of course, and woven into their anger was an inescapable sense that they, like millions of other parents, had been fools to accept so readily the standard inoculation doctrine. They debated for some months whether to initiate a legal action—aware that the drug companies commonly settled pertussis vaccine cases out of court, but cognizant as well that the facts that much time had lapsed since Ian's vaccination and that he had not been taken to an emergency room or even back to his doctor's office, where signs of a serious reaction might have been documented, meant their case would be a precarious one at best. It seemed probable that much money would be required to care for Ian over the course of his lifetime, and funds from a damage judgment obviously would have been welcome. But that outcome, in court or out of it, could result only from a vast expenditure of their time and commitment, commodities they decided they couldn't spare.

Claudia and Boyce quickly abandoned the possibility of suing anyone, and they also soon surrendered the outrage those revelations had bred, in part perhaps because at last they possessed an explanation, and that *was* something of some value. Ian's brain had been disabled and their lives had been turned totally on end by an agent and a process they could identify at last, and there was something curiously consoling in that understanding. Ian had suffered an accident, they now knew—one initiated not without clear negligence, one that *was* avoidable—yet accidents somehow happen.

Eighty percent of all people with autism are severely allergic, researchers now know, and that finding is consistent with the long-term understanding in the medical community that "encephalitis, especially from vaccination, can give rise to an allergic state, while conversely, the existence of an allergic state predisposes to the development of encephalitis after vaccination," according to Coulter. And if allergy is indeed a common component of postvaccination encephalitis, then one more piece of autism's intricate puzzle begins to fall into place.

During the years I spent observing Patrick Sternberg—who still tends to be the pseudonymous Dr. Ferrier when I think of him at his work—I met many patients with multiple sclerosis and a few with a far more rare disease called Guillain-Barré syndrome, the two diseases quite distinct but nonetheless sharing several features: Both are autoimmune diseases, in which the body's immune system mysteriously attacks its own tissue as if it were a foreign antigen. In the case of both diseases, it is the insulating myelin sheaths surrounding and protecting the axons of nerves that fall prey to attack. In MS, however, myelin is selectively destroyed in the central nervous system (the brain and spinal cord), and the symptoms—numbness, blurred vision, loss of motor control, in particular—tend to follow a chronic relapsing/remitting pattern, the symptoms improving or disappearing before they return, sometimes permanently. With Guillain-Barré, in contrast, only myelin surrounding *peripheral* nerves (those that project from the spinal cord to innervate the body's muscles) is attacked—suddenly, dramatically, but usually only temporarily—with patients sometimes left in total paralysis for weeks before they return to normal health.

In sharing that autoimmune component, the two diseases can be grouped with many others—diseases during the course of which the body turns against itself—and which together comprise perhaps the least understood of all disease mechanisms. What long has been suspected, however, with multiple sclerosis and Guillain-Barré syndrome, as well as with a variety of other autoimmune disorders affecting other organs, is that their courses are set in motion by a bacterial or viral agent—but it is a process that may result less in a straightforward infection than in the triggering of an allergic response, one in which the immune system mistakes one of its own key components for an antigen that summarily must be dispatched. Although no such agent ever has been proven to initiate multiple sclerosis, it is in this autoimmune arena that most MS research currently is focused. About half of all Guillain-Barré patients, however, report that they did indeed suffer flulike respiratory or gastrointestinal infections in the weeks before their neurological symptoms first appeared. And intriguingly, in a rare outbreak of the disease in 1976, a large percentage of the cases reported were people who recently had been vaccinated against the swine influenza virus.

The myelin that these two diseases seek and attempt to destroy is a tough, white, fatty material whose role in its coating of central and peripheral nerves is similar to that of the plastic insulation that surrounds electrical cables. During gestation, millions of nerve cells and their axons throughout the brain and nervous system are almost entirely formed, but by birth their myelination has just begun, and it is only this slow myelinating process that allows virtually every developmental step to ensue—electrical conduction through the nerve fibers too slow prior to their coating with myelin, too faulty, too prone to short-circuit to allow smooth or efficient movement, clear or distant vision, the sharp discerning of sounds.

Within the brain, myelination begins in the brain stem, the brain's oldest, most primitive part, and continues in a kind of hierarchical order until finally, at about eighteen months, the showcase cerebral cortex begins to myelinate, the process patiently continuing in that speaking and thinking center until about age six. Anything that interferes with myelination at successive stages or locations during those several years—preventing myelin from being deposited, or somehow removing it once in place—can profoundly hinder neurological development of every kind. And it may be, come the close of the day, that an allergic, autoimmune, *de*myelinating process—similar to what is suspected to occur in multiple sclerosis and Guillain-Barré syndrome, and initiated by postvaccination encephalitis—is the pathological explanation of much autism.

I already have wondered whether brain stem impairment in a child with autism somehow does not allow the left cerebral hemisphere to begin its latent linguistic patterning. My suspicions about the myelinating process are no more provable, but I'm captivated nonetheless by a possibility that closes something of a circle, and that connects in more than merely symbolic ways my friend Patrick and his patients, whom I still hauntingly recall, with my nephew Ian and the baffling disorder with which he is much beset.

It now seems sure to me that those cases of autism that are *not* prenatal, which clearly are not caused by minute kinds of damage to the brain occurring prior to birth, are, in fact, often initiated postnatally by an allergic reaction to the pertussis vaccine. Particularly among hyperallergic children, it seems very probable that the vaccine acts as an agent that not only initiates encephalitic swelling and its attendant trauma but also, whether separately or concurrently, initiates an autoimmune response, putting myelin at catastrophic risk and subsequently impeding myriad kinds of neurological development. If this possibility is one with some real substance—and it *is*, I want to shout—then aren't there several attendant issues that begin to make some sense?

Wouldn't diffuse and unpredictable demyelination in the brain and the cranial nerves help account for autism's wide array of symptoms? Wouldn't demyelination in the brain stem's cerebellum help account for the sensory impairments and sensory overloads that cruelly characterize the disorder? And wouldn't demyelination in the cerebral cortex—coming, in Ian's case, at *precisely* the moment when his cortex was beginning to myelinate the nerves that would form a nascent linguistic network—go some distance toward accounting for autism's deficit of symbols, its deficit of the most intricate kinds of neural patterning, and the miracle of speech?

As far back as 1951, Isaac Karlin suggested in the journal *Pediatrics* that two separate language disorders—stuttering and the deficit in understanding speech that sometimes is called "congenital word deafness"—tended to be caused by "delay in the myelinization of the cortical areas in the brain concerned with speech." In the late 1980s, magnetic resonance imaging research conducted at the UCLA School of Medicine's Department of Radiological Sciences by Rosalind Dietrich and her colleagues found in comparative MRIs of normal and developmentally delayed children that the brains of those who were delayed showed "immature patterns of myelination." And Charles M. Poser, senior neurologist at Boston's Beth Israel Hospital, explained in a 1987 paper that "almost any . . . vaccination can lead to a noninfectious inflammatory reaction involving the nervous system. . . . The common denominator consists of a vasculopathy that is often . . . associated with demyelination." This much *does* seem capable of being stated with real certainty: Vaccination can be the cause of a demyelinating process in the brain and nervous system. And demyelination can lead to a wide array of sensory, motor, and linguistic deficits. But do neuroscientists know enough yet to bridge successfully those two separate understandings with the contention, with the strong conviction, that a pertussis-induced demyelinating mechanism plays a central role in autism?

Among the many things I learned some years ago as I stood, wide-eyed, at Patrick's side, was that in the enterprise known as medicine, questions long have been a richer harvest than have answers. And that was something Claudia and Boyce now knew intimately as well—whether the question was why Ian had run perilously away that day, or precisely how his brain had been compromised, or why, despite the Hippocratic oath, medicine sometimes does do harm. It is an understanding that all of us have, at least to some degree, I suppose, a realization that much of living conscientiously has to do with discerning what we do not know.

5
IAN GOES
TO SCHOOL

If language is, in fact, the symbolic system with which we begin to furrow and wrinkle our brains, if it is the single, improbable seed that spawns a network of cortical neurons almost as intricate and complex as life itself, if language is the means with which we discover ourselves through thinking, it is also our sole means of meeting the world. "Language is social," linguist S. I. Hayakawa wrote in 1940. "Cultural and intellectual cooperation is, or should be, the great principle of human life [and] coordination for the functioning of society is of necessity achieved by language, or else it is not achieved at all." It is in the act of speaking, of conversing—one of us solely with one other or with thousands—that our brains can meet and then miraculously commingle. It is in conversing that we fleetingly can crawl outside ourselves.

So while language is structural, representational, and systematic, it has also been essentially social since sounds first seemed to mean something, and that process commenced a very long time ago. The safest assumption about the time when true language emerged has long been pegged to 30,000 years ago—the first Cro-Magnons too sophisticated, too successful in several endeavors, to have been able to thrive without a vibrant language. Yet there are some—paleon-

tologists, anthropologists, and linguists among them—who are eager
to push language back many more millennia, to date its first florescence as early as 100,000 years ago. Anatomically modern remains
of the earliest known Neanderthal-era people have been unearthed
in contemporary Israel, and DNA analysis confirms that they are a
hundred millennia old—the remains of people with modern supralaryngeal vocal tracts and brains quite similar to ours, people capable
very probably of speech and abstract thought, capable of cooperation
and social altruism of several kinds. But whether complex and creative language dramatically began to alter human life at about the
time those first Neanderthals emerged or only as they died away, it
seems sure that the sort of language the first fledgling speakers spoke
was a direct precursor of the languages we speak today.

Unlike the kinds of archaeological records that are set in stone
and bone, however, prehistoric language left no evidence of itself,
no clear clues of any kind regarding its structure or its breadth. Our
linguistic common denominator, our true mother tongue—usually
called Proto-Indo-European—may never have been spoken, in point
of fact. But late Stone Age people, certifiable *Homo sapiens*, did
speak a complex language, dozens of them perhaps, that evolved
over many epochs into what is known as Indo-European, a language
that almost certainly *did* exist—its constructions, its phrases, some
of its very words still spoken today.

It was the English jurist Sir William James who initiated the fuzzy
science of historical linguistics by teaching himself the long-dead
Hindu language Sanskrit—kept alive solely in sacred hymns—following his posting to India in 1783, and by noting how strangely
similar many Sanskrit words were to their equivalents in other languages. He noted, for instance, that the Sanskrit word for "king,"
raja, is curiously comparable to the Latin *rex* and the Spanish *rey*;
it fascinated him that the Sanskrit word for "birch" was *bhurja*, and
that the number ten, *dasa* in Sanskrit, was so much like the Latin
decem. James eventually was bold enough to contend, in a widely
influential speech delivered to the Asiatick Society in Calcutta, that
Sanskrit, Greek, Latin, Gothic, Celtic, and Persian all surely evolved

from the same source, a contention that led later to efforts on the parts of people around the world to verify a parent language.

During the subsequent two hundred years, however, no empirical evidence has been found—no tablets, no scratched or scribbled slates—that inarguably links all languages to a single source, but neither has anyone realistically expected to find such a palpable sort of proof. What has emerged is abundant anecdotal evidence—the words *tre* and *trai* for "three" in two languages spoken in ancient times in the Chinese province of Sinkiang, for example—as well as the growing understanding that any language inherently is a mongrel mix of other tongues. To suppose that a language ever did develop in absolute isolation, in fact—distinct groups of primitive people somehow concurrently coming to terms with syntax and with words—now seems to be by far the bigger leap.

We might well know a bit more, it is true, about the shape and style, even the *sound*, of Indo-European if the Greeks or Romans had taken much interest in the origins of *their* languages. But neither culture's scholars ever exhibited real interest in that evolution, the Romans leaving untranslated even many writings in Etruscan, a language that obviously is ancestral to Latin, one they surely would have been able to decipher. But despite that early indifference and admitting that the view in retrospect is still quite cloudy, it appears probable that this tongue called Indo-European eventually spawned a dozen offspring, twelve broad groups that included Greek, Italic, Celtic, Indo-Iranian (whence Sanskrit), and Germanic languages among them.

Not every one of these major groups fared equally well over the long linguistic term, nor did each group subsequently sire similar numbers of tongues. The separate Armenian, Albanian, and Greek languages produced only themselves, for example, while the Balto-Slavic root eventually evolved into ten major idioms spoken from the Black Sea to the Baltic. Some root languages, like Celtic, flowered early and achieved great influence before beginning a long decline—this tribal tongue that once was spoken throughout Europe now limited in our era to fewer than half a million people in the

British Isles, the Gaelic spoken in Scotland largely incomprehensible to the Gaelic speakers of Ireland or Wales. The Italic root, on the other hand—and with the indispensable aid of the advancing Roman Empire—readily evolved into two Latin tongues, one a classical form used almost solely for literature and scholarship, the other a popular, so-called vulgate derivation that ultimately gave way to Italian, Romanian, French, Spanish, Provençal, Portuguese, and Catalan, each still alive today and very vibrant.

The Germanic root spawned three branches early on: a relatively short-lived eastern branch comprised of the Gothic, Burgundian, and Vandalic languages, each one long dead and gone; a northern branch that included the four Scandinavian languages that still thrive; and a western branch that eventually gave rise to German, Dutch, and Flemish, as well as an obscure idiom once spoken solely in the spur of land separating the North Sea from Kiel Bay of the Baltic, a region once called Angeln, a language now called English.

In about A.D. 450, the tribal people of Angeln, together with related Jutes and Saxons, began a long-term migration across the North Sea to the island of Great Britain. There, Roman colonization had come virtually to a close, leaving a long-established and rather civilized Celtic people to fend for themselves against the growing numbers of these base intruders. Despite their cultural advancement, and despite the fact the island had been their homeland for a thousand years, the Celts plainly and simply were overrun by the Germanic tribes during succeeding decades, forced to retreat westward to Wales, north to Scotland, many to a broad peninsula on the European mainland that came to be known as Brittany.

History grows hazy here, the Dark Ages shedding little light, but the invaders of Britain somehow flourished—or at least the Saxons did, most impressively. It may be that they simply subsumed the tribal Jutes and Angles, or perhaps the social, cultural, and linguistic distinctions between them slowly paled, then disappeared. But however it happened, the Saxons did indeed make a successful home for themselves in a place they came (for reasons we do not know) to call *Englaland*, their common tongue a robust and greatly variable one that, equally curiously, had come to them from the Angles—a language that shamelessly lacked purity, refinement, or restriction, but a language that rather prospered.

No one has reasons that explain it, and none really are needed, but since she had been very small, Sarah Drummond had escaped the tumult in her household by retreating into history as well as fantasy. The westward migrating, covered-wagon period in America long had held her parochial interest, but otherwise, the truth was that Sarah was an Anglophile, and she steeped herself in Britain's history. She was fascinated by the bold Arthurian legends and was a frequent and enthusiastic visitor to swashbuckling Renaissance fairs; her tidy, frilly bedroom carefully reflected Queen Victoria's time; her interest in things contemporary proceeded not a bit farther than the televised reminiscences of James Herriot's rural, prewar Yorkshire; and surely she could be forgiven if she saw her Scottish heritage too as part of a similar and seamless British piece.

It was impossible to know, of course, whether Sarah would have been equally consumed by story and by history if imagined worlds into which she could escape had not been so essential for her. She was very bright, that much was certain early on, and imaginative, and it made sense to assume that living without ready backyard access to other children also had played a role in the development of her rich inner life. But her brother's agonies surely had propelled her as well into worlds she could not know firsthand, and you often could see delight and real relief register on her face when trips with parents, grandparents, or friends took her far enough away from home for a day or several days so that home too became a kind of fantasy, a place she knew so well, but which for a bit seemed blessedly distant.

Public school had immediately offered Sarah an analogous sort of escape from the explosive environment of her home, and for a year—in a kindergarten in a tiny rural school fifteen miles away—she had reveled in her interaction with other children as well as in the scholastic challenges. The perfectionist streak she had inherited from her father had spurred her to do well—no, perfectly—at everything she attempted, and that dedication, even in kindergarten, a total concentration on required tasks, successfully had diverted her attention from the brother she quietly loved and cared for, but for whom she could do so little. In the summer of 1988, Sarah was poised and eager to begin first grade in the Woodland Park school where her mother taught. Ian—who still could not enter a supermarket, a shop, or even a fast-food restaurant without engendering pandemonium— similarly was scheduled to begin his preschool year. But in the process of preparing for school, which would commence following Labor Day—Sarah surely so eager she barely would be able to contain herself on that first overwhelming morning, Ian's attitude far more problematic—they also had to prepare to move to town.

It was a decision that had been some time in the making, yet it was one that had seemed inevitable. Someday down the line, Sarah's long bus ride likely would not work for Ian, and surely there would be days—many of them, perhaps—when Ian's deliberate and inviolate schedule would mean he wouldn't be ready for school until midmorning, days when something would go awry at school and he would have to be taken home. Claudia and Boyce had made long, cataloging lists before their decision was set, noting the pros and cons of staying at the research station, listing too what moves to Colorado Springs or Denver or even Claudia's hometown of Cortez might mean. And then there was the possibility as well of a less disruptive move of only twenty miles into Woodland Park.

In the end, that possibility had seemed to make the most sense. Claudia liked her job and the people with whom she worked; they all liked living in the mountains and making use of Colorado Springs's several amenities only as much as they chose to do so. Living in Woodland Park would allow Boyce to retain at least peripheral contact with the research station and with Sandy and Laura Sanborn. Owners of the ranch, the research station, a conference center, and two venerable summer camps, the Sanborns and their extended family had been kind and supportive in so many ways since Boyce and Claudia had arrived four years before from Illinois. Boyce still would be able to teach and consult for the Sanborns on occasion, yet giving up the directorship of the research station would allow him more time to write, to take on projects he long had promised himself, as well as to assume more of the household duties that tended to go begging. In July, they found after much investigation a house in town they liked, one that met the rather exacting requirements that Ian now imposed—a yard with trees, his bedroom near the kitchen but well separated from Sarah's so she could sleep, a bathroom he alone could use. And although they did so with some trepidation, absent a clue, for instance, whether Ian *ever* would grow at ease in a house other than the one he'd always known, they struck one of those real estate deals that bring you starkly face-to-face with indentured servitude, then immediately began to take Ian for daily visits to the new, tree-surrounded house on Redfeather Lane, the introductions brief at first but then successively longer. By early August, with a seemingly endless series of trips to town in loaded trucks soon set to commence, the move had become a chaotic reality and an anxious and uncertain new era for the four of them was about to get under way.

There had been two distinct phases in Ian's life till now. One spanned the eighteen months from his birth until the day he received that last DPT booster, months of much delight and the attainment of successive milestones in what surely would be a legacy of splendid days for him, a time that abruptly ended as he began to scream. The second phase of this blond boy's life had endured for more than three years now, years characterized by his constant shrieking fright, and, in counterpoint, by his wordless silence, years for his family of the starkest kind of catastrophe, but which at last had begun to evidence some hope. Ian's third era, now nearly under way, would be one about which little could be supposed yet, except that— whether easily or wrenchingly—he soon would be pushed out into a larger world, at least, if not out of silence.

Although he had been fiercely protected by his parents in the time since his brain had been assaulted, defended as best they could manage against those myriad things that induced in him such terror, neither Claudia nor Boyce ever had seemed reticent for Ian's school years to commence. In part, Ian's public schooling represented to them some real assistance at long last, a welcome way for each of them daily to shed for some hours the constant pressure his care entailed. But more important than those considerations, school would be the setting in which Ian would achieve some semblance of a social life, if such a thing were possible, the best means imaginable for him symbolically and literally to strike out on his own. He long since had proven his abilities to attend to tasks, if only for short periods; he had shown an eagerness to learn and an appropriate pride in his accomplishments. He seemed well suited, his parents noted with some humor, to the dull demands and socializing routines normally imposed on children at his age: hanging his coat on the appropriate hook each morning, putting his lunch box in its proper place, or falling into a queue before recess could begin—those things he would do daily without the slightest deviation. Although it seemed doubtful that Ian truly was reading, his early vocabulary training with flash cards, his bombardment with books, his use of picture boards, the computer, and the VÒIS all had given him great familiarity with symbols, with letters and with words. Yet he still interacted only with his parents and his sister, and even with them only in his own curious and complex way, and it was hard not to imagine that the clutter and commotion of his classmates would make him crazy, or alternatively, that perhaps he always would seem oblivious to them and to everything that transpired in the classroom. Yet they dared too to hope that as a third, though probably less likely, possibility, those kids he would meet and spend his days beside somehow might draw him out.

As a classroom teacher and a specialist in curricula for gifted students, Claudia also was well versed in current methods for meeting disabled children's needs, and she had been a fierce proponent since well before Ian entered her life of what once was known as mainstreaming but now more commonly was called inclusion—the notion that children with disabilities and special needs, as well as their normal peers, were well and valuably served by sharing the same classroom and by undertaking virtually all school activities together. Almost everyone currently involved in public education agrees that inclusion is an ideal worth striving for, but one that of necessity isn't always practical; however, there are those militants like my sister who view that perspective as plainly spineless, the worst kind of waffling. Claudia could not imagine a child who would not benefit from the experience of a regular classroom, a child whose presence would not be important for his or her peers. And now it seemed inescapably ironic that her own son soon would test her strong conviction.

But Ian simply could not be escorted down a long hallway one day come September, then ushered into a chaotic classroom in a kind of hold-your-nose-and-jump approach to this concept of inclusion. The process would be a slow and painstakingly careful one; it would be a full year before Ian would spend more than the briefest time in a regular classroom setting. Claudia herself would take a leave of absence from teaching that first fall to help ease Ian's traumatic transition from home to school, and the transition would begin while summer thunderstorms still blackened the sky by noon every day, while the building called Gateway Elementary still was utterly quiet except for a custodian or two, a time when a precarious boy could get to know the place at a pace that seemed to suit him.

My two sisters and I grew up in the 1950s in the kind of backwater town where anything flushed with creativity was invariably dubbed "strange" or "kooky" or, as our more tolerant parents tended to demur, "different." Like people in dozens of other western towns set amidst geographic splendor, the denizens of little Cortez curiously seemed to shun any beauty they might make themselves, as if perhaps it would seem some sort of flippancy, a showy distraction from the truly important things like elk hunting and auto mechanics. There were exceptions, of course, and our parents' backyard garden was one that actually garnered some renown, but by and large we lived in a community where the annual beautification campaign meant getting the grade-schoolers to pick up all the beer cans beside the roads, and where seemingly half of your friends' fathers spent their weekends atop their yellow backhoes—those much beloved and obviously indispensable pieces of machinery that are capable of tearing the holy hell out of *anything* in under twenty minutes.

But despite its unadorned and rather unappealing visage—I've referred to it as "rat-ass" in other contexts and subsequently have been scolded—ours was a town where people felt so secure in those days that they virtually never locked their doors or took the keys out of their cars' ignitions, where seats on the town council were filled based on whose turn it was this time, where all the ministers met for breakfast once a week, and where the Rotary Club's annual Fourth of July fireworks extravaganza seemed to draw double the population. You didn't know everyone in town, of course, but you recognized most faces, and you'd heard entertaining stories about nearly everyone to whom you could attach a name. With all its shortcomings out in the open for observation, with its isolation and its intransigence always too apparent and pervasive, it was, nonetheless, one of those towns that somehow served its citizens' needs and that was oddly endearing in the end, and I probably should confess that I can see Cortez—at least the tall radio tower and the silos at the flour mill—from the window as I write these words.

Over a span of fourteen years—if my notoriously poor calculations are correct—Claudia, Carol, and I attended an elementary school that was perhaps a quarter the size of the school that Ian soon would attend—a single classroom for each grade, maybe twenty kids per classroom. Modest, boxy, red-brick Downey School was situated in a north Cortez neighborhood that allowed every student to skip or run or loiter en route and still arrive in seven minutes, a school where teachers tended to spend their whole careers, priding themselves on remembering quite clearly that your sister also had had a tendency to talk too much, a place inhabited as well back then by magical Mr. Nordling, the Norwegian-born custodian who made a pair of stilts for all one hundred plus of us one spring, and as many "Indian drums" out of old inner tubes stretched across the rims of fat tin cans, who played his musical saw at regular assemblies and on the occasions when we were visited by dignitaries, and who was our Christmas Santa Claus (I know, because I got to be his helper, and saw him dress, and therefore officiously had to try to keep that stupendous secret from the little kids).

Downey School didn't offer any of its students rigorous early educations, I don't suppose. The curricula no doubt were outdated, and probably few of us met our true potentials. But as I have looked back in recent years and have tried to ascertain the roots of my good fortune—meaning my ability and opportunity to write instead of *work*, meaning too a kind of dumb audacity I have in believing that I can confront an empty computer screen each morning and fill it, by the end of the aching afternoon, with words of any consequence— I can't help but focus on something anchored in that innocent time that has to do essentially with security, with constant reassurance, and with being told I could do it, in a context in which *it* meant almost anything.

I don't remember wanting to become a writer in the same way that my friend Patrick, raised in distant Denver, had known since he was five or so that one day he would be a doctor. I lacked that singular sort of focus. I suppose that, despite ample evidence to the contrary, I dreamed that my talents best belonged to baseball, then subsequently to ski-racing as Jean-Claude Killy's exploits and successes (and glamorous girlfriends) began to assume a certain allure. I did want to be a priest for a time, I remember with some certainty—in part because *Episcopal* priests didn't have to deny their carnal natures, but also because I conspired to think that if I promised God that the priesthood would be my calling he just might spare me the tragic early death that seemed sadly inevitable about the time I became pubescent and awkward and ugly as a stump.

Mathematics utterly baffled me—from multiplication tables to my first frightened skirmish with algebraic equations—but for reasons I cannot explain, I always was facile enough with words. I wrote plodding, imitative stories, which I remember with a shudder; I wrote maudlin poems with subjects such as the arrival of the Pilgrims and the migration of kinfolk of mine from Arkansas; I wrote lavish, overly long reports about exotic places, such as a verdant land called Vietnam, where some sort of conflict had begun to draw American attention, my carefully composed, handwritten pages accompanied by maps I redrew from those I'd seen in the *World Book*. I was a pint-sized, grinning raconteur, a bullshitter in the regional vernacular, and I was fairly good, I've got to admit, at talking my way out

of trouble with teachers as well as with bigger, tougher kids like
Toby Lobato, who finally befriended me when he learned that my
ready rap could be his ally. I was a ham on proud parade when I
stood on Downey's little stage, whether to recite the Gettysburg
Address or to play the part of a Wise Man in the Christmas pageant
(in *our* corner of the country, the separation of church and state
seemed like a trivial sort of detail), and there was the day I still recall
when, at the close of some important performance, I heard a friend
of my mother tell her she could imagine me as a valedictorian one
day, and I thought to myself, Okay, then that's what I'll be, although
I didn't precisely know what kind of work valedictorians actually did.

In the end, I performed with words and wrote with words, made
my friends laugh and told the bad guys they were buttholes in
an easy slurry of words, basically because I had been so steadily
encouraged. There had been some subtle but surely consequential
familial examples set for me, it was true—aunts and great-aunts in
my mother's family whose literary gifts were locally renowned; the
admonition of my maternal grandfather, a redheaded and ruddy-
faced farmer and sheepman, to make sure I made my way in life
with my head instead of my shoulders; and the image of my father,
every evening of the world, reading the *Rocky Mountain News* so
attentively and completely, the first page to the last—evidence obviously to me that printed, *published* words were things of substance
and importance. But more than anything else, I think, I was drawn
to words and the web of language that they wove because my mother
and my father and a caring coterie of teachers so repeatedly assured
me that I was good with them, that they were a costume that seemed
to clothe me well. I was the kind of boy who plainly wanted to pan
out one day down the line, to be liked and praised and somehow
deemed successful, and I think perhaps I latched onto language in
those early years, as well as in the tumultuous time that followed
them, not because I knew where it would take me but because
wherever language led, surely that place would be rich with creative
possibility as well as the kind of security and comfort a kid from a
small town could hang on to.

—

It was a similar sort of reassurance, it seemed, that might well come Ian's way at school. And school too might propel him toward his own goals, whether they were the command of quantum physics or one day simply speaking. Gateway Elementary would be, we hoped— every one of us for whom Ian by now had come to represent something more than the sum of who he was—the setting where he might gain a meaningful measure of his disabilities and his strengths, how they limited him and how they engendered possibility. For Ian, as with every child, these years he would spend in school would be his fundamental early means of encountering independence and of making as well that sometimes difficult discovery that he was only a very small yet nonetheless important part of a large and many-layered social whole. School would enrich his life in myriad ways, we all wanted very much to believe in that sanguine summer of 1988. On the other hand, if after many attempts and trials school simply did not work for him, we were also starkly aware that his life likely would turn toward far bleaker prospects.

It was with those kinds of companion hopes and fears—their son's life and important aspects of their own lives in the balance—that Boyce and Claudia readied Ian for a ride on August 8, a few days following his fifth birthday. The move to town wasn't yet completed, so it was from the house at the research station that Claudia and Ian drove at noon, despite his immediate and insistent protest that their route was not the proper one. In Woodland Park, Ian long ago had learned to like the drive-up windows at Wendy's and McDonald's, where French fries always were forthcoming, but the huge red-brick building in front of which his mother parked that day was utterly new to him and terrifying, and he shrieked and kicked in terror as she carried him inside. They remained at Gateway for seventeen minutes that afternoon—Claudia keeping careful track of the time— before Ian's anguish was too much for him or her to bear and that first day's introduction to his future was finished and deemed successful.

Ian was able to remain inside the school for twenty-three minutes

on the second day, and for twenty-eight minutes by the third; on
the fourth day of his school career, he arrived and simply acquiesced,
casually investigating the nooks and crannies and countertops in the
special-education resource room where, in days to come, he would
spend most of his time, wandering the building's quiet hallways,
reveling in the playground that was ringed by a fine fence he could
run beside and which offered slides and swings and climbing structures he was familiar with, slides particularly capable of inducing his
smile, his happy giggles, and his eager ascents.

A week into this new routine, Claudia began to introduce the
"worktime" Ian had known each day at home for nearly three years
now, and although he fussed a bit and was inattentive, he accepted
that change without undue commotion. At the end of two weeks—
with hundreds of other kids soon to join him—Ian already was
attending school for the full three hours they had hoped he could
manage sometime before the autumn was out, his schedule commencing with thirty minutes of various games and exercises intended
to enhance his attention and motor coordination, followed by a half
hour's recess where he could spend his time as *he* chose, which
normally meant running beside the fence. Next, he would watch a
movie and (with some prodding) eat a snack for thirty minutes before
beginning a half hour of unstructured downtime, during which he
often flapped the pages of books in front of his eyes as a means,
perhaps, of keeping in control; and then he would end his short
academic day with a half hour of structured prereading activities that
were led by his mother for now, and likely would be for several
weeks to come before she could begin to back away.

Although school administrators remained more than a little leery
of taking responsibility for a child whose disabilities and potential
for disruption were as enormous as Ian's, and despite the fact that
several teachers who one day might work with him still openly voiced
their dread of having to attend to his diapers as well as his daily
tantrums, the experiment *was* working, working splendidly at the
start, just as Claudia and Boyce so fervently had hoped it would.
They had known that Ian was capable of accepting new activities and

environments if he was eased into them over time—or in only a day or two, for that matter, if round-the-clock screaming was reckoned worth the price—so his growing acceptance of the building hadn't been surprising. His willingness to do work he'd never done before outside his bedroom did impress his parents, however, and it also helped allay the anxious concern of the teachers who soon would begin—equally slowly, just a minute or two at first—to join Ian and his mother in the classroom. Yet for all the meticulous planning and careful forethought, the attempts to head off every obstacle, there was one aspect of Ian's new schedule that hadn't been attended to: the school week was five days long while Ian's own week counted seven days. He was willing to go to school, he liked going almost from the start, but if school was part of his life now, then for heaven's sake, he *had* to go to school, and Saturdays and Sundays weren't exceptions.

Ian didn't sleep his first night in his new house, even though his father and a friend had flown into action and meticulously re-created his bedroom there as best they could during the short hours earlier that day while Ian and his mother were at school. He had flown into a rage as his mother drove to Redfeather Lane instead of the research station, then had been more puzzled than angry when he saw his new bedroom—things so much the same, Snoopy and Pooh posters hung exactly as they had been, the television in its proper position relative to his bed, yet seeming still quite different. He remained very unsettled as he conducted his late-afternoon and evening routines, and despite preparing for bed exactly as he always did, he stayed restlessly awake all through that long night. But what Ian simply couldn't contend with in any way, in contrast, what *was not acceptable*, was this thing his parents were calling a "weekend" as they attempted in vain to calm him on the first Saturday in October when they tried to keep him home from school. The hours of that afternoon and evening, ten hours or so of constant screaming, seemed tantamount, they remember, to hundreds—surely close to a thousand now—of tantrums Ian and his family had experienced so far, more horrific than his first visit to Children's Hospital had been,

worse even than those several times when the power had failed and
Ian had had no movie; yet they did not relent, and Ian did not go
to school that Saturday.

This was something plainly no one had foreseen, but now, of
course, it made much sense: How was Ian supposed to intuit or
immediately accept the fact that the rest of the world operated on a
schedule that included two shutdown days, days when things were
different? On the other hand, how were his parents and his sister
going to contend with weekends racked by screaming? They desperately did not want to—and realistically could not—re-create the
school day for him each Saturday and Sunday, but neither would
they simply surrender and abandon this bright prospect: Ian's introduction to school was succeeding far too well for them even to
entertain that possibility. This unforeseen complication (apparently
there would be no gains without attendant setbacks) would take
some thinking and some time, but *surely* they could find a way to
alert Ian to what the day held in store for him, whether school or
more familiar ventures. Surely Ian could acquire *some* flexibility if
he so successfully could adapt in other ways.

A partial solution, not complete but helpful from its outset—
one Boyce and Claudia remember with rolling eyes and sheepish
smiles—was invariably to sing "the school song" as they drove Ian
to Gateway, the ditty obviously omitted however on the mandatory
drives they took on weekend days. Five days a week—first Claudia
committing its sparkling lyrics so much to heart that she could sing
them without thinking, then Boyce assuming the lead voice once
she returned to work—they would take up the tune to "Three Blind
Mice" as they drove out of their garage and along graveled Redfeather Lane, singing cheerily to their son:

> *Ian goes to school,*
> *Ian goes to school,*
> *Go inside, go inside,*
> *Play with Play-Doh and have some fun,*
> *Do a puzzle and go out to run,*
> *Ian goes to school.*

Although weekends remained problematic despite the absence of that song, and notwithstanding special "cow rides" Ian could count on on Saturdays and Sundays, the weekdays continued optimistically, and it was obvious right from the start of his foray into that public world that he too wanted to do well, to succeed, and to be as best he could be a regular kid at school.

Ian fussed at first as two new teachers briefly began to join him and his mother in the classroom; next he tried to take them by the arm and escort each of them back out of the room; and finally he simply ignored them. But as they remained determined, staying longer on each successive day, he in turn began to study them with what seemed to be a mix of curiosity and suspicion. As Charmaine Thaner, who would be Ian's special-education teacher, and Mary Lou Krueger, the paraprofessional to whom would go the role of aide and surrogate mother, began separately to sit at his table and accompany him outside, there were plenty of times when he would try rather matter-of-factly to push them out of his way, attempting to tell them that their presences really weren't required, yet he seldom screamed in objection, nor did he refuse to attend to tasks as they sat nearby watching him with fascination. Slowly, careful never to push him too quickly or too far, Mary Lou began to assist Claudia with Ian's exercises and games, to sit close beside him and touch him in ways he liked, even to assume Claudia's duties on occasion, and sometimes he even would greet her and Charmaine with his strained but unmistakable smile as he arrived in the afternoon, the two new teachers now with him constantly throughout his abbreviated day.

On the morning of Tuesday, September 6, four hundred kids with new shoes and shirts and haircuts, toting new and unmarked notebooks and the latest Snoopy and Bart Simpson lunch boxes, poured into Gateway, and by noon had filled the building with the kind of rambunctious energy that made it feel truly like a school. But Ian seemed far more intent as he arrived that momentous afternoon on meeting the several routines he by now had made inviolate—*his* lunch box in its proper place, his jacket hung where it belonged before he took his seat at the low round table, ready to go to work—than he did on that day's dramatic changes. The playground was inhabited by children for the first time when he went out for recess, and he did have to move a few of them out of his way as he went about his ritual recreation, and yes, there were a few kids in his classroom now as well, kids who would enter the room alone or in groups of two or three, working with Charmaine and speech therapist Jill Hoover before they left and other curious kids replaced them. Yet Ian remained unperturbed for the most part throughout that afternoon, paying this onslaught only grudging attention, or so it seemed, intent instead on what had become his essential and invariable business—kneading dough and happily hammering with a mallet, stacking colored blocks and reading books, playing finger games with Claudia, playing with balls and plastic trucks, watching movies while this time he flapped the pages of a book in front of his eyes, delighting in the games of Tickle Bee he played with his mother and Mary Lou, pointing at their prompting to his proper body parts, pressing each key on his VÔIS that announced the activity that would follow, then finally, and often with noticeable relief, pressing the key that declared the school day done.

In only a month, Ian had grown fundamentally at ease at school for the few hours planned for him; he had learned to accept the playground, the special-education room, and the long hallway that connected them inside the cavernous building; he had acquiesced to the presence of the few adults who appeared to inhabit it, and now, after a bit of time, a few other children had become equally acceptable. As was the case with most of his fellow five-year-olds, the big-kid stuff of school actually attracted him, and it seemed probable as well that over the long term, public school's particular rituals and regimentation would provide him with the kinds of security and structure he thrived on and indeed could not survive without. *It would work: Ian could go to school*, Claudia and Boyce now assured themselves with cautious confidence—weekends already easier and perhaps worth the price in any case, his school song one they knew they could sing for days and days to come.

—

For fifteen hundred years, the language Ian now was learning despite his inability to speak, the language in which these collected words are written, had been able to adapt with the ease and suddenness of a chameleon's colors. English had been a language enormously amenable to influence and to change in that time, an idiom that seemed to welcome innovation. It was a tongue that had survived and spread so successfully in part because it was widely spoken by common folk—and indeed and wonderfully because its grammar and its lexicon had been the handiwork of children.

One among the many reasons for our scant understanding of the way in which the language of the Angles became dominant among tribal intruders into Britain during the Dark Ages is that virtually no information from that time was recorded. People did scratch inscriptions into totemic stones, called runes, with what has become known as the runic alphabet, and a farmer's field in Suffolk yielded in the 1980s a small gold medallion dated sometime prior to the year 500, one which bears a runic inscription believed to read, "This she-wolf is a reward to my kinsman"—the earliest extant sentence written in our language. Yet neither the Angles nor the Anglo-Saxons—as the confederate, then conglomerate tribes became known—were great scriveners or even scribblers in metal or in stone, and at least as far as we know, they never wrote on paper, so few details of their nascent years on that great island have survived. That absence of recorded words, and hence recorded culture, began to change and change dramatically with the arrival in 597 of Saint Augustine and forty fellow missionaries from the European main-land. Within a year, the Anglo-Saxon King Ethelbert of Kent was converted to Christianity, and following that first formidable conver-sion, the religion, together with the peripheral importance it placed on literacy, spread rapidly west and north across much of England. By the year 700, England largely was a Christian realm and it rivaled several longer-established European states as a seat of culture and learning—its dense and elaborate language quickly transformed from a minor tribal tongue to one that even boasted scholarship.

Yet *Englisc*, what now is referred to as Old English, truly was labyrinthine in its grammatical complexity. As Bill Bryson explains in *The Mother Tongue*, his 1990 history of the language,

> Nouns had three genders and could be inflected for up to five cases. As with modern European languages, gender was often arbitrary. *Wheat*, for example, was masculine, while *oats* was feminine and *corn* neuter. . . . Old English had seven classes of strong verbs and three of weak, and their endings altered in relation to number, tense, mood, and person (though, oddly, there was no specific future tense). A single adjective like *green* or *big* could have up to eleven forms.

But although it was grammatically intricate, even knotty, Old English's complexity made it capable as well of impressive subtlety and flexibility. Its era of erudition and early scholarship was short, however, and that era presaged momentous change.

In the summer of 850, a fleet of wooden Viking sailing ships, perhaps 350 of them in number, sailed ominously up the river Thames to the settlement of London, sparking three decades of periodic skirmishes and occasional open battles for control of the island. A treaty that finally ended the fighting granted the invading Norsemen control of most English territory north of London, the Norse language subsequently assuming cultural dominance there and in Scotland, but inserting its strong influence as well throughout all of Britain—introducing rather fundamentally the pronouns *they*, *them*, and *their*, for example—Norse words less often replacing those in Old English than joining them as synonyms. Then, two centuries later, it was the French language that similarly came ashore, this time in company with the Norman conquest—the Normans also early Scandinavians who had colonized the region now known as Normandy, and who had entirely abandoned their Nordic tongue for a rural dialect of French.

In the decades that followed the fateful Battle of Hastings in 1066, Norman French became most widespread in England among the immigrant royalty and aristocracy who had ascended to power, its societal influence focusing therefore on matters of court, government, fashion, and aesthetics, while the Anglo-Saxon peasant classes continued to conduct their lives in English. And in the same way that they had two hundred years before, English speakers simply added Norman words, *French* words—many thousands of them—to their existing lexicon rather than surrender their speech to the conqueror's tongue. That Old English now was relegated to commoners meant, in fact, that a dramatic process of grammatical simplification could ensue unchecked and unobjected to, changes that marked the advent of Middle English—gender gone, declensions and conjugations greatly reduced in number, spelling simplified despite the flood of exotic words the language by now had made its own.

Middle English was, as historian C. L. Barber notes, a language characterized by "a chaos of dialects, without many common conventions in pronunciation or spelling, and with wide divergences in grammar and vocabulary," but probably foremost for those very reasons, it heartily survived. By the time the French crown had taken command of Normandy in 1204, isolating the Norman rulers in Britain to the extent that they began to consider themselves British, the mongrel English language slowly had begun to reassert itself. Already, children of privilege had to be *taught* French before they could be sent away to school; French was dropped as the official language of Parliament in 1362; and by the end of the century, students at Oxford University were required to be instructed at least partially in that tongue "lest the French language be entirely disused."

When William Caxton—the first person to print a book in English—noted a hundred years later that "our language now used varyeth ferre from that which was used and spoken when I was borne," he was making reference to a contemporary idiom that still utterly lacked orthodoxy, but which once again had become the sovereign idiom of the realm. And the linguistic changes that had occurred in his lifetime were scant in comparison with those that had been under way for a thousand years. Scholars estimate that during the centuries of occupation by Norsemen and by Normans, fully eighty-five percent of the preexisting Anglo-Saxon lexicon was lost. Only about forty-five hundred Anglo-Saxon words have survived to the present—one percent of those collected in the *Oxford English Dictionary*—yet this, nonetheless, is still a language rooted in the early speech of the Angles: every one of the hundred most commonly used words in contemporary English is of Anglo-Saxon origin. English obviously was hugely altered and intricately shaped by the languages with which it was commingled over time, but it seems sure as well that those influences were welcomed rather than prescribed or imposed, that the telltale genius of the Angles' tongue was that it and its descendant speakers were drawn to variety and creativity in the ways in which things could be said, that they delighted in the dozen ways something could be scribbled down.

Are proximity and time the sole sparks that engender change as languages collide? Did a bit of Norse syntax and hundreds of Norse words worm their way into English only because they long were spoken on English soil? Did the English language become so infused with French simply because French speakers ruled an English-speaking populace for some generations? Linguists long have been curious about the ways in which one language can influence another, or even subsume it, how languages resist certain kinds of change at the same time they eagerly welcome others. While no language is static, unchanging even in isolation from all others, every idiom is prone to undergo substantial, sometimes tumultuous transformation when another language becomes current in its midst. Yet on a personal and individual level, how *do* the curious sounds that two speakers of disparate languages make ever come to mean something, one to the other? What is the mechanism that allows the two even to borrow words in time? And why, on occasion, does a *third* language emerge from their meeting?

During the 1970s, University of Hawaii linguist Derek Bickerton looked at these kinds of questions in an extensive study of the crash of languages that occurred as the Hawaiian islands were colonized,

and he came to a remarkable conclusion not only about how permanent linguistic change commences and in what it results, but also
about which members of society most directly influence those
changes. Bickerton's investigation focused on an era that commenced
in 1876, and during which sugar growing in the islands underwent
rapid expansion and thousands of field workers were imported from
Japan, Korea, the Philippines, Portugal, and Puerto Rico in order
to facilitate the export of sugar. By the 1880s, the islands were a
multilingual mix of many tongues, the huge plantations and service
towns crowded with workers who could understand neither each
other nor the English-speaking plantation management—nor native
Hawaiians, for that matter, whose language was a form of Polynesian.
And as had happened countless times in similar immigrant contexts
throughout history, a basic means of communication slowly did
emerge: a "pidgin" language came to life amidst that jumble of
other idioms—the word *pidgin* believed perhaps to be a Chinese
pronunciation of the English *business*—not a true language but a
convenient collection of words borrowed from among the assembled
languages, an amalgam of words and phrases lacking grammatical
structure, every pidgin around the world only a *protolanguage*, to
use Bickerton's own term.

A pidgin speaker in turn-of-the-century Hawaii, Bickerton explains in *Language and Species*, might have commented to a friend,
"Aenu tu macha churen, samawl churen, haus mani pei," a sentence
that could be translated literally as, "And too much children, small
children, house money pay"—its meaning understood by the pidgin-
speaking friend despite the absence of the grammatical elements
that would have transformed it into something like, "And I had many
children, small children, and I had to pay the rent." Bickerton is
impressed by how primitive the Hawaiian pidgin had been—linked
four-word utterances, often absent verbs, its sole dependable
shape—yet every one of the workers who relied on pidgin to communicate had, nonetheless, complete and fluent command of at least
one *true* language—his or her own native tongue. Why, he wonders,
did people who spoke syntactically in their own languages find it
impossible to employ structural elements when speaking pidgin?

And there was another fascination: did pidgin languages change when they were spoken over time?

Bickerton's ready answer to the former question relates pidgin to the kinds of communication of which apes, small children, and anomalous cases like the adolescent girl called Genie are capable—each of the four forms inherently *proto*linguistic—and it is Bickerton's strong conviction that protolanguage is never a precursor of complete, syntactic language, the two springing from distinct language-forming mechanisms.

His response to the latter question is nothing less than arresting: if pidgin, he proposes, "is the only common language of a community, as it was in many tropical colonies, it will be acquired by locally born children and will then become a fully developed language, called a creole language." Imagine: the fully realized language that is now called Hawaiian Creole emerged when a second generation of children spoke their parents' pidgin among themselves during their critical language-acquiring years, bringing to life in the process a *new* language complete with inviolate syntactic rules and a large lexicon of words derived from among the islands' native and immigrant tongues, an idiom at ease with abstraction and capable of expressing great subtlety, a language as sophisticated in every respect, Bickerton contends, as any with which you might compare it. But even more amazing was the kind of structure that the children's creole idiom had assumed:

> [T]he grammar of the language that resulted bore the closest resemblance not to grammars of the languages of Hawaii's immigrants; nor to that of Hawaiian, the indigenous language; nor to that of English, the politically dominant language; but rather to the grammars of other creole languages that had come into existence in other parts of the world. This fact argues that creole languages form an unusually direct expression of a species-specific biological characteristic, a capacity to re-create language in the absence of any specific model from which the properties of language could be "learned" in the ways we normally learn things.

A creole language, by way of Bickerton's own elemental definition, is a "nativized pidgin. It is what results when a pidgin, created
by adults, is learned by the children of those adults," and if he is
correct, of course, his conclusion clearly buttresses the claims of
linguistic "nativists" like Chomsky, who argue that some sort of
inherent language lies inside each one of us and who contend that
we don't need to *learn* language so much as simply to start speaking.

It is easy enough to latch on to the notion that much of childhood
is *for* learning language, a time of awestruck discovery and oddly
purposeful play that lingers long enough for complex language to
assume its shape and perhaps even to shape similarly all abstraction
in our brains. But to go one step further and imagine that children—
quite innocently, without the slightest sense that they do so—create
language not only for themselves but also for *society* is an idea that
begs a question or two. Very long ago, for instance, was it children
who made some sense of their parents' snorts and glottal sounds,
then linked them in the several ways that began to signify a whole
array of things? Did children unwittingly play with words and their
meanings, generations in succession, in the creative kinds of ways
that ultimately turned the Indo-European language into twelve new
tongues and then twelve dozen more? Did children on the island of
Great Britain, their parents Norse speakers as well as speakers of
Old English, meld the two languages in ways that interrelated them
forevermore? Was it children, rather more specifically than an amor-
phous mass of "common folk," who, along about 1100, first mixed the
Normans' Romance French with their own still-Germanic speech,
creating as they did so a language that seemed to revel in both roots,
one far richer for the mixture?

"If Bickerton is right," offers physician, essayist, and "word-
watcher" Lewis Thomas,

we have a new possibility to consider in speculations about the
origin of human language, whenever it was that that landmark
event for the species took place. We are born . . . with centers
of some kind in our brains for formulating grammar and manu-
facturing metaphors. Moreover, we become specialized for the

uniquely human function in the early years of our childhood, . . . the period in which our brains are so immensely
productive for the survival and further development of our
species, learning to speak and acquiring new ideas about acquiring ideas.

If Bickerton is right, then what it means to be a child perhaps
grows more complex. Maybe childhood isn't merely a kind of patient
practice, a blissful sort of tuning up in preparation for years of substance that lie ahead; and perhaps childhood's inherent language-
learning process isn't solely private, the province of each individual.
Instead, it just may be that although evolution has tricked the wee
ones into thinking they're having *fun*, children actually are doing
essential social work that adults simply cannot do, work that must
be done as long as we are gregarious creatures linked by language.

Bickerton is careful to make clear that *new* languages emerge in
the sociable midst of children only when their parents' sole communal speech is a protolanguage and when children in turn, and somehow magically, shape syntax from its raw materials. When true
languages are spoken in a multilingual culture, however, an utterly
new language never will spill out of the attendant linguistic stew.
Rather, the dominant language will be transfigured in fateful ways
by its intercourse with those languages that flank it or surround it,
and the minority tongues will be altered too. Language is, by its
nature, too malleable, too amenable to change, too receptive to
innovation for it to resist the seductions of new words, new ways of
saying things, despite dozens of resolute attempts throughout history
to keep one language or another chaste, uncompromised, chauvinis-
tically pure. And again, it seems very likely that it is children who
turn linguistic vagaries, quirks, and fashions into adopted forms,
children who in time transform novel usages into lingua franca.

You can imagine, for example, how Anglo-Saxon children born
in about 880 might have heard their elders employing novel yet
nonetheless quite useful Norse words like *rotten*, *dazzle*, *scream*, or
sky, and who would have noted nothing exotic or unusual about

them, the children in turn adopting those words, *speaking* them just as they did all the others that flew from their tongues, firmly fixing them in the Old English lexicon in only a generation. You can imagine how this process similarly occurred as thousands of French words and phrases became current along about 1100, and it's easy to imagine too how, by Elizabethan times, when both *shoes* and *shoen*, *houses* and *housen* (plus hundreds more) were commonly and variously used as plurals, it was in the playful speech of children that the orally simpler -*s* form emerged as standard—except, of course, in the curious case of *children*.

In my own corner of the world, where just a few generations ago English and Spanish first collided in a region of canyons and mesas and desert plains, this inexorable process similarly continued— words like *lariat* (from *la riata*), *buckeroo* (from *vaquero*), and even *canyon* (from *cañon*) that first were the bastardized Spanish of English speakers, later emerging as words in their own right in marvelously mongrel English, the process complete as soon as a subsequent generation of children put them to daily practice without knowing or caring about their etymology. The English spoken contemporarily in the American Southwest is flush with Spanish influence, and you could select hundreds of word-specific cases like this one that relates specifically to me: my mother and her brother and sisters using *savvy* as a synonym for *know* as they grew up because they so often had heard their father inquiring, "*Sabes?* Do you understand?" as he sought to communicate with his Spanish-speaking herders; my sisters and I in turn giving *savvy* little thought, *no* thought except at those times when we announced that there was something we simply didn't savvy.

There is a substantial difference, I understand, between the admission of slang words into a generally accepted lexical canon and the creation of an entire language out of only a few common protolinguistic words and phrases. Yet both processes make rich use of language's ability to find ever-new ways of representing abstractions and describing what has been observed or undergone; both highlight the fact that language is as ephemeral and changeable as sound itself, as music is; and surely both are also partial proofs that the verbal music made in childhood is the point from which all other linguistic art and communication commence, then make their way.

In his widely influential book *Language in Thought and Action,* first published in 1940, the late S. I. Hayakawa tangentially addresses this linguistic social work of children in his focus on what he calls *presymbolic* language, a kind of speech rooted in that ancient time when human sounds possessed only the vaguest kinds of meanings, yet too a kind of speech we still engage in every day. Long before our ancestors developed symbolic, representational speech, they, like other animals, made much use of expressive cries of several kinds—grunts, growls, coos, and shouted sounds that denoted hunger, fear, triumph, or sexual desire. But although those social sounds somehow evolved over time into symbolic language, Hayakawa is convinced that a human need to express internal conditions through nonsymbolic noise has remained constant for those hundred millennia or more. The result, he posits, "is that we use language in *pre*symbolic ways; that is, as the equivalent of screams, howls, purrs, and gibbering. These presymbolic uses of language coexist with our symbolic systems, and we still make constant recourse to them in the talking we do in everyday life."

Spoken conversation among adults is often largely presymbolic, Hayakawa contends—ranging from the most basic shouted warnings, in which volume and tone of voice are far more important than is the meaning of specific words, to the kind of cocktail party chatter at which each of us is variously adept, the kind of conversation in which topics or commentaries really matter not a whit. What *is* important in the latter context, according to Hayakawa, is what he calls "communion":

> Human beings have many ways of establishing communion among themselves: breaking bread together, playing games together, working together. But talking together is the most

easily arranged of all these forms of collective activity. The *togetherness* of the talking, then, is the most important element in social conversation; the subject matter is only secondary.

Yet if adults are decent presymbolic speakers, children are true masters. If you ever have watched in amazement as two four-year-olds who haven't met before—or two strangers at eight and ten years, even—get under way with fort building or jumping rope or an ear-piercing battle of televised Nintendo within only seconds of being introduced by their parents, you have witnessed children's ability to "commune," to use Hayakawa's word, at its most immediate. Until they are beset at eleven or twelve with the kind of self-consciousness that presages puberty, kids are remarkably capable of achieving this communal togetherness, whether with family or friends *or* with fellows newly met, in very large part because their whirlwind of speech is seldom encumbered by concerns about what is being *said*.

Kids, as well as adults, often speak for no other reason than to stave off silence, yet it seems that at the core of children's essentially presymbolic prattle—a flurry of subjects shifting moment to moment—is precisely the kind of process that allows them to become the language makers that Bickerton contends they are. It is their ability to shed the weight of subjects as they speak and to focus their subconscious instead on the shape of the language itself—its vocal inflections, its fluidity, the relationships of verbs to objects, the myriad clever linkages that are the province of prepositions and conjunctions—that allows them to grow so at ease with language's inherent creativity that before long they are eloquent creators themselves. The presymbolic speech of children is analogous to finger painting in that respect, I suppose—an accurately represented subject far beside the point; color and shape and the sensuous feel of each successive swirl the enterprise's actual raisons d'être; a sure sense of how you paint far more important than any *thing* that is represented. Or indeed that is spoken while at play.

—

To everyone's great pleasure at Gateway Elementary, the playful presymbolic chatter of Ian's several classmates didn't unduly disturb him that first fall. Nor did their energetic antics in the classroom perturb his precisely set routines, in large part because the kids themselves quickly learned to give him ample space. And the thing that perhaps seemed most remarkable about the advent of Ian's public life was that, if you knew him well and watched him carefully, you couldn't help but be convinced that he *loved* being old enough— and, yes, ordinary enough—to go to school. He would rush into the classroom in great anticipation each day and invariably greet Mary Lou with a wide smile. And there were other, subtler responses: a kind of obvious pride in what he was accomplishing, the pleasure he evidenced in being part of something large and shared and success- ful, and rather more specifically, the excitement and discovery— though masked by his autism—that surely were attendant with the likelihood that he was learning how to read.

In the same way that Claudia very slowly had eased Ian into school life with her by his side, late in September she subsequently had begun to remove herself from the special-education classroom where he spent most of his time—disappearing first for just a few minutes before the school day ended, then earlier each day until she simply would arrive with him, then leave. By Christmastime, Ian had become such a standard sort of student that he even had received his first report card, this one written by Charmaine Thaner, high- lighting his achievements and addressing rather kindly and euphe- mistically those areas where he indeed was deficient or unacceptably "unique," Charmaine outlining his progress as it pertained to several skills:

> *Interaction skills:* Ian engages in parallel play with other stu- dents at the water table. He is able to remain in the same area as a group of four students during a language activity for approximately ten minutes. He has begun to do worktime at

a table while a peer is present. He has swung on the tire-swing twice with a peer for approximately five minutes each time.

Augmentative communication skills: Ian can press the correct level button on his VOIS with a verbal prompt. He can press the correct picture with 90% accuracy. Ian can sign "open" [in ASL] at appropriate times. He often needs prompting to sign "all done" and "up."

Reading readiness skills: Ian currently is reaching for the correct word card when given two choices with nearly 100% accuracy. He can correctly place seven puzzle pieces together. He is beginning to match magnetic letters to the outline of those letters to spell names and words.

For some time, Ian had been successfully selecting the proper picture from among the several options offered him. "Show me the picture of Daddy," he had been asked hundreds of times, for instance, and invariably he had selected the photograph of his father. In much the same way, he now could demonstrate he knew his numbers and the letters of the alphabet and he also could reach for the movie he wanted to see by selecting from among the single large words written on the spines of videocassettes. So this new ability to point to the requested word from among two choices offered him on separate cards wasn't, on its face at least, a spectacular accomplishment, yet together with his growing interest in having favorite books read to him at home as well as at school, something rather extraordinary did seem to be under way: despite his inability to speak, the totality of language clearly had not been lost to him. Whatever Ian's neural deficits specifically included, they did not involve an entire inability to make sense of linguistic symbols. He long since had demonstrated that he could comprehend spoken speech, at least at a basic level; it had seemed easy for him to memorize the written English alphabet; and now, when presented with cards that read *goat* and *duck*, or even *car* and *cat*, he could point to the proper word when requested to do so. His facility with these skills surpassed the majority of his kindergarten peers, and by the measure of most every scholastic indicator only one conclusion could be drawn: Ian, like an ordinarily wondrous five-year-old, was on the verge of reading.

Apart from the voice his VÔĪS gave to him, he still could express almost nothing, but imagine what could come his way if ever he truly could *read*! If books could become as elemental as his movies were, then wouldn't the length of Ian's reach beyond his isolation become nearly limitless? If he could read, wouldn't he experience vicariously the very things from which autism kept him otherwise at bay? If Ian could read the printed words and stories that captured his interest as well as understand what was spoken to him, then even absent speech, surely he would live a life alive with language.

When Charmaine reported on Ian's progress again in the slow-commencing, snow-shrouded spring, she noted that he had to be challenged with new word cards often nowadays because his vocabulary was growing so rapidly. Intriguingly, he had begun to touch his teachers' mouths when he wanted them to pronounce a name or when something specific needed to be said as part of an important school-day ritual. And accompanied by what must have been over-whelming kinds of encouragement, Ian also had begun to try to vocalize the sounds that animals make as he encountered their pictures in books: "Oi, oi, oi," he would struggle hard to say when he saw a picture of a pig; the sounds "Mumm, mumm" now often emerged from his mouth as he encountered a treasured cow.

For three hours each day, five critical days a week for seven months, Ian had been something of a model student, not because he had been easy to contend with or the kind of self-starter you could nudge then leave alone; Ian in fact needed constant attention to help him stay on task, and he remained every bit as vulnerable as he always had been to catastrophic explosions. He still wore diapers, to everyone's dismay; he couldn't wash his hands or take off his boots or coat, nor could he put them on again; he still would attempt to push strangers (the school's principal among them) out of his classroom and would scream at the top of his lungs, for instance, if a particular green chair had been pushed against an improper table. Yet too, Ian had shown determinedly, his parents could attest, a subtle but real desire to do his best at school. He somehow could endure disruptions at school that would make him crazy anywhere else; at school he could stretch his attention span to a point far beyond where it normally broke at home; and you could see it in his tongue-tied endeavor to enunciate the growls and honks of animals— a kind of *trying* that was new and remarkable and which enormously endeared him to his teachers and to the children whom he sat beside each day, kids with obstacles to contend with in their own right, of course, but all of whom could talk, kids who lately had taken to hollering in happy excitement each time Ian accomplished something new, something *they* could do, something some of them still couldn't.

Already a productive *pre*reader, Ian had thoroughly convinced Charmaine, Mary Lou, and other staff at Gateway that soon he would be reading, their convictions billowing, of course, as he began to distinguish readily between words like *about* and *among*, their buoyant support of this intriguing boy mounting commensurately, the huge amount of extra work and care he demanded, the intense stress he inevitably transferred to them at times, worth the connection, the curious *communion*, they declared. Come first grade, his teachers averred, Ian, like other kids at five then six and seven, would begin to glimpse the way in which language really did link everyone—a kind of touching as real as hugs and holding hands—as well as the truth that although he might be mute, he never had to be languageless, absent that link between himself and a public world he had begun to open to. Come first grade, they knew as they observed him now, Ian, in companion with his classmates, would begin to take a kind of personal command of the social English language—in his case, at least as it was written—to discover not just the English that had come to each of them through time, but a language too that always was brand-new.

6

A CLEAR AND ORDERLY
ARRANGEMENT

Although perhaps most parents would argue otherwise, human children grow up slowly. Unlike our close kin the apes, whose offspring remain dependent on their progenitors for as little as three months following birth for many monkeys and only as long as four years or so among the long-lived chimpanzees, children in every human society need nurturance at least until puberty, until they have lived and grown for thirteen, fourteen, even eighteen years. And the principal reason for our lengthy, leisurely childhoods has far less to do with societal or even parental altruism among our species than it does with human biology and its evolutionary basis.

It is a curious fact that fetal and infant apes bear a close resemblance to adult humans. With their flat faces, long necks, round heads, small teeth, and massive brains in relation to their body weight, prenatal apes appear more *Homo* than hominid. There is little hair on their bodies at birth, the ridges on their brows have yet to develop, and their spinal cords still enter their skulls directly beneath their brains, allowing erect postures. But apes mature quite quickly after birth, their bodies changing dramatically as they approach adulthood, the physical distinctions between them and humans ultimately becoming quite pronounced. The evolutionary rift that now separates humans and hominids did not begin with a speeding up of the apes' development, however. It came, rather, with a pronounced *slowing down* of *Homo*'s rate of maturation, a process known as "neoteny."

Literally meaning "holding youth," the notion of neoteny was first proposed by Dutch anthropologist Louis Bolk, who developed a theory of "fetalization" in the early years of this century. Although much of Bolk's work soon became discredited, his idea that an evolutionary slowing down of physical development can allow a species that has become overspecialized—too good at too few endeavors—to return to a more general, less specialized form has remained academically important. In the context of human evolution, it is now widely agreed that the most significant aspect of the DNA-regulated slowing down of postnatal development was the formation of the big and complex brain. The brains of large apes are three-quarters complete at birth and are fully, entirely formed by six months of age. The human brain, in contrast, doubles its weight during the first year of life, then increases it again by twenty-five percent in the second year and fifteen percent in the third. "Such an altered program of growth," Jeremy Campbell explains in his wide-ranging book *Grammatical Man*,

> so important for human uniqueness, is under the control of the algorithms, or rules, contained in the DNA message. Clearly, these algorithms have changed during the course of evolution, and they have changed in ways which enable humans to become neotenous, retarding the timetable of maturity for the brain. This means that the schedule for the formation of the brain does not come to an end immediately, or even very soon after the infant leaves the womb of the mother. The brain goes on growing after birth at a rate almost as rapid as before birth. The result is that the neural circuits are still being laid down at a time when the child is growing up and coming to terms with its world. They are open to the full impact of information pouring in from the outside.

An obvious consequence of the uniquely slow development of the human brain, Campbell points out, is that humans are much less bound by automatic or instinctive mental responses than are related species, the brains of humans made malleable, inherently creative, and receptive to novelty by the dramatic process of discovering and learning that accompanies brain growth. A 1979 study by Peter Huttenlocker, professor of pediatrics at the University of Chicago, has determined, in fact, that by age six a human brain, which has at last grown virtually to full size, possesses more complex neural circuitry in its cerebral cortex than it ever will have again, yet the electrical firing within those circuits remains slower and more irregular than do impulses in an adult brain—those two coincident conditions, Huttenlocker maintains, making possible a six-year-old's enormous capacity to acquire, manipulate, and remember abstract information and the symbology of language. "One of the most interesting aspects of the six-year-old brain," he says, "is that a child who has had little educational experience in this crucial year has tremendous difficulty in catching up later, even with very good effort. Six seems to be a critical period, a time when the brain is especially receptive."

And so it had seemed with the six-year-old Ian Drummond. If the year when he was five had been his coming out—and it had been in greatly encouraging ways: the emergence of a heretofore pathologically private boy into a world occupied and animated by other people—the year when Ian was six became a year of commensurate discovery, of engagement, and even of nascent speech. Although he was dramatically different from other children in so many critical respects, his own developmental timetable now seemed to approximate normalcy if indeed that seventh year of life was so seminal. His brain, though undeniably unique, appeared to be maturing in much the same way and at the same time as the brains of other boys and girls, and Ian was growing from infancy into full-fledged *kiddom* at long last, each day still very difficult but nonetheless laced with hope.

On the morning of August 2, 1989, Ian's sixth birthday, his sister, Sarah, excitedly had presented him with a box wrapped in festive paper and topped with a bow. Although he never had paid attention to packages before, this one somehow captured his interest and he seemed to know already that he would have to strip away the paper to look inside. With Sarah's help, the wrapping came away and Ian instantly was engaged by a plastic truck in which rode Winnie-the-Pooh and Tigger. Those two figurines were critical to his attraction, of course, and trucks too were becoming something of a big deal these days, but whatever the several reasons for this present's appeal, the larger import of the moment was not lost on Sarah or her parents: this was the first time Ian *ever* had taken immediate interest in an object with which he was unfamiliar. The toys and figurines he had grown to treasure over the years all had been part of his bedroom environment since before the time when his life had so catastrophically changed. And up till now, new toys or objects of any sort had received either his utter disinterest—a kind of looking through them as though they didn't exist—or, as much more commonly was the case, a screaming rejection and the attendant certainty that they would have to be taken away.

Ian had spent much of that summer he turned six at Gateway Elementary. A nine-week summer program had been devised solely for him and one other special-education student—a small, physically delicate little boy with a sunny countenance and constant smile whom I'll call Leroy, a boy who had befriended Ian during the preceding school year and to whom Ian by now had returned his affection, sometimes touching Leroy's shoulder or leg as they sat listening to a story, hugging him as well on those unpredictable occasions when a hug somehow was warranted. Five days a week, Ian and Leroy would go to school happily, eagerly, as though summer holidays were for sissies, accompanied in that cavernous building solely by Mary Lou Krueger, the teaching assistant to whom Ian by now had formed a special bond. Claudia clearly was the most critical person in Ian's life; Boyce was indispensable to him in several very specific as well as ineffable paternal ways; and to Mary Lou Ian now had given a commensurate kind of trust—he now seemed similarly dependent on her for security and solace, for help and steadfast affection.

It was Ian's ability to express affection—I think I can call it love—
that in turn so readily had endeared him to so many of the people
he had begun to know. Although his autism had to be considered
severe in terms of his speech deficit and his needs for exacting ritual
and self-stimulation, he by now had become more able than most
children with autism to make social and emotional connections with
others. Ian still needed to spend an enormous amount of time utterly
alone and in the solitary domain of his bedroom, and apart from the
quick, fleeting appearance of his smile, he never demonstrated that
he was excited to see anyone—the moment the smile faded he
invariably would continue alone about his business. Yet he *had*
grown social nonetheless: He clearly held his sister, Sarah, in a
younger sibling's sort of awe, and people like me and his four grandparents had begun to be important to him as well. At school, Mary
Lou was his loving surrogate mother, Leroy his best buddy, and a
remarkable high school student named Jenefer Elsea, who first had
volunteered in his classroom and who lately had begun to visit Ian
at home as well, had forged with him a fast and special friendship.
Even Sheila, the long-suffering family dog whom Ian hadn't seemed
to notice for so many years, now was undeniably *his* dog: he loved
to push his nose into her dense coat, to lie on her as if she were a
pillow, and he even had begun to feed her as his first official enterprise every morning.

Although Ian still could venture into only a few specific buildings,
he loved to walk anywhere and everywhere outside, to wander according to his instincts, and he could travel in the car some distance
now—just as long as the destination was his grandparents' house in
distant Cortez and as long as the route didn't deviate in the slightest
during the six-hour drive from the one he readily had memorized.
At his grandparents' house, Ian could adopt a strange bedroom for
a span of several days—provided it was overhauled into a near
facsimile of his room at home—watching his movies and completing
his routines there as if nothing were terribly out of the ordinary; he
could come out to the country where Karen and I lived and run
beside *our* fences, and the playground equipment at a park in town
was an acceptable substitute for the swings and slides he loved at

Gateway. And it was in Cortez on an abbreviated summer vacation that followed his birthday and the close of summer school that Ian began to spend several hours kicking, splashing, and giggling in a swimming pool, delighting in the water—appropriately cautious but unafraid—floating alone for the first time, an inflated tube wrapped around him, jumping from the tiled lip of the pool into his father's open arms, appearing for all the world like a kid who'd just turned six.

If all his heady, hopeful progress in recent months hadn't been enough to buoy his parents' spirits, to give them a glimpse of a family life filled as much with pleasure and accomplishment as it inevitably would remain racked by crisis, Ian enormously pleased them in mid-August by becoming basically toilet-trained at long last. Claudia and Boyce had been struggling toward that fairly fundamental goal for four years, trying every trick they could muster, seeking the counsel of experts of several sorts, offering food and favorite music at those occasional times when he would perform appropriately, trailing him for hours, inside the house and out, carrying a heavy potty chair that battered and bruised their legs, his father even offering demonstrations, yet nothing had worked till now. Toilet-training had seemed somehow beyond Ian for so long—serial sensations and responses he just couldn't grasp, couldn't understand or be bothered with—until at last a Mickey Mouse "Touch and Discover" toy began to appear, as if out of nowhere, only at those times when Ian successfully peed in the proper place. The toy so delighted him that it took him only a day or so to connect the toy with the toilet and with his fitting response, a huge leap at last accomplished, a subsequent series of telephone calls going out from the house on Redfeather Lane announcing great good news.

Ian now was ready for first grade, ready to continue the odyssey outside his bedroom he so successfully had commenced the year before. Following many hours of meetings in the spring—consultations that included his several teachers, Gateway counselors and administrators, therapists and psychologists from the Board of Coop-

erative Educational Services, and his parents—a decision had been
made to increase the length of Ian's school day from three hours to
five and to include him each day in a regular first-grade classroom
for math, story time, lunch, and the recess that followed lunch. His
day would be lengthened gradually, to be sure, and his introduction
to the classroom would proceed cautiously as well, but despite what
still appeared to several of the professionals involved in his schooling
to be Ian's overwhelming disabilities, and despite the potential for
myriad attendant problems, at last it was agreed that this next experimental step should be taken.

Prior to Ian's actual introduction to his classmates in September,
Claudia, Charmaine Thaner, Ian's special-education teacher from
the year before, and first-grade teacher Barbara Myers had decided
it made some sense to discuss with them the unique new boy who
soon would spend part of his day inside their room. One morning
Charmaine came to Gateway and showed the attentive, curious,
still-shy first-graders in Barb Myers's class a videotape Claudia had
prepared—a collage of images of a kid who looked normal enough,
a blond boy running through a stand of ponderosa trees, swinging
and sliding on the same playground they had gotten to know, images
too of Ian reading books in a kind of funny way, quickly flapping the
pages just inches from his eyes, pictures of Ian using his VOÌS
instead of his mouth to talk, and impressive proof as well that *he*
already could use a computer. Claudia explained on the videotape
that she was Ian's mother, that he also had a dad and a dog and a
sister named Sarah; she told them that Ian liked to take hikes, that
he liked animals and stories about animals, and that he loved to
watch all sorts of movies. He was good with arithmetic, she said,
and, like them, he was eager to learn how to read—a pretty regular
kid, it began to seem. Yet the kinds of sounds Ian would make when
they began to get to know him, she explained, wouldn't quite be
words, and Ian wouldn't say anything they actually could understand;
sometimes he would move them out of his way—like he was mean
and pushy—but it only would be because he really *needed* to go
where he was going. He would get very upset sometimes, crying
and screaming for reasons that wouldn't seem to make much sense,

and at other times more understandable things like loud noises would disturb him; he would spend lots of time by himself, even when they wanted him to join them, but it would be only because he needed to be quiet and not because he didn't like them. Claudia closed by saying that although it probably didn't count since she was his mom, she nonetheless liked Ian a lot, and she knew that other kids would too. Following the video, Charmaine answered just a question or two about whether Ian was into Ninja Turtles and if he could ride a bike before Barb thanked her for coming, adding as well that she already had met Ian and that she agreed with his mom that he was pretty cool.

When Ian first came to the room a few days later, his classmates were excited—some a little afraid, others quite eager to meet him—but within an hour or so his presence was little more than a matter of course, and Ian too took this new step in his own kind of stride. He could eat his lunch of rice cakes and peanut butter at a table with other kids in the cacophonous cafeteria; with the help of his aide and advocate, Mary Lou, he could remain peripherally attentive during math, and he loved sitting in a big circle on the floor to listen as Barb read wonderful stories. He still spent about half his day with Leroy and other kids in what was called the resource room, and his clockwork coming and going between the two seemed to suit his ritual needs. During his individualized language sessions, he ably demonstrated with word cards how his reading vocabulary had grown during the summer just ended, and by early October he could successfully identify from among several choices a variety of two-word phrases—a subject paired with a verb—that formed simple sentences: Mommy laughs, Sarah laughs, Daddy sings, Ian swings, Ian *dances*.

Every one of the world's estimated twenty-seven hundred languages is built on the structural foundation of the sentence, and every sentence in every language contains a subject and a predicate. That elemental truth is responsible in large part for the several curious dichotomies that are inherent to each language: each is at once startlingly simple and intricately complex; each is tightly bound by unbreakable rules yet made limitless by possible combinations of words, messages, and ideas; each is an utterly abstract and artificial construction that is the only means at our disposal for informing and describing the nuts-and-bolts business of reality.

It is equally intriguing to consider the fact—an indisputable sort of certainty—that a "primitive" language never has been spoken. Zulu, Bantu, Cherokee, and Kiowa are languages that are every bit as sophisticated as Latin or its descendants, as richly etched and multifaceted as English; even very recent languages like Hawaiian Creole are as structurally complex as those that have endured throughout the epochs. As languages come into being or undergo substantial change, their structures, their grammars, indeed evolve, but they never do so in ways that can be measured hierarchically or qualitatively. As linguist Robin Lakoff explains,

> languages have an internal rationale for what is going to change and in what way. As the case system went out of Latin, for example, Latin started to impose a fixed word order, and these changes went inexorably together, because there must be a way of giving information about structure, and if cases no longer do so, then the order of the words in the sentence must take on that task. . . . There is no reason why language should decay, any more than the human mind should decay. The conceptual structures of the mind that are responsible for the universal forms of grammar do in fact keep language running.

Languages are structured in a multitude of ways, and the structure of a given language is its *grammar*, a word we unfortunately tend to associate with junior high school and the nasty certainty that education could be cruel. Yet regardless of whether any of us ever learns to identify past imperfect tenses or those tricky subjunctive moods, we employ our grasp of grammar in every sentence that we speak, that grammar composed of two principal components: morphology, from the Greek *morphe*, meaning "form," is the structure of words themselves; and syntax, a variant of the Greek word for "arrangement," is the positioning of words into sentences. But in part because so many of us cannot help but conjure an image of a spinster teacher with an attitude when we think of *grammar*, the term *syntax* often is used to encompass both morphology and syntax, and the word *grammar* in turn tends to be reserved for that kind of woeful study that once gave you and me the willies.

So there are *two* grammars to consider—the larger definition a referent to the inherent shape that every language assumes, the narrower one the sort of academic construction, under way for centuries, that attempts both to catalog and to regulate that shape. And perhaps the principal reason that latter grammar has confounded so many earnest young English speakers for so long is that the grammars first devised for our marvelous but mongrel idiom not only were based on the intricate grammatical structure of Latin but were *written* in Latin as well, a notion that made much sense during eras when it was deemed natural, indeed necessary, to build linguistic models on classical, albeit sometimes dead, languages. English, complained poet John Dryden in 1660, had "not so much as a tolerable dictionary or a grammar; so our language is in a manner barbarous," and for that misfortunate reason, Dryden explained that he could only endeavor to improve his English sentences by translating them into Latin, then revising and polishing them to a classical fare-thee-well before translating them back into English.

The fact that the English language had little in common with the structure of Latin didn't concern grammarians for many centuries, in fact, and so-called traditional grammar was devised, espoused, and taught as inviolate into the middle of this century, finally relegated to the linguistic rag heap only as widening studies of non-European languages made it ever clearer that at the subsentence level, languages could be quite different: Japanese, for instance, is a language that treats pronouns, verbs, and adjectives in ways that seem bizarre to most of the rest of us; nouns and verbs in Chinese and Vietnamese are not inflected by declensions or conjugations; and the Inuit language intricately combines constituent elements to the point that single words are often whole sentences themselves. In an attempt to address these varieties of form, so-called structural grammars at last began to be introduced, attempts to analyze each language in terms of its particular and unique structure by focusing on its external form. Yet while structural grammars succeeded admirably in terms of their ability to dissect languages into their component parts without the kind of pigeonholing that theretofore had gone on, they approached language rather formally, statically, tending to ignore its constant changes and seemingly unconcerned with the fact that languages somehow were acquired in all their complexity by little children who had as yet to become licensed grammarians themselves.

It was the issue of the acquisition of language, one that became the focus of Chomsky and his colleagues in the 1950s, that finally led to the development of what are now known as generative or transformational grammars, and which indeed gave a new general definition to the term—grammar no longer a rulebook but rather a theory, an attempt to be scientific, yes, but also to come to terms with essences and the biggest possible picture of what language *is* and how each of us comes to claim it. The new grammarians, with Chomsky in the controversial lead, wanted to address language with the same enormity of scope that modern physicists used to approach the subjects of matter and energy. They wanted to pose comprehensive propositions about the nature, use, and acquisition of language, then to test them with empirical data. In that context, the sentence rather than its many parts became the distilled focus of their study, and they collectively undertook the challenge to describe successfully the parameters of all those sentences that are acceptable, hence "grammatical," to native speakers of any given language. Although modern grammarians—more commonly now identified as linguists—still employ some of the terminology first introduced with traditional and structural grammars, they toil in a weedy field nowadays, one far more abstract than any Dryden could have imagined, their manipulations of concepts like P-rules and T-rules, X-bars and cyclic conventions, enough to make your head hurt, enough to make that world of interrogative pronouns and subjunctive clauses seem indeed like kid stuff.

Although Ian's ability to point to specific sentences was brand-new, he had been fascinated with the sequential words that made up books for some time. He would object when his mother or father skipped a word in a familiar story, sometimes pointing it out as a means of insisting that it be read, proof as well that the story's words were more than merely memorized, and he had begun to demonstrate a real affinity for stories written in rhyme, the books of Dr. Seuss in particular, the cadences of his sentences and the surprise of the rhymes themselves obviously appealing to Ian's ear, to a brain that seemed to seek out structure of every kind.

As Ian began to enter his first-grade class near the end of every morning, he would circle the perimeter of the room while Barb Myers read aloud to her students. It wasn't long, however, before he had begun to sit on the floor at the flank of the cluster of kids who sat crowded around her, and lately he even had begun to move well into their midst, simply wanting to join them now perhaps, perhaps needing a clearer view of the pictures that she showed, the books' pages opened wide, or was it that he wanted to hear better, Barb's words seeming to come directly at him where he sat, words that so well described those Cats in Hats and Whos? In addition to the entire oeuvre of Dr. Seuss, Ian's tastes in books ran readily toward animals—stories about animals occupied with regular barnyard business, tales of animals in the wild, as well as those fanciful sorts of stories about critters like Pooh and Tigger and cranky Eeyore, whose lives seemed a lot like people's. Ian made a point, Barb had noticed, of investigating as soon as they caught his eye the new books she would display on a chalk tray, and his own book box that sat beneath his desk was full of favorites he often chose to peruse during the silent reading time that preceded lunch.

On a day in early November, hard on the heels of the Halloween festivities that hadn't seemed to interest him at all, Ian and his classmates sat at their desks in the minutes before the lunch bell rang, each student quietly attending to a book, an illustrated story called *The Farm Concert* open in front of Ian. Her students that year tended to be a very vocal, high-energy kind of class, Barb remembers, but everyone was quiet by chance at the moment when Ian openly but rather nonchalantly said "cow." He spoke in a kind of throaty whisper and he said "cow" a second time—audibly, distinctly—before the room erupted in excitement, classmates shouting "Ian said 'cow'! Ian said 'cow'!," most of them rushing to his desk, surrounding him, pushing in on him in ways he might have hated, Barb beside him as well now, tears streaming down her face, a few girls teary too, and the jubilant boys whooping it up as though Ian had scored a touchdown. "Say it again! Say 'cow' again," the buoyant, blended voices encouraged him, and so he calmly said "cow" another time, the *ow* he shaped with his small mouth stretching out for a second as he softly spoke it, far from filling the room with sound yet heaping it high with accomplishment and then with commensurate amazement.

"Cow," Ian said that autumn day not long after he turned six, and was it only anecdotal, simply the most curious kind of coincidence, that the last time he spoke a word—four and a half years before—"cow" had been what he said? Or could you explain it by pointing out, accurately enough, that Ian had been fascinated by cows at eighteen months and so he remained at six, on both occasions cows therefore simply on his mind? Or—and this too certainly seemed a possibility—had the word *cow* and the means of pronouncing it been imprinted in Ian's left cerebral cortex long ago, the abstract word and the neural patterning that might have reproduced it lying latent until his brain somehow had redeveloped linguistic capabilities that the onset of autism had assaulted and destroyed?

It would be impossible to know the answer to that query, and for now at least that single spoken word seemed phenomenon enough, Ian's breath pushing "cow" out again as his buddies slapped his back and cheered, his face expressionless, outwardly unappreciative of their praise, yet Ian at six now clearly speaking, speaking just as he had some chaotic years ago, speaking that word he owned again in the seconds before the liberating lunch bell rang, before his delighted classmates rushed to the cafeteria to spread the incredible news.

Words did not begin to come in a fast and jumbled flurry following that remarkable November day, but other words nonetheless did start to issue out of Ian's mouth—slowly, one at a time, each the product of a tangled and difficult physical effort. A few of the new words he could enunciate easily, readily—*Mom, ball, good night*—while others were only the most liberal approximations of their usual sounds: *Sarah* was "Eesha"; *Tigger*, "Guhguh"; *eat* was "ee"; both *Kanga* and *donkey* were simply "kuh"; and *Leroy* consistently was "Bee." By Christmastime, Ian could pronounce, fairly intelligibly, the numbers from one to fifteen; he could say "go" and "bye" and sometimes "hi" quite clearly; "Dad" was more difficult, "Sheila" a true challenge, and "Mary Lou," despite its obvious utility, was a name he seldom attempted.

Years before, at the suggestion of staff at Denver's JFK Center, Claudia and Boyce had begun to speak to Ian in a kind of clipped and abbreviated fashion—saying "Ian go for ride" each time they climbed into the car; saying "Ian eat French fries" and "Tigger take bath too" and "Watch pig movie once more" as those phrases were appropriate—that recommendation, one they still adhered to, based on the assumption that highly filtered speech, speech reduced to its barest components, might well be easier for him to understand and one day even imitate. It was impossible to know, of course, whether years of addressing Ian in a kind of speech absent conjugations, sparing adjectives, adverbs, prepositions, and conjunctions, had helped him decipher what was being said, and neither did anyone know now whether his own budding, labored speech had been assisted by the simpler language he so long had heard. His first words tended to be names, just like those of a regular two-year-old, and if his speech was beginning to emerge in a commensurately normal progression, it seemed unlikely that it would be dependent on hearing a boiled-down sort of speech any more than would a normal child's. Yet as always, neither Ian's parents nor his teachers knew as much as they would have loved to have known about this boy's basic cognitive and linguistic abilities.

Ian was not classically retarded: his precise, seemingly photographic memory; his intuitive grasp of arithmetic and quick mastery of puzzles and computer games; and his burgeoning ability to select appropriate sentences all pointed toward average or even above-average intelligence. Yet still, Ian could not manipulate a fork or spoon; he had been partially toilet-trained only very recently; without constant supervision out-of-doors, he remained blithely willing to run away; and he still was terrorized by so many things that to any other child would have seemed benign, if not inherently intriguing. So it was hard to know just how to contend with this new surge of development, these many new milestones he had begun to reach. Should Ian be treated and taught much like a normal six-year-old, his ritualization and his absence of speech peripheral albeit important issues? Or was he to be considered highly, even profoundly, handicapped, although possessed of selectively impressive skills?

Claudia and Boyce long had championed Ian's right to a comprehensive public education, and they worked to make his childhood as richly ordinary as it could be within the constraints of his obsessive necessities and his constant crises, yet it was inescapably ironic that it increasingly fell to them these days to make the case to school psychologists, administrators, and even teachers that despite his terrific progress, he remained a dramatically disabled boy. Ian was capable of remarkable things at school, it was true, but increasingly he had to pay a traumatized price for his public achievements in the late afternoons and evenings he spent at home. His attentiveness and plucky attempts to be flexible at school were countered at home with an even greater than usual fragility and need for precision in everything from food to movies to the placement of furniture. The books he calmly, carefully read at school, his finger following each word, he simply flapped in front of his eyes at home, and although he was able to spend the school day in the close proximity of dozens of children and adults, their attention often focused intently on him, at home he craved, and indeed demanded, the solitude of his room for hours on isolated end.

The case Claudia and Boyce ultimately tried to make—and at which they basically succeeded—was that Ian rather completely and uniquely embodied those two extremes, and he probably always would. He likely would remain a kid for whom multiplication tables would be a snap but for whom using a pencil would be impossible; although using a computer for many tasks clearly would be common-place for him, fire drills or impromptu assemblies that altered his school-day schedule surely would continue to make him crazy. And the same kids, such as dear and tiny Leroy, with whom Ian would hold hands and whom he even would hug at school, he curtly would close out of his room if they tried to visit him at home. Despite his progress and the basic dependability of his socialized behavior, Ian surely would remain confoundingly difficult at times. And although his growing ability to identify sentences might burgeon next into an ability to create them himself from word cards or even to speak those sentences eloquently and clearly, Ian's parents and the people who directed his days at school did their best to recognize and remember that brains beset with autism seldom ceased to demand idiosyncratic kinds of structure, and that they always were needy of much that others could not understand.

"Go cows," Ian said out loud in midwinter, the first time he had linked two words together, a spoken sentence of sorts, but one far less sophisticated than the sentences his VÓIS still vocalized for him as he pressed a single key: "I am thirsty for some juice"; "I want to play on the slide." Ian's spoken words seemed characteristic of what Derek Bickerton calls protolanguage, a communicative use of lin-guistic symbols that precedes true language in all children, but which, he contends, is largely unrelated to it. In contrast, the sen-tences programmed into the VÓIS's circuitry, although still simple, were grammatically *linguistic*; they contained readily identifiable subjects, verbs, and objects, as well as the prepositions and conjunc-tions that link words with some subtlety and begin to offer infinite possibility for the creation of similar kinds of sentences. "Language seems to have so much that is missing from protolanguage," Bickerton explains,

> infinitely recursive processes; the binding of anaphors and the traces of moved constituents; government, the "proper" as well as ordinary; case assignment; the processes by which null elements are identified; constraints on movement; adjunction, conjunction, and the embedding of constituents . . . From where can all these principles and processes have sprung? The mere fact that they have all, at one time or another, been proposed as concepts indispensable for the proper understanding of language argues that language is itself an immensely complex, multifaceted, and essentially mysterious thing. This is not necessarily the case, however. It should be borne in mind that the structure of language was, to all intents and purposes, a new field as recently as the 1950s, since only taxonomic studies of syntax had been conducted until then.

It was Noam Chomsky, of course, who began to look at syntax, née grammar, in revolutionary ways in the 1950s, and although there is no denying that his and his colleagues' discourses on syntax did then and often still do appear as impenetrable as modern number theory to those of us positioned outside their particular academic loop, at the heart of Chomsky's theory of syntax is the notion, rooted in observations of how children acquire language, that all language surely possesses innate and abstract structure. That structure, Chomsky's "universal grammar," is the source of regularity and order that underlies the noise and muddle of ordinary speech, acting as a filter, in effect, screening out vocal errors and myriad spoken tangents, preventing a kind of utter randomness to which language otherwise would fall prey, allowing spoken or written language to be understandable person to person because each of us inherently knows the rules, those rules preprogrammed in our brains.

An infant child—a child absent speech—hears every manner of haphazard, irregular, informal language as it is spoken by parents and siblings. If that child were dependent solely on the surface of what he or she hears for the deduction of grammatical rules, guessing at larger principles from bits and pieces of spoken data, that child necessarily would need to be something of a genius to master a language in only five or six years, Chomsky contends. Instead, he posits, the child's own innate language-ordering principles, as native to him or her as arms or appetites, allow first the making sense of the muddled speech, then soon its creative reproduction, virtually everyone capable of acquiring a first language. Jeremy Campbell elucidates Chomsky's thinking in *Grammatical Man*:

> Universal grammar . . . is not a grammar itself, but a theory of grammars in general, a set of hypotheses about them. And it is an observation worth repeating that the whole point of any theory, whether in linguistics or in physics, is that it does not merely account for the limited number of facts already known, but predicts the existence of additional facts which are still unknown. In short, a theory generates new information. It makes a lot of knowledge out of a little data. From the sparse and chaotic information given in the form of adult speech, children arrive at the grammar of their own language in a leap, as it were, rather than by a slow and painful process of learning and instruction, because a theory of grammar is in their heads as a gift of nature.

It is that ability to use language *theoretically*—to generate much that is new from only a little data—that ultimately distinguishes language from protolanguage. If protolanguage, the kind of speech that Ian now was gaining day by day, was communicative—and it was, of course—it was not inherently generative, productive of myriad new forms. As soon as Ian had succeeded in saying "go cows," you can imagine that he quickly might have begun to say "go school," "go Wendy's," and "go walk" as well, to transform one phrase into many, but he did not. Each new acquisition, each subsequent spoken word or group of words, he seemed to acquire independently of those he already commanded, and it appeared that at the root of these new skills was a fundamentally phonetic process—an imitation of word sounds, the nascent practice of pronunciation—along with an important but necessarily simple neural process of labeling, rather than something spurred by an unconscious application of syntactic rules.

Although he was six years old now, it was curious that this proto-linguistic stage—normally the province of two-year-olds—was not one he could somehow skip over as he began to speak. If Ian were to become a speaker, it seemed, he would have to leap from protolanguage to language just as younger children did, but now, at least, the possibility of true speech actually existed—words manifestly stirring in his brain, words transforming themselves from neural impulses into sputtered, gargled sounds while he was still young enough, still neurologically athletic enough, to make that leap to language.

Yet something most intriguing was also undeniably under way: At his teachers' prompting, and using cards instead of aural symbols for words, Ian by now *had* begun to reproduce sentences taken from his favorite books—sentences that were far more complex than those he could enunciate. He could, for example, arrange five cards into a linear order to create the sentence from *The Farm Concert* that read "Moo, moo, went the cow," then could replace three of the cards with others to create "Wuff, wuff, went the dog." And he even could improvise a bit, finding the place where the cards could be spread apart and the word *brown* could be inserted into the sentence, for instance, so that it became "Wuff, wuff, went the brown dog."

As Ian's *spoken* lexicon steadily grew larger that year—*bathroom, book, movie, morning, kiss, tickle,* and something more clearly approaching *Leroy* now instead of *Bee*—and as that first two-word phrase, *go cows*, was joined by a dozen others and even by three three-word phrases—*go to lunch, play the organ, time for snack*—it became increasingly obvious that much of Ian's spoken speech was echolalic, the repetition of words or phrases he had newly heard, a pattern of speech very common in people with autism. If Mary Lou asked, for example, "Ian, do you need to go to the bathroom?" then "go to bathroom" somehow could spill out of his mouth rather easily. And "It's time for your movie" similarly tended to prompt a spoken "your movie." Words seemed stuck oftentimes without that aural prompting, and Ian's verbal vocabulary seemed to grow in direct relation to questions commonly put to him. Yet in comparison, the kinds of sentences he could arrange with cards seemed to his teachers to be far more than merely echoes of the sentences in his books. He had to be encouraged to create them, it was true: he had to be at his specified table during his regular, daily language session, the cards spread in front of him, Mary Lou getting him settled, focused, and under way, but once those preconditions were met, he could arrange the cards with what appeared to be a budding sense of what was grammatical. He could substitute one adjective for another— *brown* becoming *gray*, for instance—and too, somehow he knew that "Quack, quack, said the duck" could be rearranged to read "The duck said, quack, quack," but that "Said quack duck the quack" simply wouldn't do.

At the same time that Ian's spoken speech remained protolinguis-tic, the normal kind of talk of a two-year-old, the manner in which he could arrange cards linguistically appeared rather distinct—a separate but coincident process perhaps, the latter employing a cognizance of syntactic order, Ian's expression via the word cards seemingly akin to the emergence of true language. In a normal child, these two linguistic stages virtually always would be sequential, developmentally separated by several years, but in Ian's case, they seemed simultaneous—yet how could that be so? How could a boy whose language skills had been so compromised, so completely lack-ing for so long, nonetheless show signs of having a six-year-old's good hold on English grammar? Why were the words he spoke so crudely limited, so terribly difficult to disgorge, while the words he manipu-lated on a table like some card shark evidenced a clear and orderly arrangement?

Were they to visit Woodland Park's Gateway Elementary one sunny winter morning and to observe Ian struggling to speak, few words at his tongue's command, and to observe him as well writing grammatical sentences with printed cardboard squares, I can imagine linguists Derek Bickerton and Noam Chomsky quickly taking keen and reinforcing kinds of interest. Although he might note that Ian's card manipulation might be little more than memorization, surely Bickerton would be tempted as well to see Ian's two distinct kinds of linguistic skills as evidence that language and protolanguage are largely unrelated and independent, with Ian, most unusually, possessing both forms at once—a case study not unlike the protolinguistic girl called Genie. Ian's speech was at least as limited as hers, but quite unlike Genie, he seemed capable of comprehending grammar's strictures and its freedoms, and he appeared on the verge of employing true language in a visual, written form. Surely Chomsky, on the other hand, would seize Ian's complex case as substantial proof that language and speech had far less in common than others of us tended to assume. Surely in his measured, soft-spoken voice he would attribute Ian's still-fledgling and faulty speech to some sort of compromise in the neural circuitry that linked his brain to his vocal tract, whereas his nascent written language skills were the product of an *uncompromised* language faculty elsewhere in his brain, its organizing and generating mechanisms successfully at work, syntax taking shape and assuming the subtlest kind of control, as it should, true language beginning to emerge via the sole symbolic avenue available to him.

But if Bickerton and Chomsky came to school, it would be less than cordial not to invite Philip Lieberman to join them for observation in Ian's classroom, Lieberman's perspectives often antithetical to theirs, yet equally elucidating, it seems to me, grounded fundamentally as they are in the evolutionary process and the theory that speech surely *is* language's prime catalyst. Lieberman does concede in *Uniquely Human* that "Noam Chomsky's intuitions probably are, in part, correct—human beings undoubtedly have brain mechanisms that genetically code some aspects of the possible syntactic rules of all human languages. However, the biological 'language organ' must conform to the general properties of biological organs—variation, maturation, and an evolutionary history," something Lieberman says is starkly lacking in Chomsky's basic theory. And if Lieberman were to take a turn assessing the roots of Ian's linguistic deficits as well as his nascent abilities, he might begin by comparing Ian's halting and ungrammatical few words to the kind of speech common to patients who have suffered strokes in Broca's area of the left temporal lobe.

Researchers have long understood something of the role Broca's area plays in the production of speech. But in recent years they have begun to amass much clearer evidence that, although Broca's region of the left cerebral hemisphere indeed is critical to several aspects of language function, its role is played only in concert with a variety of other brain structures. According to neuroscientists Donald Stuss and D. Frank Benson, damage to "the Broca area alone or its immediate surroundings (a lesion that could be called 'little Broca') is insufficient to produce the full syndrome of Broca's aphasia, at least not permanently. . . . The full, permanent syndrome (big Broca) invariably indicates larger [left] hemisphere destruction . . . including the area of Broca but extending deep into the insula and adjacent white matter and possibly including basal ganglia."

A "big Broca," generally defined, is a type of aphasia that results in greatly inhibited spontaneous speech, in speech that is hesitant, labored, distorted, the timing of the complex, sequential motor activity that is necessary to produce smooth speech somehow impeded. Many patients with Broca's aphasia are able solely to repeat simple words and phrases in the seconds after they have heard them and otherwise are mute; some speak ungrammatically, seemingly forgetting to use simple "function words" such as *the*, *by*, or *to*, or neglecting to conjugate verbs into tenses, for example, and their comprehension of speech, dependent as it is on syntactic cues, similarly tends to suffer. In addition to encountering problems with the motor aspects of speech—the coordination of the many essential movements of the mouth and throat—virtually all people with Broca's aphasia curiously suffer at least minor motor deficits in their faces, hands, arms, and legs as well, a kind of chronic clumsiness and weakness that tends to be right-sided and that often is most pronounced in an inability to coordinate fine motor movements involving the thumb and forefinger. This is a finding that corresponds with neurologist Doreen Kimura's contention that the brain mechanisms making possible the fluid production of speech probably evolved from mechanisms that first facilitated skilled hand movements, those mechanisms that first made possible precise tool-making movements evolving in time into gestural language systems before finally giving way to hand-freeing speech.

In Kimura's studies, conducted in the 1970s, she was able to show that several patients who had suffered a range of left-hemispheric speech damage also had difficulty performing precise thumb-finger movements, particularly if those movements were new or unusual rather than simple or stereotyped. That latter finding in particular has further piqued Lieberman's interest in two specific aspects of Broca's aphasia: first, the growing likelihood that it is the result of damage to *multiple* brain structures rather than damage isolated solely to Broca's region, and second, the possibility that Broca's aphasia also fundamentally involves an inability to coordinate *new* motor activity—whether new sentences or new movements of the fingers—mechanisms for the processing of novel motor activity localized in an area called the prefrontal cortex, located directly behind the forehead.

The human prefrontal cortex is twice as big as any ape's, having grown so large as part of that process of neoteny—evolution's slowing down and expansion of brain growth—children's brains becoming physically larger and ever more intricately capable from the time of birth until they are six or so. Yet the prefrontal cortex appears to perform similar tasks in both human and nonhuman primates: it helps regulate behavior as wide-ranging as blood pressure and heart rate, social interaction, emotion, and the processing of novel experience via sensory input. According to zoologist Hans Markowitsch, author of *Comparative Primate Biology*, damage to the prefrontal cortex "leads to a limited capacity in dealing with tasks that demand either that complex interacting variables be kept in mind simultaneously or that behavioral strategies or tendencies be switched, re-planned, or restructured."

In a solely human context, the prefrontal cortex is among the several brain structures that continue to grow long after birth, and it seems logical enough that this should be if it does indeed play a critical role in the processing of new information as a child slowly, wondrously comes awake to the world. In both children and adults, say Stuss and Benson,

> the prefrontal cortex is the anatomical basis for the function of control. . . . The frontal lobes are imperative at the time a new activity is being learned and active control is required; after the activity has become routine, however, these activities can be handled by other brain areas, and frontal participation is no longer required. . . . The control functions of the prefrontal cortex become more and more obvious [in] language, memory, and cognition, reflecting the greater complexity of the functions.
>
> The ability to take information extracted from other, higher brain systems, verbal and nonverbal, and to anticipate, select goals, experiment, modify, and otherwise act on this information to produce novel responses represents the ultimate mental activity; all available data indicate that these executive functions are prefrontal activities.

Citing numerous studies of the etiology of Broca's aphasia, Lieberman is convinced that the prefrontal cortex does play a vital role in the production of smooth speech and also, in particular, in the production of novel speech: in the enunciation of new, unmemorized kinds of sentences. Conversely, he contends, it is damage to the prefrontal cortex or to the subcortical nerve pathways connecting it with Broca's area in the left temporal lobe—as well, perhaps, to deep structures such as the basal ganglia and brain stem, which also play a role in making motor activities of many kinds smooth and sequential—that results in the syndrome that formerly was believed to involve damage solely to Broca's region.

Recent innovations in imaging—positron emission tomography (PET scanning) in particular—impressively have demonstrated intense prefrontal activity in the brains of normal volunteers as they

are asked to respond to a variety of unusual questions, neural activity
that is *absent* when the same people simply offer rote or memorized
responses, and which is absent as well when they repeat sentences
that are put to them. Patients with Broca's aphasia, in contrast, show
drastically diminished neural activity in both Broca's area *and* in the
prefrontal cortex as they attempt similar novel responses. "Broca's
area clearly is not *the* human language organ," writes Lieberman:

> It probably should be regarded as a multipurpose higher-level
> association area that is specialized to access subroutines for
> certain sequential operations. It appears to enter into different
> aspects of behavior through different circuits. . . . Through
> connections to the prefrontal cortex these automatized subrou-
> tines are applied to perform a novel manual act [or] utter a
> syllable . . .
>
> The [evolutionary] enlargement and complexity of the hu-
> man prefrontal cortex undoubtedly derive, in part, from the
> specific contributions of language to biological fitness. But the
> prefrontal cortex is also involved in all new, creative activity.
> It integrates information and appropriate motor responses,
> learns new responses, and derives general abstract principles.
> It is the brain's "think tank." We don't need it when everything
> is running smoothly and routinely, but it comes into action to
> solve problems and learn new responses.

As I read Lieberman, then imagine him appraising Ian's speech
and word card arrangement there at Gateway, I can't help but assume that he would note, as I now have with some amazement,
that Ian's verbal production is *remarkably* similar to that of Broca's
aphasics—the few words, the labored effort even to get them out,
the echolalia, the absence of syntax, the inability to say anything
that is new. And I can imagine Lieberman suggesting to Chomsky
and Bickerton—the three men appearing rather awkwardly out of
place near the long, low coatrack at the back of Barb Myers's classroom—that this youngster apparently had encountered such difficulty with speech because areas of his brain's Broca's region, his

prefrontal cortex, and the circuits that connect them somehow had been compromised. I doubt that either Bickerton or Chomsky would choose to argue much with that assessment, and Chomsky, perhaps, might well suggest that indeed Ian appeared capable of understanding written syntax because syntax somehow was coded at a deeper level. I wouldn't be surprised if Bickerton in turn balked a bit at that suggestion, noting that the evidence before them only suggested that the representational system that is linguistic speech and the linguistic arrangement of visual symbols—the thing we normally call writing—were rather less intimately related than we tended to assume they were. Lieberman, you subsequently can imagine, might respond that surely that was so—that syntax clearly was controlled to a large degree by Broca's area, but that that particular "syntactic structure" also was interconnected—directly, critically—to other language regions and motor-initiating centers via myriad neural circuits, some of those circuits probably severed in the brain of this most intriguing blond boy, others still intact and operating with normally miraculous precision.

I didn't really know the earliest, then-still-healthy Ian. Oh, I knew his tiny laugh was always quick to commence, and I knew he loved the security of his parents' enfolding arms; I knew he listened to them read to him and played with his sister with curious kinds of attentiveness, as if even in the midst of the purest pleasures there was much to learn. Yet few uncles really *know* their nephews or nieces at that age, not in the way parents are attuned to nascent personalities, to the kinds of common preferences, responses, and resolves that later will so completely shape them. It wasn't until Ian had been assaulted by the pertussis bacterium, then had retreated to his bedroom and to a place deep inside himself, that, rather ironically, I truly began to get to know him.

I saw Ian only briefly, three or four times a year during the years that spanned his second birthday and his sixth. Like other visitors, I could walk into his room only at those times that he somehow deemed acceptable, and once there, I could begin a simple soliloquy—if I chose to—as he went about his set routines or I could sit in silence. Unlike his parents or his teachers, who had abided by expert advice, I didn't address Ian in that clipped, contracted, abbreviated sort of way, and neither did I endeavor to say much in particular. I would tell him that I'd heard he was really into *Charlotte's Web* these days, or I'd note how cool it was that he could swing so high. I'd tell him what I'd been up to lately—which was always pretty boring and usually had to do with writing books—and I'd say that Karen and Nana and Grandad had wanted me to say hello and to give him a big hug for them. In those days I seldom tried to hug him, however; I didn't tousle his hair or pretend to punch him in the stomach in an uncle's awkward way, and sometimes I'd quite comfortably opt for silence in the few minutes before he would usher me to his door, then matter-of-factly close it behind me, alone again in his sanctum. It was in that very brief and casual context that I nonetheless began to develop a curious kind of rapport with Ian, driven largely by my interest in his welfare but also by an ineffable but budding relationship between us. And like the grandparents and the few of his parents' friends whom he occasionally and similarly sought out, I can tell you that when he would steal unexpectedly into the living room, then take my hand and lead me back to his bedroom, I would go with him suddenly flooded by pride, a more profoundly flattering gesture difficult to imagine.

People who know me well would respond with sneers and noisy guffaws if I tried to convince you that I'm a sucker for children. That clearly isn't the case. In much the same way that I don't expect to like every adult I meet, neither am I entranced by every kiddo. Yet my nieces and nephews have always engendered in me something of that effusive familial attraction that is blind and deaf and utterly forgiving. My sister Carol's children, clever and comical Laurel Hatch and her irrepressible brother, Silas; Claudia's sweet, complex, self-expressive daughter, Sarah; and even a lad named Zane Russell Sternberg, to whom I bear no blood connection but who has been granted express nephew status by virtue of his having been born on my birthday, are all young persons possessed of remarkable wit, talent, and humanity. But it is Ian Drummond—who has never called my name nor once come to spend the night—to whom I'm sure I have been most ineluctably drawn over the ebb of years. In part, I understand, I have wanted to reach out to Ian simply because he has been so unreachable, and because it is that inexpressible sort of space between people, rather than absence, isn't it, that causes hearts to grow fonder. Like Ian—but surely for different reasons—I often have difficulty expressing emotion, and for many years now I have understood his wariness as much as I have been attracted by his sudden smile. Wordy, even windy as I can be, Ian's contrasting silence has always fascinated me and made me long for clues about his conscious thoughts—whether they are catholic and convoluted and hence very ordinary in the end, or whether they're as repetitive and rigid as are his rituals. But at the nub of things, I think, it also has been Ian's disability itself—his brain's complex and incredible functions and malfunctions, his autism, his utter singularity—that forcibly has lured me to him.

Wanting early on just to get a basic sense of this syndrome—a selfism that now appears to me to be much more akin to terrible entrapment—I know I've grown successively more obsessed over the years with snaring some sort of layman's hold of this predicament that seems so cruelly unaccountable. But for reasons that have more to do with my own uncertainties than with a desire to protect collective privacies, for the longest time I didn't entertain the idea of writing about Ian's disorder or Ian himself, and even once I finally had begun to try to write, I discovered that I was as strangely mute as he was—there seeming nothing more to say so often except that the disorder was etched with mystery and that his life was hard. I hope therefore that you can understand how this enterprise—these sequential words captured on these pages—often seemed to be as self-absorbed as Ian's flapping pages, as fruitless as his screams. And I hope, conversely, that you'll forgive this foolhardy kind of confidence when I say that in the maddening midst of arranging them I think I actually have stumbled on a basic picture—albeit foggy, one that flickers like a kinescope—of how the brain of this

boy I love was severely compromised, a picture of the neurological
root of his speechlessness, and even of his horrible need for sameness
day to day to day.

I am as convinced as I can be, absent empirical proof, that Ian's
syndrome was set in motion at eighteen months when he underwent
an allergic, encephalitic response to a whole-cell pertussis vaccination. I believe that the direct result of that allergic response was the
demyelination of nerve pathways within, as well as those that critically interconnect, Ian's cranial nerves, his brain stem, and multiple
areas of his cerebrum—diffuse demyelination that accounts, in large
part, for his wide array of symptoms. I believe that the demyelination
in Ian's cerebrum came at exactly the time when, like any child, he
was beginning to myelinate the cortical and subcortical pathways
that normally would form a nascent linguistic network, and rather
more specifically, that the demyelination affected at least two fundamental language-production centers: Broca's area of his cerebrum's
left temporal lobe and the frontal lobe's prefrontal cortex. I believe
that a similar demyelinating process also damaged "association fibers" in the dense white matter of the interior cerebrum, nerve
fibers that unite those two language regions in its cortex, as well as
"projection fibers" that similarly link the brain stem with numerous
cerebral sites.

That, in short, is everything I think I know about the etiology of
Ian's autism. I am not a neurologist—I've never played one on TV
nor even pretended to be one in a book—yet I'm oddly, perhaps
presumptuously, sure that something very much like what I've outlined did indeed befall him back when he lived on the remote
periphery of that rolling ponderosa forest, when he was young and
open to all that he encountered, at a time when language had begun
to bud in him but had not yet laid down its intricate and encompassing kind of patterns. And if there *is* something approaching
accuracy in my few contentions, then I think they begin to cast, at
long last, a rough sort of sculpture that reflects the boy Ian has
become—describing why his language skills have been so compromised and why he cannot contend with anything that is not routine.

It seems odd and perhaps even far off track at first to compare the general aphasia that is common with autism with the aphasias that follow strokes—speech or comprehension, or both, disappearing as select areas of the brain are destroyed by the occlusion of blood vessels or by their hemorrhaging—and it seems exceedingly unlikely that Ian's brain ever underwent those kinds of trauma that physicians refer to as cerebrovascular accidents. Yet the parallels between the form and character of Ian's early speech and the syndrome of language deficits known as Broca's aphasia are nonetheless unmistakable and they intrigue me enormously—not only because they shed substantial light on what specific regions of Ian's brain may have been destroyed by demyelination, but also, and amazingly for me, a comparison of Broca's aphasia with Ian's aphasia for the first time seems to offer a tentative yet very likely link between his speech deficits and his terrible, crippling need for sameness—a connection that heretofore has seemed remote.

If the cerebrum's prefrontal cortex is indeed "the anatomical basis for the function of control," and is intimately "involved in all new, creative activity," and if, as Philip Lieberman persuasively contends, the prefrontal cortex is as fundamental a component of the smooth and novel production of speech as is Broca's region itself, then doesn't it straightforwardly follow that the demyelination of nerve cells and nerve pathways in Ian's prefrontal cortex accounts, at least in part, for his much belated, paralytic sort of speech *and* for his inability to filter, organize, and control new stimuli, new experience? If one of the roles played by the prefrontal cortex is the deciphering and organizational sense-making of novel sensory impulses passed to the cerebrum from the brain stem—and it increasingly appears that that's the case—and if the prefrontal cortex subsequently relinquishes its control of those impulses as soon as they have become familiarized and are imprinted elsewhere in the cerebrum, then doesn't it seem very plausible in turn that it is prefrontal damage that accounts, rather fundamentally, for Ian's inability to contend with what is new? Is it a compromised, demyelinated prefrontal cortex and its connecting pathways that chain Ian to what is endlessly routine? Has precisely the same neural damage also made creative speech very difficult for him—and until he turned six indeed made it entirely impossible? And does damage by demyelination to his prefrontal cortex—long understood to play a significant role in the regulation of emotion—similarly begin to account for Ian's apparent unresponsiveness, on the one hand, and his hair-trigger terrors on the other?

I believe the answer, though unprovable, is *yes*, that word which Ian in the first grade still was entirely unable to say. And it seems to me as well that if linguist Susan Curtiss is correct—remember that she speculates that as language develops in a child it simultaneously determines the ways in which the cerebrum will become organized and specialized for other tasks—then it may well be that the prefrontal cortex serves rather specifically as that organizer, transferring processed stimuli of every sort—sensory, cognitive, linguistic—to reservoir sites throughout the cerebral cortex, effectively patterning the brain as it separately but similarly patterns the production of speech.

Imagine, for a moment, the large frontal lobe of a normal child, ever increasing in size until age six or so, its neural circuitry more intricate than it will remain, those circuits still firing more irregularly than they will in future years, the primordial role that its prefrontal region once played in organizing vital sequential motor movements of the hands long since generalized to include as well novel linguistic and cognitive endeavors of every kind. Imagine language centers of the left hemisphere that are capable of producing protolinguistic speech without input from the prefrontal cortex, but that are utterly dependent on it for sequential, syntactic, inherently *novel* speech, for the clear and orderly arrangement of grammar. Imagine that the still-forming, still-malleable prefrontal cortex plays a role in the instantaneous emotional swings that are inherent in all children. Imagine too that it is precisely this burgeoning prefrontal cortex whose role in marshaling every manner of new stimuli has become absolutely critical in every six-year-old, and that perhaps the prefrontal cortex is specifically responsible for the way in which normal children so freely contend with experiential and linguistic novelty—turning pidgins into true languages by precisely patterning them, for example, effortlessly incorporating the kinds of changes that over the centuries have so completely characterized the evolution of English, making sense of, making *grammatical*, everything that is new.

Then imagine Ian Drummond.

And in doing so, isn't it soon simple to assume that the wrinkled arc of gray matter that is *his* prefrontal cortex has never served him as it should? Surely that fragile and fundamental part of Ian's brain, together with several other sites, began to malfunction at eighteen months, then continued till today. It is an argument that itself is "grammatical," it seems to me, yet despite the distance it may overcome in linking Ian's speech deficits to his profound ritualization, it does not explain how, unlike his speech, his nascent word arrangement actually evidenced something of an inherent sense of syntax. It is a lone conjecture, solely mine to advertise and defend, that attempts—in the manner of Campbell's definition of the meat and structure of theories—to generate new information from a limited amount of data, yet it is data in Ian's case that had begun to evolve rapidly, excitingly, by the time he was a schoolboy six years old, data dependent too on my, on *our*, still ill-defined and dusky understanding of the ordered grammar of the brain.

7
THE DECIPHERING OF
SPOKEN CODES

The move to town two years before had been easier for Ian Drummond than anyone had imagined it might be, and it had provided vivid proof that he didn't need *specific* settings or activities—his bedroom at the research station, say, or the animated movie *Dumbo*—so much as he desperately demanded stalwart sameness. He would watch one movie till the end of time, it seemed certain, until the day when his parents at last decided—for his sake as well as theirs—to force a new one on him, sending him into a cataclysmic state for about two days, long enough for the replacement to become routine and for the *new* movie now to matter more than anything. And the same thing had happened quickly with the new house: he had hated it the first time or two he was taken there for familiarizing runs; he had screamed in disapproval on the day his mother first drove him there after school; he had refused to sleep his initial night there, and he barely slept for several more, but then he simply seemed at home—apparently as rooted there on Redfeather Lane as he ever had been anywhere else.

It was Ian's father, rather ironically, who had had a more difficult time adjusting to his new surroundings and to the new life he led in town. With the move, Boyce had severed himself from a structured kind of connection to a school, a degree program, a teaching position, or the daily complexities of a job for the first time in forty years. As Claudia had returned to work full-time, Boyce in turn had assumed an essential house-husbanding role—cleaning, cooking, and attending to Ian for several hours each morning prior to driving him to school—and those chores he met with ease and equanimity. But for the first time since Ian's disorder had commenced three years before, Boyce also spent much of his time alone, his schedule his own, at work on a variety of writing and consulting projects, his office burrowed into the house's windowless basement, and as that autumn turned to winter, Boyce at last had time to confront his son's predicament, his family's, his own.

In ways his schedule never had allowed before, Boyce's thoughts now could linger at length on the realities of their situation: for the next dozen years or perhaps for many more, he and Claudia would be unable to see a film together or share a quiet dinner in a restaurant; there would be no family vacations, no camping, no ski trips with the kids. Ian had regressed rather drastically the last time Boyce had been away on a two-week trip to Costa Rica—a severe enough setback, in fact, that now Boyce no longer would return to the tropics to do the research he loved and which so invigorated him. And even at home, the hours Ian demanded of him, of them, inarguably meant that Boyce's work would suffer, meant that money likely always would be tight, meant that the daily sameness Ian had to have also might nearly drive his housemates mad.

It was curious—and fortunate, it seems to them in retrospect— that it was only as Claudia's anger ebbed on her return to a full teaching load that Boyce's rage at last was loosed, his sense of frustration and entrapment aimed at her sometimes because it had to be vented somewhere, but directed inward as well into a depression that endured for nearly two years before it began to wane. Despite Ian's successes at school, despite his beginnings of speech and the toilet-training, which had come as a real benevolence, Boyce had been numbed since moving to town by a forced acquiescence to a life he never had imagined, as well as his commensurate surrender of a far different life he once had hoped for himself and for his family.

But by now, with Sarah turning nine that fall and Ian at seven, with the four of them settled into the house in town for two years already and routines of every kind well established and dependable, at least, Boyce's spirits had lifted significantly. He had accepted seats on several civic boards and committees as means of getting himself out of the basement and briefly into different frames of mind; he had begun to work on children's disabilities issues; and in the midst of one of my short visits, he and Claudia even *had* gone to a movie together: they had dashed out of the house one spring evening after both children were asleep to see *Rain Man*, ironically, a film about a man whose autism endured, of course, well into his adulthood.

Faced with their unique and sometimes bleak circumstances, several critical decisions they had had to make with much uncertainty by now seemed to have been the best ones they could have made. It *had* been a good plan for Claudia to teach full-time and for Boyce to freelance as well as manage the household; Ian had thrived in school, and so had Sarah, of course, and now that she lived in town she was developing important friendships. The four of them spent far less time in transit these days, and they liked their house and its surroundings. Its purchase too seemed to have been the right decision, despite the fact that neighbors were nearer than they would have liked them to be, and despite their discovery that each neighbor seemed to own ten or twenty dogs.

It wasn't that Ian didn't like dogs: he loved the collie who was three years his senior and who calmly suffered his unusual kinds of attention. It was the *barking* of dogs that he simply couldn't bear. The shrill noises made by vacuum cleaners, blenders, and police and fire sirens were equally horrible for him—each noise immediately sending him into shrieking, thrashing fits, his hands pressed over his ears for as long as they endured—and the noises the neighborhood dogs made were no worse in and of themselves. It was the fact that, unlike those other dreadful sounds—which were short-lived or simply never were initiated in his presence (vacuuming done while Ian was at school or never done at all)—dogs with too much time to kill would bark for hours on hideous end along the length of Redfeather Lane, and Ian *never* could go into the yard to play without inducing their maddening chorus, forcing him to return immediately to the house. There was the golden retriever pup—dumb as a post— who belonged to the family in the house that lately had been built just behind them; there were the two yappy dachshunds, "show dogs" purportedly, who lived just across the fence; and now that Ian's sixteen-year-old friend Jenefer Elsea had taught him how to take walks—the two of them ritually stopping at each intersection to look both ways for cars—there were dozens more dogs to contend with, mountain homes always as surrounded by dogs, for some bucolic cultural reason, as they were by four-wheel-drives and stacks of drying firewood.

As the dog situation got truly untenable about a year into their residence, Boyce and Claudia seemed to have exhausted every conceivable possibility for correcting it, and lately they had even tried one of those expensive dog-silencing devices that emits a sound the critters cannot stand. Then, when the silencer showed only very spotty success, they tried—despite their better judgment, really— to talk with their neighbors, offering them a much-abbreviated story of Ian's circumstances, asking them if they might keep their animals inside during the two times of the day when Ian wanted to be outside or, barring that, simply do whatever they could think of to kindly try to limit the barking. The owner of the puppy—one of those modern young fundamentalist preachers with the perfect hair and the pearly smile—was as nice as he could be about their request, but he immediately was far more interested in curing Ian and saving Ian's family members from eternal fire and lamentation than he was in silencing his dog. In fact, he assured them, if they would join his New Day Redeemer Joyful Faith Bible Fellowship, just about every problem they could think of would quickly fall by the sinners' way. A neighbor down the street simply sat on his porch and watched one day as his hound went into barking apoplexy behind a fence and as Ian writhed and screamed on the adjacent street. And the owners of the dachshunds, nice enough people it initially had seemed to Sarah and Boyce, who had chatted with them from time to time, now accused Boyce of trying to harm their weenie things with the silencer. When he tried to explain to them in more detail about Ian's

disorder and his incredibly sensitive ears, the retired couple averred
that, in that case, the boy probably needed to be in an institution.

Then, on August 17, 1990, a Social Services caseworker knocked
on their door, explaining that those same neighbors had alerted his
office to the possibility of child abuse at the Drummond residence—
it seeming, so he understood, that at least one child, maybe two,
constantly screamed as if in awful pain. Boyce was in Denver for the
day, and although Claudia steeled herself to be civil with the social
worker—keeping herself under control as best she could as she told
him she understood, of course, that he had to investigate every
allegation, and referring him as well to the local school officials who
would be happy to explain Ian and his situation in some detail—her
outrage was immediate and enormous. By the time Ian was ready
for his afternoon ride, she already had spoken to several realtors and
had scoured the classified ads, she and her son driving by several
houses that were for rent as they went to visit the cows that afternoon
and on the way home again as well, one of them, a big house at the
end of a quiet cul-de-sac, appearing perfect at first glance—perfect
enough, at least, that once home again, she began to pack.

Claudia and Boyce had suspected that Ian was deaf, or partially so,
back in 1985 as his behavior first became unusual. Although his
hearing had appeared quite normal very early on, over the course
of just a few weeks in the catastrophic spring of that year it began to
seem as though he heard nothing at all. He would no longer turn as
his name was called; he wasn't interested in his parents' voices, and
neither would he startle at loud noises. Yet as Ian's symptoms grew
more pronounced and as autism became a diagnostic certainty,
noise—certain noises—now appeared to bombard and cruelly batter
him. The high whine of the vacuum cleaner was the first sound that
tormented him, then Sheila's occasional barking binges also began
to throw him into terrors that seemed sparked by physical pain. And
for five years now, this was what you invariably would observe each
time he encountered some sound with which he could not contend:
Ian falling to the ground or to the floor as if felled by a bullet, his

hands cupped over his ears, his body writhing in agony, Claudia or Boyce, or both of them, flying into immediate action to do whatever they could to quell the noise, or barring that, to cup their larger hands over Ian's in an attempt to further muffle the sound that was causing him such terrible distress.

Sound—outward-rushing waves of molecules of air initiated every time an object moves: a feather, a freight train, the taut steel strings of a piano—travels rather slowly to Ian's ears and to everyone's, where its pulsing pressure causes the eardrum to vibrate, that vibration in turn setting three tiny bones in sequential motion, the third bone pressing in its turn against the soft, fluid-filled inner ear, where those waves of air are transformed into waves of fluid—a rolling ocean in utter miniature—that travel through a passageway in the snail-shaped cochlea, in turn exciting tiny cochlear hairs that are attached to as many as thirty thousand nerve fibers, the pulsing of the waves transformed finally into electrical impulses that travel the pathway of the acoustic nerve to the brain stem. It is along the acoustic nerve, perhaps, where Ian's hearing first may be impaired, but it is more probably in his brain stem that something initially goes awry. Just prior to his second birthday, he had undergone separate brain stem auditory evoked-response tests, one interpreted as showing significant brain stem abnormalities, the other indicating only subtle damage, but whatever the true degree, his hearing abnormalities clearly had been borne out in the ensuing years.

In a normal brain, it remains unclear how extensively the brain stem "filters" auditory impulses prior to relaying them via projection fibers to auditory perception centers in both temporal lobes. What is sure is that impulses from the left ear are delivered to both the right *and* left cerebral hemispheres, as are those from the right ear, meaning that if the auditory center in one hemisphere is damaged, deafness in the opposite ear does not result. Cerebral damage to that initial sound-decoding center can result in a variety of other impairments, however. Certain sound frequencies can become undetectable, while others remain normally perceived. Separate sounds can blend indistinguishably together, akin to the jumbled noise of which hearing aid wearers often complain, words uttered at their shoulders perceived at the same intensity as are conversations across the room. And shrill sounds, which normal brains somehow modulate, can, in cases like Ian's, be perceived as piercingly, painfully loud even at decibel levels far too low to damage the ears themselves.

That ability to modulate the perception of sound—and of all other sensory stimuli as well—is the result of the normal brain's capacity to suppress the firing of neurons that normally would be initiated by those stimuli. Far more cerebral neurons are switched "off" than "on" at any given moment, and some neuroscientists speculate that as much as eighty percent of the brain's total neuronal capacity normally acts to suppress electrical activity rather than excite it. We are bombarded by far more auditory stimuli than we can contend with, in other words, and when our brains function as they should, we are able to select and manipulate those stimuli according to their familiarity, novelty, or utility. Sounds that are recognized as words are relayed by association fibers from the initial sound-perception centers in the brain stem to Broca's area, Wernicke's area, the prefrontal cortex, and related language centers; and nonspeech sounds are similarly recognized and relayed—sounds that signal immediate danger traveling only to the hypothalamus, for instance, where fight-or-flight responses are initiated. And whether Ian's auditory deficits lie solely in his brain stem or diffusely throughout his cerebrum as well, this much clearly seems to be the case: unlike normal brains that can decode delicate aural messages caught inside a windy flurry of noise, and that, conversely, can ignore messages that are meaningless and suppress those that are received with too much screaming urgency, Ian's brain lacks much of that critical ability to modulate, to filter, to listen only to the messages he wants to hear.

In the same way that the color white is the blending of all colors, noise, technically, is the presence of all frequencies of sound. In the applied communications sciences, noise often is defined as anything that corrupts or destroys an intended message: radio static, garbled print, a snowy screen. And in rather more theoretical terms, noise can be considered entropy—disorder, scatter, chaos, formlessness. The antithesis of noise in those three contexts is, therefore, a discrete sound, a message successfully received: shape, arrangement, order. The opposite of noise is *information*, not just the nightly news or filed facts of every kind but a force as real as are matter and energy, a force that "informs" the world, creating pattern, dependable kinds of repetition, *form* despite nature's tendency toward entropy.

It was in the postwar 1940s that a Bell Laboratories engineer named Claude Shannon first proposed the notion of information as a physical reality. The subject of the two landmark papers he presented in those years was ostensibly the technical problem of transmitting messages quickly and efficiently. But as Jeremy Campbell explains in *Grammatical Man*,

> the wider and more exciting implications of Shannon's work lay in the fact that he had been able to make the concept of information so logical and precise that it could be placed in a formal framework of ideas . . . establishing laws that hold good not for a few types of information, but for all kinds, everywhere. . . . In spite of the fact that the theorems of information theory were intended chiefly for radio and telephone engineers, they can be used to investigate *any* system in which a "message" is sent from one place to another.

Prior to Shannon, classical communication theory treated messages as single events, unrelated to any others. But what Shannon proposed—together with others who soon began to amplify this rather revolutionary sort of thinking—was the notion that any given message sent by whatever means must be received and considered in the context of all those theoretically possible messages that are *not* sent. In any system, information truly is transferred only if it changes the receiver's store of knowledge, whether in subtle or dramatic ways: a message that is not somehow *new* is not a message. The receiver, therefore, must be uncertain about what will be received—because of the message's inherent novelty—but must not be entirely ignorant of what the message *might* be or else it inevitably will be interpreted as only noise, as something incomprehensible. A person picking up a phone in Woodland Park, Colorado, for instance, is uncertain about what message he or she will hear, yet is quite confident nonetheless that it will be one of those billions of messages that can be created with the words of the English language. If that person hears only the loud squeal of a fax machine, on the other hand, no message is received because the listener is ignorant of the language of that machine.

A message, any message, may be most improbable (*Ian woke up this morning entirely cured*) and hence very hard to predict, or it may be highly probable (*He had another bad day today*), one the listener might well have predicted. The more improbable a given message is, the greater the amount of uncertainty it resolves and, correspondingly, the more information it conveys: *Ian is unchanged* is a message that conveys only the smallest bit of information; conversely, *Ian can sing today* is a message that is etched with novelty, one that is quite improbable and is therefore rich with information.

Messages—and all instructional systems—effectively lower the universe's tendency toward entropy by producing structure: the serial squeal of that fax machine, for instance, its yes-no binary sequences shaping a coded kind of order; the similarly encoded clicks of a telegraph, outmoded though they are; the words of a sentence ordered by syntax into a meaningful form. Any sentence, any message, any form of information is inherently more complex, more valuable, if you will, than the muddle of noise out of which it arises, and the most valuable kinds of information are those that are most complex. Along with Campbell, we can envision in that regard a search for a specific book—let's say, *Grammatical Man*—in three separate libraries, one organized very much like those libraries with which you are familiar, the second a library in which books are arranged solely according to the colors of their covers, the third some sort of science-fictional House O' Books where volumes are placed at random on available shelves. In the conventional library, *Grammatical Man* can be found in only one very specific location and no others; that library's arrangement is intricately structured and hence highly informed. The second library is ordered, to be sure, yet its order conveys far less information, and *Grammatical Man* can be found anywhere within the section that corresponds with its color, assuming that that color can be ascertained. In the library out of "The Twilight Zone," in contrast, each of its thousands of books is "arranged" in a sequence, it is true, and *Grammatical Man* is there in solely one specific spot, yet since the sequence is unknowable, that library offers its patrons only noise. Its entropy is enormous and it is an archive absent information.

Although Claude Shannon initially was concerned with issues pertaining expressly to telecommunications, and although information theory by now also has become the province of physicists, geneticists, and scientists of every stripe, it is with regard to the functions of the human brain and its facility for language that information theory perhaps has become most readily accessible. "The proper metaphor for life," says Campbell, in fact, "may not be a pair of rolling dice or a spinning roulette wheel, but the sentences of a language, conveying information that is partly predictable and partly unpredictable. These sentences are generated by rules which make much out of little, producing a boundless wealth of meaning from a finite store of words; they enable language to be familiar yet surprising, constrained yet unpredictable within its constraints."

Our brains themselves are information devices, even absent language—sending constant regulating messages to vital organs, receiving important sensory messages that describe the exterior environment, relaying motor messages to the nerves that innervate all muscles. Memory, cognition, emotion, sleep, and sexual response are the results of information processes as well, one neuron *informing* a neighboring neuron via an electrochemical spark, then it in turn informing a third, and so on, millions of neurons firing in intricate sequence as a head turns toward sunlight, as the smell of grass is perceived, as spirits rise on clear spring mornings. Each brain—yours, mine, Ian's—is an example of the most complex information-coding and -organizing system known, and language surely is the brain's showiest, most dynamic subsystem. Language is an informational process whose "messages"—the sounds and scratches that represent words, which themselves represent ideas—are symbols rather than nerve impulses, yet they are symbols that only can be conveyed, of course, if corporeal neural circuitry functions as it should. "Symbols can be decoupled from physical reality," Campbell writes. "Words are not deeds, though they often lead to deeds. Symbols can be manipulated to form new statements and expressions which are only tentative, playful, figurative. Symbols are at liberty to be a little irresponsible and experimental." It was the manipulability of symbols that first allowed, long ago, a grunted sound to signify an action. It is their separateness from physical reality that permits linguistic symbols to rein in abstractions that otherwise would be as uncontainable as wind. It is the experimental nature of symbols, surely, that makes it possible for children to turn pidgin speech into richly grammared languages. And it is grammar, to be sure, that provides the framework that makes the symbolism of words inherently accessible to each of us, its messages merely uncertain—hence filled with informative possibility—rather than unknowable, inaccessible, impossible to understand. It is grammar that lets language shape its novel arrangements in the midst of what otherwise would only be noise.

And it is in this context as well, it seems to me, that Ian's several deficits can be envisioned as breakdowns of key information systems. His inability to say "I'd like to wear my red shirt today" is a specific message that cannot be sent or received, obviously. But at the neural level, the absence of those spoken words also represents the failure of cortical and subcortical circuitry to make informational connections, to send essential electrochemical messages between Broca's area and the prefrontal cortex, for instance, between the prefrontal region and the basal ganglia, a failure in the relay of convergent neural messages from several language sites to the brain stem perhaps, or from the brain stem to the mostly mute speech organs in his throat. Similarly, Ian's inability to contend with change—*Pinocchio* today instead of Pooh—can be perceived as a problem anchored in the receipt and deciphering of messages, anything new somehow always unknowable for him and therefore absent the *form* of information. And the physiological root of that ritualization is likely the absence or malformation of intricately patterned circuitry that otherwise would be capable of making sense of new experience in the same way that, say, a television can create order—a clear and pixelated visual arrangement—out of the novel electromagnetic messages it receives at millisecond intervals from a transmitter on a mountaintop or from a VCR, information successfully transferred as the set displays a moving picture of a pudgy bear instead of simply snow, instead of the blurry entropy you can also call noise.

The neighborhood dogs were sending incessant messages—their barking, as usual, enough of a grating, maddening cacophony that Ian was buried in blankets in his bedroom, the window closed and a movie's volume turned to a booming level—when Boyce returned home on that August evening. Soon after Claudia had outlined the day's events for him—a daylong chorus of dogs again, of course, the social worker and the allegation, Claudia's discovery of a rental house in a subdivision on the southern edge of town where there appeared to breathe some blessed quiet—Boyce briefly left again to reconnoiter the house himself. By chance, the owner was looking after the empty house as Boyce parked his car in the cul-de-sac, and as soon as he expressed his interest in the place, the owner invited him inside.

And the house *did* seem to suit them in several important ways—enough potential privacy for Ian, a bedroom that might well be transformed into an aboveground office for Boyce, one whose windows displayed a splendid, if surely rent-inflating, vista of Pike's Peak, space enough in general despite a rather Lilliputian kitchen, and most importantly at the moment, enough territory separating it and the nearest neighbor that resident dogs on protective patrol would not be alerted to their every move outdoors. There *was* a dog at that neighboring house, the owner acknowledged to Boyce, but it was a little thing that lived in laps, and it seldom ventured outside. Cars only infrequently came and went in the cul-de-sac, he said, and although two tranquil llamas did live two houses away, the immediate environs were otherwise free of domesticated critters prone to yelping conniptions. When the owner agreed that he would pay for the materials to fence the property in exchange for a higher rent, the move seemed more feasible still, and within a day or two the deal was done and another change of residence, together with a search for renters for *their* house, was under way. School was starting in just two days and the move would demand energy and time that the Drummond and Martin clan didn't have or couldn't spare, yet it already seemed clear to them that the neighbors' contemptible call to Social Services had provided, at least, a stimulus for the true resolution of the barking crisis that otherwise might have lingered a very long time. Although they joked that perhaps it would be fitting to barbecue a couple of dachshunds on their last evening on Redfeather Lane, in fact they approached neither the dogs nor their lower-life-form owners again before they moved away.

Friends and colleagues who had been equally outraged by those recent events on Redfeather Lane rallied around them on the first weekend after school commenced, and with perhaps a dozen people pitching in, most of the move was made in an intense and chaotic Sunday flurry. Ian left his bedroom in the house on Redfeather Lane for the final time on an early September Monday morning, then discovered it relocated and precisely repositioned in the basement of the house on Ponderosa Court that afternoon, the rest of the house an utter shambles but his bedroom dependably, critically intact. Unlike the temporary trauma that his family's move had induced in him nearly two years before, this time Ian adjusted to his third bedroom in his third house with a seamless sort of ease and with an almost visible relief. He even could contend with newness, his demeanor seemed to say, if it was accompanied by some silence. And although neither Claudia nor Boyce ever sat on the edge of Ian's bed and explained in detail the reasons for the move, they remember that each of them was curiously certain as they slowly settled into the new house on Ponderosa Court that he understood the move entirely and that he heartily endorsed their quick decision.

Although Ian's lexicon of spoken two- and three-word phrases had continued to grow during the preceding summer—his ability to make reference to ever larger numbers of objects and actions subtly, sometimes significantly, chipping away at his isolation—it was with regard to those rather more intricate kinds of communication that Ian and his family still shared few communicative tools, few means of making their complex messages intelligible, truly informational. Claudia and Boyce retained the substantial hope that his protolinguistic speech—each word painstakingly enunciated by employing what seemed to be every muscle in his body—would give way one day to fluid and syntactic speech, yet statistics applied to people with autism argued heavily against that possibility, they realized. Some years ago, Ian had seemed a poor candidate to become proficient at sign language, and nothing had changed over time to alter that assessment, principally because of his chronically poor hand and finger coordination, a disability that also seemed to preclude handwriting or any kind of typing other than the single keystrokes he could manage as he employed the VÓIS or played instructional games on the computer. Yet didn't there have to be *some* means, his parents continued to ask themselves—something that simply hadn't crossed their minds yet—that would allow Ian to express his feelings as well as his immediate needs, his perspectives, even his aching desires? Although spoken speech might not ever offer him that symbolically coded channel, and although writing, for now at least, remained unlikely, wasn't there some way, somehow, for Ian truly to inform his world? How *could* he someday send the messages that surely swelled inside him?

Among Boyce's numerous enterprises these days was a part-time position as editor of the quarterly newsletter distributed by PEAK Parent Center in Colorado Springs, a federally funded support facility providing training and information of many kinds to parents of children with disabilities throughout Colorado and surrounding states, and lately he also had begun to chair the Governor's Interagency Coordinating Council, a group that oversaw a variety of state programs aimed at improving the health and well-being of the state's infants and toddlers. It was via this network of people involved with children's and disabilities issues, which Boyce and Claudia increasingly had become connected to, that they first had heard tall tales—fanciful, impossible stories, surely—of a special-education teacher in Australia who had devised a technique with which people

with autism supposedly were typing intelligent, grammatical, astonishing kinds of statements, explaining in flash floods of pent-up information that they were *not* retarded, that they *hated* being treated
as idiots, that they liked pizza and ice cream like everybody else
did, and that the fact they couldn't talk didn't mean they had nothing
to say. And although the stories that were current at the moment
were laced with much of that same too-good-to-be-true quality that
tended to accompany the periodic announcements of ennobled kinds
of recovery from autism in the popular magazines, an article detailing
this new technique, as it happened, had been published, unbe-
knownst to them, in the *Harvard Educational Review* just as they
were in the harried midst of moving. "Communication Unbound:
Autism and Praxis," the lengthy journal article was titled; its author
was Douglas Biklen, a Syracuse University special-education professor who had made repeated trips to Australia to observe the technique in application and who had become convinced that the
technique was far more miracle than chimera, that it *worked* for
reasons he remained at a loss to explain.

Biklen first had read about the technique that rather clumsily
yet appropriately had been labeled "facilitated communication" in
Annie's Coming Out, a 1980 book coauthored by Melbourne, Australia, educator Rosemary Crossley and Anne McDonald, a woman
with severe cerebral palsy who was Crossley's friend, protégée, and
housemate. Institutionalized at Saint Nicholas Hospital in Melbourne for many years, her mental development presumed to be
little more than that of an infant, McDonald had met Crossley in
1975, when she was fourteen, as Crossley, a recent college graduate,
had become a "play leader" at the hospital. Within two years, and
with the help of Crossley's constant attention and support, McDonald had become able to write and to solve math problems by pointing
to letters, numbers, and words on a language board with the aid
of Crossley's hand firmly supporting her forearm, steadying and
restraining the spastic muscles that otherwise caused her limbs to
flail uncontrollably.

When McDonald petitioned in 1979 for the right to leave the
hospital, it ultimately fell to the supreme court of the state of Victoria

to decide that McDonald's facilitated statements—her proof of her intellect and her desired independence—were her own and not Crossley's conscious or even unconscious manipulations. McDonald's messages, her statements of every conceivable kind, were her own, the court ultimately ruled. And Biklen—who met Crossley and McDonald in 1985 while in Australia giving a series of lectures on the integration of disabled children into conventional schools—had no trouble believing as he observed that a person like McDonald, limited by cerebral palsy yet possessing normal intelligence, could indeed communicate by pointing or by typing if she somehow was assisted with the control of fine motor movements. But when he read in a letter from Crossley the following year that she had begun to have remarkable success as well using facilitated communication with people with autism, Biklen grew extremely skeptical. "From what I knew about autism," he explained to the *New York Times* a few years later, "and I knew quite a bit, it just didn't make sense to me." People with autism were presumed to have massive personality and cognitive defects, and their language deficits were so extreme in so many cases that it seemed impossible for them to be "speaking" by any means whatsoever.

On two subsequent trips to Australia in 1988 and 1989, Biklen observed Crossley and many of her students at work at Melbourne's DEAL (Dignity through Education and Language) Communication Centre, and this time he came away puzzled, to be sure, by how the simple procedure worked, yet utterly convinced that it did and that it therefore held the very real potential for unlocking the desperate door of mutism for many thousands more people round the world. "It was important for me not only that I could in some way prove what I had seen," he explained. "But I also felt an absolute moral obligation to get it in place in the United States."

Biklen's fascinating assessment of facilitated communication ultimately had to be written "qualitatively," a term applied to studies in the natural or social sciences that don't depend on controlled or replicated data, and which are structured and supported instead by narrative observation—a type of investigation that can be cumulatively convincing but which necessarily lacks the kinds of controlled testing on which science must depend. Yet the stories Biklen told were credible and often quite compelling—like this one about a troubled preteen boy with autism who regularly screamed, vomited, and scratched himself and others as he attempted to escape from their close contact:

That afternoon [a few years prior to Biklen's visit], after watching Jonothan's stereotyped repetitive play with a squeeze mop, Crossley managed to settle Jonothan on her sofa, first interesting him in a speech synthesizer and then in a Canon Communicator. With wrist support, he pressed buttons that she touched. Occasionally he pressed buttons without any assistance. She typed "JONATHAN," followed by "MUM," and then asked him for "DAD." He went straight to the *D*, without any wrist support and then to *A*, where he hesitated. . . . [Then] she merely supported his wrist as he moved his hand toward the letters. She typed "JONATHAN," whereupon he typed "JONOTHAN." Crossley later checked the spelling with his mother. Jonathan had been correct. . . .

Coincidentally, on the afternoon I interviewed Crossley about how she had discovered that this method worked with Jonothan, he came to visit DEAL. Crossley told him that we had just been talking about the first time he had typed on the Canon. She asked him if he remembered what his first word had been. As she asked the question she held out the Canon Communicator. Independently [with no physical support from Crossley this time] he typed "DAD." Then he typed, "JONOTHAN NOT JONATHAN." This is one child who remembers his first words.

The fact that Jonothan by now had become able to type on the small, calculator-sized Canon Communicator, which prints letters onto a narrow paper tape, without any form of second-party assistance, offered inarguable proof that his words were his own. Yet Biklen also observed at DEAL dozens of other people with autism who only could type intelligible phrases when a facilitator's hand virtually enveloped their own, or only when their index fingers were extended and held firmly by others, and proofs of the genesis of *their* communications were far more problematic. Biklen was quite willing to admit that some speechless students were successful with facilitated communication only some of the time; a few succeeded only with one specific facilitator and no others; and although virtually everyone's output included numerous typographical errors, sometimes what was typed was indecipherable as anything but gibberish. Yet time after time, Biklen observed situations in which students responded to simple questions whose answers the facilitators could not have known; and phonetic spellings and novel usages of language also seemed to contribute to the mounting likelihood that the facilitator was not directing the output, that *only* the person with autism could, in fact, have "spoken." And as he attempted to explain at the end of his article, this astounding but inexplicable communicative process, one in which both physical support and emotional support somehow seemed to be the prime components, Biklen could posit little more than to say, "It is as if this group of people, labeled autistic, by *not* communicating except with certain facilitators and in certain, supportive circumstances, is saying what all students at one time or another have said, if less obviously: We will reveal ourselves, we will show our creativity, when we feel appreciated, when we are supported."

Imagine that suddenly the barks of dogs were words, or that for the first time there were messages in the rustling branches of tall trees; or ponder, with a bit more probability but no less a sense of magic, hearing Alexander Graham Bell call "Watson, I need you" through a wire; imagine watching, as perhaps you did with some astonishment a quarter-century ago, live television being broadcast from the surface of the moon: Surely they engendered commensurate surprise or incredulity as mute and—it had seemed—largely mindless children in Melbourne began to type, saying what they wanted to say for the first time in their lives. IM NOT RETARDED, one plaintively had explained. MY MOTHER FEELS IM STUPID, said another, BE-

CAUSE I CANT USE MY VOICE PROPERLY. Yet they were anything but stupid, these youngsters who until then had lacked only a means of sending messages, and this new ability to type—their wayward hands and fingers held in helpful check—must have been an opening of floodgates for them, a release from a heretofore hopeless imprisonment, an opportunity to interact finally, to inform their worlds with words.

Biklen readily had acknowledged in that 1990 article that facilitated communication would seem to some "no more real than a Ouija board" at first, but the phenomenon nonetheless was *very* real, he reported, and thirdhand accounts of its success began to speed their way around the United States and Canada—erroneously trumpeted as a *cure* for autism, oftentimes, or made to seem as simple as setting keyboards in eager laps, then getting out of the way as literature spewed forth like a geyser's spray. It was heady stuff, to be sure, and the snippets of information that educators and parents like Claudia and Boyce began to hear made facilitated communication seem like the sort of thing they might hang some hope on, but the uncertainties too were many. In their particular case, Ian long ago had proven his ease with picture boards and keyboards—touching number or letter keys in response to verbal prompts, typing memorized and long-practiced words and phrases when he was helped to do so with physical support—yet he never had typed spontaneously, absent a computer's or a person's prompt, and it was hard to imagine that he might begin to do so one day, in large part because spontaneity was an attribute Ian simply didn't own.

When another school year started in September, Ian was nominally a first-grader again, "held back" because in prior years—and owing to his August birthday—he had been the youngest in his class, and as one of the oldest now, it was presumed that his progress would better match his classmates' skills. At a computer keyboard, with a teacher's hand-over-hand support, he could type these words these days, each word spelled correctly except for persistent typos: *cow, chicken, rabbit, lamb, horse, mouse, pig, duck, bird, turkey, cat, dog, Mom, Dad, Sarah, Ian.* He could add and subtract the numbers from one to ten, and his card-based reading vocabulary, growing larger with each day, included such words as *tunnel, out-side, mountain, swings,* and *school.* School remained an environment in which Ian was successfully challenged and in which he was often clearly happy; and in addition to stretching his attendance close to a full seven-hour day, much of that time now spent in a regular classroom, he even had begun to ride a school bus—a new routine he readily had accepted as the school year commenced. Evidently, it had seemed to him that the small, special-education bus was simply the conveyance by which people traveled from Ponderosa Court to school.

Since Ian had begun to go to Gateway two years before, an important bridge between home and school had been the figurines that accompanied him as he journeyed back and forth—small facsimiles of the Pooh characters, Tigger most importantly; the four Berenstain bears, whose family members mirrored his own; several of the Peanuts gang, among them Snoopy mattering most; plus assorted others he had garnered over the years in McDonald's giveaways or had pilfered from his sister's bedroom—all of them, surely twenty or more, collected in a clear plastic produce bag. Ian's "friends," as Claudia, Boyce, and Sarah referred to them, accompanied him everywhere he went, in fact, and although he seemed to ignore them much of the time, they offered a kind of constancy he desperately depended on. He could assess in only a glance whether one was missing, and if it was, life was clearly complicated until it could be found. At home, Ian's "friends" sometimes were scattered widely around his room or were carefully grouped atop a dresser, where they played roles that weren't always easy to ascertain, but at school—especially as his group of "friends" grew ever larger—they tended to stay inside the bag, in part because the school day was filled with other concerns and distractions, and in part, perhaps, because Ian increasingly was making other friends.

Mary Lou Krueger was Ian's close companion, of course, but her role was unmistakably maternal, Ian becoming a son of her own in many respects; and Charmaine Thaner, the special-education teacher with whom he had developed a special rapport during his kindergarten year, now was his classroom teacher in this *second* first-

grade year. Ian and Leroy, buddies from the beginning yet capable
as well of minor conflict, lately had begun to share toys successfully,
to take turns with computer games and other enticements, and after
Ian had had a run beside the fence as each recess commenced, he
and Leroy often would swing and slide together, each boy clearly
an important ally of the other. But this year, and really for the first
time, Ian had begun to make fast friendships with kids in the larger
class as well. There were Daniel and Tristan and Kalyn and a half-
dozen other kids who were drawn to Ian for reasons they couldn't
quite explain. He was "cool"—that much they were sure of—and
they were blithely unconcerned when he often acted as though they
weren't sitting there beside him, or when he regularly would move
one of them out of his way to do something he simply *had* to accomplish. It plainly didn't matter to them that Ian could say so few
words, or that the words he could pronounce sounded sort of funny.
And with Ian's friend Eddie—a towheaded sprite who spoke nonstop, who was as rough-and-tumble as any of the other boys, but who
also somehow had assumed for himself the role of Ian's champion and
intuitive confidant—a one-way flow of words seemed more than
adequate. Right from the outset of that year and only very soon after
he had met Ian, Eddie seemed to develop an uncanny ability to
sense what Ian could tolerate and what he could not, to know what
Ian needed well before a crisis commenced, even how to push Ian
a little, to get him to try some new and varied stuff, to have some
regular kinds of fun.

"Eddie and another friend gave Ian potato chips at lunch," Mary
Lou wrote in Ian's logbook one day in late September, "and he ate
them! At recess, he watched Eddie play tetherball, then he actually
hit the ball twice at Eddie's request." And a few days later, Eddie
had made Mary Lou's notes again: "Eddie *always* eats lunch with
Ian these days, and now several others want to as well. Today Eddie
opened his arms for a hug (Eddie's own idea) and Ian obliged him—
a real hug! I was very impressed—with both of them." This new,
more adaptive, far more socialized phase Ian seemed to have entered
at school—with Eddie's and other kids' help—now was evident to

everyone, and it engendered real delight in the people who had seen Ian remain so private for so long. On the last day in October, Charmaine included a special note in the logbook that traveled between home and school in Ian's pack:

Claudia & Boyce,

I went to watch my class & Michelle's sing Halloween songs & do some movement activities today during PE & Music time. I was so pleased with how well Ian did! I got teary eyed watching him stand on stage with the other students. Annie helped him with some of the hand motions, but he remained standing with the group for the whole 10 min.

The best part was when they went down on the gym floor for songs & movements. One song about cats Ian was able to participate in totally independently. The kids sat against the wall & at a certain point in the music, the "cats" all crawled to the center of the gym, and later they scampered back to their "homes." As Ian scampered back, he turned his head to look at me with this huge grin, as if to ask, "Did you see me & how well I did?" Yes, I did see!

But although his progress that year kept to an accelerated pace—Ian advancing beyond his classmates in math, his reading vocabulary also above the first-grade level (at least as best it could be ascertained), a new ability to "sing" now during music and to play ball games with Annie Carter's subtle assistance, his several vital friends—the progress was not without its price. More than ever before, Ian's steady successes at school were countered with tantrums or ritualized collapses at the end of the day at home, and unlike in previous years, there were days as well when, for reasons his parents could not understand, he rigidly balked at going to school in the morning, acting fussy and out of sorts as he awoke, then objecting strenuously, crying "weekend, *weekend*," as they attempted to initiate the rituals that set him on a course toward school.

Ian constantly was beset with colds and the common viruses that
made the winter rounds, and because of them, there also were many
days when he simply *had* to stay at home, his poor diet and the
intense stress he constantly was under presumably playing a principal role in his susceptibility to the ubiquitous bugs. And always there
were the few disastrous days like March 20, 1991, when several
issues and aggravations combined to bring him—and them—to the
very brink: "Some of you may not know what has happened during
the past days," Claudia later wrote in the logbook as a means of
filling in everyone who played a role in Ian's care, "so I'll briefly
review it and write it in here 'for the record.' "

On Wed. 3/20 Ian freaked out during the Gateway fire drill as
he's never done before. He screamed and fought as Mary Lou
carried him outside, holding his ears and crying, "Go in, go
in," repeatedly. Fifteen minutes after the siren had finally
stopped, he still hadn't let up, and he kept his fingers in
his ears as if it was still blaring. Back inside, Mary Lou put
headphones on him to try to block out all noise, but although
he settled down some, he continued to whine until school was
out for the day.

At home, he really began to scream again and continued to
cry for the next 24 hrs., holding his ears and crying "Help me,
help me" & shouting every word he knows while holding his
ears. When Boyce got him to the doctor Thurs. noon, <u>still</u>
screaming, he said Ian still had the ear infection he had had
for the previous week, caused by "mycoplasma" (not viral &
not bacterial), so the antibiotic he had been on had not been
working. The doctor started him on a new drug & he guessed,
as we had, that probably the already painful ears could not
tolerate the fire drill.

After the week off & all the drugs Ian is finally well &
seeming more like himself than he has in 2 months. What a
year for illness for him! Obviously, his immune system is now
<u>shot</u>. So it is with great fear & trepidation that we send him
back to school & more germs, but here we go.

—

Surely an ear infection is as literally painful for Ian as it is for any child, and the family-practice physician's presumption that the infection simply exacerbated his ears' chronic sensitivity to loud noises seems logical enough, an adequate explanation for the way in which Ian had been assaulted by the fire siren. Yet nothing about Ian's ears appears intrinsically abnormal, just as his vocal cords and their related speech organs evidence no abnormality despite his inability to speak. It is in Ian's brain stem, it seems far more likely, that the reception and interpretation of those specific awful sounds first goes awry, and his faulty processing of general auditory sensory input— as with the processing of stimuli he receives via eleven other sensory nerves—certainly involves a variety of other brain structures as well. Ian, in point of fact, probably is not burdened by "sensitive ears" so much as by a brain that somehow cannot contend with some of what it hears. But if *that* is the case, why then would the hearing of horrible sounds seem far worse for him at a time when his ears were encrusted with microorganisms? In the same way that a clogging head cold makes you temporarily hard of hearing, wouldn't those bugs in Ian's ears be more likely to muffle sound than amplify it? I can't answer those questions, of course, but they do remind me of Claude Shannon and the complexities of information theory.

Among Shannon's major theoretical achievements was the demonstration that in any communications system, a message can be sent and received error free, even under very noisy conditions, as long as it is properly encoded. Nature does impose a restraint on what potentially can be transmitted, but it is a limit imposed by the capacity of a given communications channel rather than a limit on the amount of noise a successful message can be surrounded by. An FM radio signal broadcast at 98.5 megahertz, for instance, is not hindered by what is being broadcast at other frequencies or by the totality of the electromagnetic "noise" that is present at any given moment. As long as a radio receiver is tuned to that same frequency, as long as it "understands" the transmitter's code, in other words, its messages can be received with great accuracy, and noise appears to disappear. Yet at 98.5, only one message—a string of words, a song, an entire symphony—can be sent and received at a time, that "channel" capable only of a kind of serial encoding that precludes simultaneous transmissions.

In a similar sort of way, normal human hearing of a given message depends not on surrounding silence but on whether that message has been encoded in a way that allows its *de*coding by the brain. Your likelihood of successfully decoding the sentence *You may play with the plastic truck that's in the closet* when it is spoken in English at the same cacophonous moment that similar sentences are uttered in twenty other languages is, nonetheless, far greater than if the sentence is spoken in a hushed room, but only in Chinese: the presence of "noise" doesn't inhibit a message's decoding or under-standing so long as the code itself can be understood.

The same holds true for the "message" a siren or a barking dog sends, and the way in which those messages are received: Sirens get our attention because they are loud, to be sure, but their volume is only one aspect of their information. It is the repetitiveness of the message—the blaring sound repeated at millisecond intervals, a single *woof* followed by fifty more—that goads us into continuing our attention. We are able to decode the warning messages of sirens, even those we've never heard before, largely because of that repeti-tion—a means of ensuring successful information transfer that Shan-non called "redundancy." Sirens are good at what they do—at creating cautionary ruckuses—not so much because they are loud but because we hear their messages, *god-awfully*, again and again and again; and even that little electronic *beep* emitted by the alarm on a wristwatch is enough to make you crazy if you have to hear it for an hour. Knowing that Ian can tolerate a variety of sounds at surprisingly loud volumes—movies and music that he is much attached to, for instance, the grinding and clanking noise of the garage door and its motor, to which he likes to listen carefully several times a day—I can't help but wonder whether it is the repetition of certain sounds, rather than their decibel levels, which so disturbs him. And I think that perhaps that *is* the case, despite the fact that Ian is a boy very much at home with repetition.

The most elemental means of ensuring that information is transferred free of error, Shannon pointed out, is the sirens' screaming
means: a message transmitted so many times in succession that,
cumulatively at least, it is received as it was intended. But simple
repetition is a clumsy and time-consuming way to achieve redundancy. It is far easier, though certainly more complex, to transmit a
message via an error-correcting code, one that effectively eliminates
noise from the message as it is sent. Jeremy Campbell explains:

> A very simple form of code is used when a clerk writes down
> the number of words in a telegram at the end of a message.
> When the cable reaches its destination, a rough test can be
> made to see if any words have been lost in transit. A self-
> healing code is a more advanced form of redundancy. It is able
> to correct errors without having to go back to the source for
> more information, as in the case of the telegram. If a message
> encoded into binary digits, 0's and 1's, is sent along a channel,
> it is possible to control the amount of errors in the message
> by adding an extra digit to the end of each string, as a sort of
> brief description of the string. A 0 added to a string, for exam-
> ple, might mean that if all the digits in the string are added
> up, they come to an even number. A 1 would mean that they
> come to an odd number. If the total is odd when the code says
> it is even, an error has been detected. A more complex version
> of this idea enables errors to be traced to individual digits by
> various forms of cross-checking. Once a digit is shown to be
> wrong, it is the easiest thing in the world to put the mistake
> right. Since a digit can only be in one of two states, either 0
> or 1, if one state is incorrect, then the other must be correct.
> The message is then self-healing.

But in contrast to computers, which speak binary languages comprised solely of two symbols, how do we ensure the accuracy of
messages sent by means of human language, made up of tenfold
more symbols that can be arranged nearly limitlessly? The answer,
of course, is that a language's redundancy is the province of its

grammar. We burden words with rules and conventions of many kinds not simply to be strict or to achieve some sort of societal uniformity but to ensure the accuracy—or something closely approaching accuracy—of the messages we send. The role of many of the words in virtually any grammatical sentence is simply to provide predictability, clarity—redundancy. *You may play with the plastic truck that's in the closet*, for example, is a sentence dependent on its grammar for its clarity, for the successful transfer of its information. The words *You play truck closet*, in contrast, far less successfully convey the intended message, and if any of those four key words is deleted, the message becomes so unruly, so unpredictable, that it relays virtually no information.

The English language is roughly fifty percent redundant, Shannon estimated, meaning that only about half of the words we speak or write are employed symbolically to represent critical elements of a given message, while the other half serve to ensure the accurate understanding of those meaningful elements. The more complex a communications system is, he pointed out, the greater the likelihood of malfunction or "misinformation." Since language is hugely complex, richly laden with possibility, it therefore follows that for any single possibility—any specific and inherently unique message—to be successfully conveyed, it must be wrapped in grammatical redundancy. Half the words we speak, in other words, harbor information, while the other half ensure that information's clear and precise reception.

As the sound waves generated by a spoken sentence enter the ear, they are transformed into electrical impulses in the milliseconds before they reach the brain stem, where somehow they are "recognized" as phonemes, as the sounds of words, and therefore are relayed to language-decoding centers in the cerebral cortex, where the sentence's meaning is separated from its accuracy-ensuring structure, where the brain first "understands" that the truck in the closet is yours to play with. It is only at that highest cortical level—at the language-comprehension site known as Wernicke's area, its circuitry firing in quick combination with other language centers such as Broca's area and the prefrontal cortex—that the deciphering of spoken codes can commence, where the myriad, melodic sounds of speech are pieced into words, and where marvelously sophisticated syntactic structures begin to discern meaning from the way in which those words have been inflected and arranged.

The brain's reception process is similar with nonspeech sounds, except that they normally are relayed by the brain stem to other decoding and interpreting sites, located in the right hemisphere as well as the left, some sounds sent to the cortex, where they are consciously made sense of—a collection of sounds interpreted as a truck climbing a hill on a nearby highway, for instance—others traveling only to one or more deep-brain centers, where they initiate automatic kinds of responses—the startle induced by a shouted "boo," the fight-or-flight response initiated by a growl or a sudden shriek. It is the brain stem, in this regard, that is perhaps the most critical component of the hearing process, its role in sending sound signals to the precise sites where they can be decoded and made sense of one that must be performed smoothly and exactingly if sound is to be interpreted as anything other than noise, if it is to be successfully received as information.

At the time he was diagnosed with autism in 1985, test results had seemed contradictory: an audiogram had measured Ian's hearing as normal while a subsequent brain stem auditory evoked-response test had shown significant hearing loss. And perhaps this finally is an explanation: Ian's ears function normally, responding to sound waves and transforming them into neural impulses, yet somehow— it seems likely and logical to me—his faulty brain stem relays them to sites elsewhere in his brain that are not capable as they should be of deciphering their aural codes.

As he could demonstrate at school these days, and as he had at home for several years now, Ian was capable of following (and there- fore decoding and understanding) complex verbal commands: "You need to go to the bathroom before you go outside"; "Push the Rewind button so the tape will start at the beginning"; "Give Sarah a hug good-night." All were commands that he could follow without the slightest hint of incomprehension. At school, Mary Lou could say, "Ian, it's computer time. Will you please turn on the computer and put in the 'Animal Kingdom' disk?" and he could readily do as he was asked. Increasingly, it appeared that despite his customary staring into space or a seemingly preoccupied focus on some object, Ian heard and clearly comprehended virtually everything within his earshot. His receptive ability with speech seemed unimpeded, his brain stem able quite normally, it seemed, to recognize and relay the multifaceted sounds of speech to Wernicke's area and the prefrontal region for initial decoding. Yet at the same time, of course, shrill and steady sounds, noises in which a single tone droned loudly and repeatedly, or sounds comprised of staccato kinds of repetition, seemed to go very haywire inside his head. I think perhaps they did so because they too—incorrectly, catastrophically—shot directly to those same language-decoding centers in his cerebral cortex, where an instantaneous and futile attempt was made to decipher them as phonemes, and where, failing that, they flashed through uncomprehending linguistic circuitry as nothing more than the most terrible, inescapable, and *conscious* kind of noise.

Imagine Ian's predicament if this hunch of mine has substance: if he indeed hears everything he hears at the conscious, cortical level—no sound of any sort modulated, impeded, or blocked by his brain stem before it is instantaneously *alive* in his cerebrum—then not only do his language centers receive and decipher the kinds of coded impulses that tell him there's a truck in a closet with which he might like to play, they are bombarded as well by myriad kinds of undecodable auditory input, neural "sounds" that he must listen to intently but whose message is nothing more than a maddening cacophony. If something like this is what Ian undergoes—his language centers forced to contend with neural signals they cannot decipher and which, in a normal brain, would otherwise be buffered by the brain stem or directed elsewhere—then several aspects of his behavior begin to make more sense.

It may be that Ian's overall hearing ability seems so acute because he hears very consciously and completely many things that the rest of us hear only automatically—in ways that allow our appropriate responses but that do not *demand* attention. His particular delight in hearing rhyming verse may be explainable, in part, by the likelihood that rhyme adds an important pattern, hence more predictability and a correspondingly greater probability for information transfer, to the words he hears. In a similar vein, one of the several reasons he becomes so attached to particular books and movies may be that their utter predictability over time is the critical reassurance that, at least while he is focused on them, he will not be met with noise. His strong attraction to music—whether children's songs or chamber music—also may be due to a brain stem that filters few or even any sounds—richly patterned chords and melodies far more vivid, more immediate perhaps, for Ian than for me. And even the chorus of several sounds that commences each time the garage door opens then closes again surely is comprised of its own kind of music, its own pleasing cadences, variations, and repetitions.

Yet sirens, on the other hand, are made up of only the crudest kinds of patterns. With their blaring one- or two-tone monotony, they are antithetical to the musical surprise and predictability that is basic to language, analogous to a seventy-word sentence that is simply a shouted "NOW NOW NOW NOW NOW NOW NOW NOW . . ." but which through ears clogged by microorganisms perhaps sounds more like "NQX NQX NQX NQX NQX NQX NQX NQX . . ."—a sound utterly absent any sense, one that may seem to Ian much more like a ceaseless shout in an unknown language than a loud and droning tone—more like a growling and garbled message he cannot help but try desperately to understand, rather than the sort of sound that is buffered and dismissed as nothing more than obvious and endless and unknowable noise.

Although Sarah attended a different school, and although she didn't witness Ian being carried screaming from the building that day during Gateway's fire drill, those kinds of terrorized responses on his part—so regular that they were chaotically commonplace at home—by now had begun to truly trouble her on the infrequent occasions when they became all too public. A third-grader already, Sarah initially had contended with her often chaotic household by creating a rich fantasy world into which she could escape, and as she grew older she began to display a rather startling aptitude for turning those fantasies into stories of her own. But as she matured—perceiving more, understanding more about her brother and his predicament—Sarah increasingly had become a girl who lived her life on tiptoe. The turbulence that Ian initiated every day was so inescapable, its stress so pervasive throughout their household, that she—rather like a child in a family racked by the turmoil that alcohol can induce—went very much out of her way to cause no commotion of her own. She was an excellent student, one who grew distraught when she received an occasional grade of B in a subject like PE and who took quiet delight in the diversions provided by summer art classes and evening ballet lessons during the long winter. Sarah virtually never acted out or tried otherwise to manipulate her parents' attentions, but in recent days she had become increasingly fragile, physically as well as emotionally—her many allergies and susceptibility to viruses, together with the psychic toll exacted by her proximity to her brother's daily trauma, often combining to keep her home from school, to hold her energy level low, and to keep her chronically on a kind of concerned but awkwardly helpless emotional edge.

Claudia and Boyce were aware, of course, of those aspects of Sarah's childhood that were being shortchanged, even cruelly sacrificed, by Ian's autism, and they did their best to provide her with special activities away from home. They had begun, early on, to include her openly in their discussions of Ian and his situation—those issues that currently were terribly wearing on each of them, the ideas that periodically seemed to offer them improvements. And as I had begun in the spring of 1991 to try to make my own sense of Ian and his disorder—of his life and the lives his family shared at his side—by writing about them (my words strangely, frustratingly, *maddeningly* as reluctant as Ian's for some time), Sarah's parents had broached my plans with her. They had wanted to seek her approval just as I recently had sought theirs, sensing, correctly, that she might well be wary of a project that would seem far too public, potentially too revealing of many things with which she still hadn't come entirely to terms.

Only a nine-year-old, Sarah never had written me a letter before.
She had sent drawings for Karen's birthday or for mine from time to
time, and she was dutiful about mailing charming, single-sentence
thank-you notes, but hearing that I might write a book about Ian
was indeed enough of a concern to her that she promptly composed
this letter in her careful cursive script:

Dear Russel,

Mom told me about your book. She wanted to know how I felt
about it. I have mixed feelings about it. The good things would
be that more people would know about Ian and understand
more. But what I'd be worryed about is that I'm scarded
thousands of people will look at Ian in a bad way.
    I would like to know you would write all the good things,
not to many difficlut things. I'm worryed that you'll missjudge
what the good things are. I don't think you will, though.

love you!

Sarah

It seemed to be a tenuous permission, one I appreciated in several
ways, and when the words at last began to come, I did my best to
write them mindful of Sarah's loving disquietude. And the "good
things" obviously *were* there to take note of, to try to scribble down:
each of Ian's milestones, his generous affections and his smile, his
brave foray into school life and the slow, laborious emergence of
language, his valiant efforts to be cooperative, to be a *kid*, his endearing impact on his teachers, his many newfound friends. And it
was a great good thing as well that same spring when Ian read aloud
to his entire class, the first time he had done so, his maiden spoken
message to his peers, the first time he had filled that bustling school-
room with information.
    It was a warm April day that presaged the end of snow, only two
weeks since Ian's return to school following the nightmare that had
been set in motion by the fire drill, a time when Boyce and Claudia

still were investigating, as their limited free time allowed, the suspicious promise of facilitated communication, the two of them careful not to lift their hopes too high, but buoyed nonetheless by every optimistic mention of the procedure in newspaper clippings or on public radio. They were confident that Ian could manipulate a keyboard with that facilitating kind of assistance, but they were also seriously concerned whether his ritualization ever could give way to impromptu typing, to unstudied "speech." They would have to learn much more, they knew; they would have to immerse themselves as thoroughly in facilitated communication as they had in autism itself and in its nearly nonexistent therapies. And on rare days like this one, it seemed very possible instead that Ian someday might use his *mouth* to send every kind of message, VÓÍSes and keyboards abandoned because he could truly speak.

Claudia and Boyce were not in the classroom where they could witness Ian's reading, but by kind design, Charmaine had set up a video camera that day to record every student's oral presentation. And by this point much later in time, of course, everyone who cares rather fundamentally about this boy has seen the tape as well: Tall and towheaded, Ian stands very calmly at the front of the room as the tape commences, a giant-sized edition of *The Farm Concert* placed on an easel in front of him, his classmates sitting on the carpet at his feet. In the loudest voice he can muster, his words spoken clumsily but nonetheless intelligibly—especially if you know the story—Ian announces the title, turns to the first illustrated page, and begins to read, his cadence, inflection, and pauses surprisingly appropriate, his left hand buried in his pants pocket, the fingers of his right hand reaching out to touch each word:

> "Moo, moo," went the cow.
> "Wuff, wuff," went the dog.
> "Quack, quack," went the duck.
> "Oink, oink," went the pig.
> "Baa, baa," went the sheep.
> "Quiet!" yelled the farmer. "I can't sleep!"

Then, mimicking the way in which Charmaine and Mary Lou, Barb Myers and his mom and dad have read the story to him a hundred times, his voice just a whisper now, he continues:

> *"Moo, moo," went the cow.*
> *"Wuff, wuff," went the dog.*
> *"Quack, quack," went the duck.*
> *"Oink, oink," went the pig.*
> *"Baa, baa," went the sheep.*
> *"Good," said the farmer. "I can sleep."*

Ian's classmates erupt in applause as he finishes, and the videotape is obviously a thing to treasure always. Before it ends, a boy seated near Ian extends his palm and shouts "Give me five!" before a dozen hands similarly are extended, the kids on their knees, some of them standing now, all hollering "Give me five!" it seems, as they press toward him. But Ian continues to stand calmly, his face still expressionless in their midst, his eyes turning to survey each of them yet appearing uncertain how to react to their loud and repeated cheers, uncertain too about this ceremonial stuff of giving five. Then Eddie jumps up to offer his help, facilitating, as it were, Ian's appropriate response—Eddie's two little hands taking hold of Ian's wrist now, guiding his hand as Ian acknowledges twenty open palms with a quick and hearty slap, Eddie saying, "Yeah, Ian, cool, *now* you're giving five!"

8

THE

EMERGENCE

OF MEANING

In the four years since that day when Ian Drummond slipped away from his father's sight and ran four miles along Teller County roads, seeming oddly desperate to get away, he similarly had disappeared six more times by the autumn of 1991. Before his family moved to town, he had run away from the research station a second time; twice he had fled from the house on Redfeather Lane; once he had vanished at Red Rocks Campground north of town, a place his parents often took him for exercise and exploration; and twice by now he had found a way through the fence that bounded the house on Ponderosa Court and had climbed up the steeply wooded hillside at the base of the Rampart Range, leaving security and his hourly rituals behind, fleeing for reasons his parents couldn't ascertain. Was Ian attempting to escape the tyranny of his routines when he abruptly disappeared? Was he trying to elude autism and all that it entailed at those times when he interrupted his otherwise inviolate schedule and headed nowhere other than away? Or was this an eight-year-old's rather more straightforward acting out, a means of causing a willful kind of trouble, Ian behaving more normally than abnormally, in point of fact, as he ran away?

For Claudia and Boyce, those questions remained unanswerable,

and in addition to everything else that Ian's care entailed, his disappearances also meant he would have to be monitored even more
closely than he already was. By now, he could open every door and
gate he encountered, save those that were padlocked, and he could
scale fences and other obstacles with ease. Although months might
pass before he would disappear again, he seemed to choose times to
take his leave when they were least expected, and as every parent
can attest, of course, there is nothing as chilling as a child's sudden,
shocking absence.

That chill still returns to Claudia as she remembers the second
of the two afternoons when Ian ran from the house on Redfeather
Lane—the day he simply left his bedroom and walked down a staircase to the basement where a closed door led to the garage, its
overhead door briefly open while Boyce carried grocery bags in from
the car. By the time anyone knew he was gone, Ian already was well
away, and police and sheriff's vehicles soon were enlisted in the
search for him. As had been the case with each of his disappearances,
it was nearly an hour before he was found—running this time down
the middle of the highway that led north from town—and Claudia
isn't sure she should be so candid as she recounts the sudden draining catharsis she underwent as she drove, alone, toward the flashing
lights and the clump of cars parked ahead on the highway. She isn't
sure she should confess to me that she didn't know what she hoped
to encounter as she approached them. If her son was *not* alive, would
that be the worst of the several possible outcomes? Surely the pain
of his death—if indeed death lay ahead—could be no more painful
than the daily pain she bore watching Ian struggle with an inescapable internal hell. Despite his progress of many sorts, the successes
of which he and everyone who knew him were so proud, all his days
were brutal days still, and so they seemed destined to remain. As
Ian grew older, his behavior inevitably would seem far more aber-
rant, she knew; puberty would impose new and difficult problems,
and already Ian had grown big enough and strong enough that his
tantrums brought new dangers. But Ian was far more than simply
her son, of course: her world necessarily orbited his; his long-term
care and immediate well-being were surely the foremost issues in

her life; and the fear that he might be dead had been so immediate and intense that she sobbed uncontrollably, she remembers, for a long time after she found him unharmed, after she took him in her arms.

If only they could *ask* Ian about these disappearances, Claudia and Boyce believed, if only he could offer some sort of explanation, then together they might find a way to prevent them. His verbal speech had continued to blossom in the year since they had made that sudden change of houses in an attempt to escape the tyranny of barking dogs. He now could say "go ways" when he wanted to fast-forward a videotape he was watching, and "go ways back" similarly meant the tape needed to be reversed; he could say "Dad go up-stairs" when he needed to be alone, and "Mom come" or "Mom come fast" when he needed assistance or was becoming impatient. "Five more minutes" were the words he used to stall for time, and "just start over" meant he had to begin a ritual again. Occasionally, curiously, he would awaken correctly pronouncing his ABCs, and regularly now he successfully read aloud the schedule his parents posted for him each morning as a means of letting him know that something slightly out of the ordinary had to happen on that day. Yet most of Ian's verbal output remained echolalic: To the question "Do you want to go for a ride?" he would respond "you go ride." "Tummy hurt," he would answer when asked if his tummy hurt, and he had begun to borrow expressions like "for sure" from his class-mates and "good grief!" from Charlie Brown. Ian would jabber aloud, quite contentedly it seemed, for hours as he attended to his routines; often his swift slurry of words was entirely unintelligible, but sometimes his family could be sure that he was reciting word-for-word the sentences from a favorite book or precisely repeating the lines from one well-known movie as he watched another.

As Ian more and more could express his basic needs—"go cows," "go Wendy's," "go ways back"—the VOÏS with which he partially had communicated since before he entered kindergarten he now used less and less. Each of the robotic phrases it spoke had to be meticulously preprogrammed by parents or teachers before he could make communicative use of it, and now that he could speak the words *French fries* with his own small and clumsy voice, there was little reason for him to reach for the VÖIS and press the key that announced "I want some French fries" on his behalf. But notwithstanding the fact that he had progressed beyond a need for that high-tech aid, and despite his swelling spoken vocabulary, Ian's ability to express himself, to speak with precision or a complex kind of meaning, remained severely limited. He still could not explain why so many things so often went awry; he couldn't offer his own input into tomorrow's schedule or the coming days at school; and still no one could be precisely sure how much personality and intellect, how much that was uniquely *Ian*, existed behind the remote expression on his face.

It was possible that Ian's three- and four-word phrases would grow into sentences in time, into spoken language shaped by syntactic complexity and rich with the subtleties of meaning, yet even at only eight years old, Ian was running out of time. If he did not progress quite soon from the basic verbal abilities of the average two-and-a-half- or three-year-old to those of a child of five or six, it was doubtful that he ever would. If he could not produce within a year, maybe two, sentences explaining "I feel too sick to go to school," for instance, it seemed sadly probable that extended bouts of screaming would remain his best means of expressing those kinds of conditions. Ian's nascent, still-protolinguistic speech had clearly opened a door that heretofore had been closed to him, but it was a door that also had offered him and his family an alluring glimpse of what a truly communicative life might be like, what it would be for Ian and for them if all his words were imbued with meaning. And in the same way that over the years they had grasped readily and optimistically each new expressive tool with which Ian might "say" more, with which he might better influence his surroundings, as he entered the second grade Claudia and Boyce found their questions and curiosities drawn ever more hopefully toward that new and controversial means of *non*verbal communication called facilitation, and they did so even as Ian's spoken vocabulary continued to swell, even as he began to speak with more meaning than would have been imaginable on that day two years before when he first said "cow."

—

In a crowded conference room at Denver's Children's Hospital, the place where Ian's autistic odyssey officially had commenced six years before, I had joined Claudia, Mary Lou Krueger, and a hundred others to listen to Douglas Biklen and fellow committed proponents of facilitated communication discuss its efficacy and its future. Although he wanted very much to attend as well, Boyce had been unable to because all three of Ian's principal caregivers simply could not leave him, even for a day.

Biklen, bearded and comfortably professorial in his middle forties, took initial pains as the conference commenced to dispel the widening image of himself as a kind of Pied Piper of desperate parents that had lately been fostered on television. Reminding us that he personally had discovered nothing, he went on to point out that Rosemary Crossley's discoveries in Australia had been independently encountered round the world—first by New York State pediatricians Mary and Campbell Goodwin in the 1960s and Illinois special-education teacher Rosalind Oppenheim in the 1970s, then by educators in Denmark (who had succeeded in using the method rather extensively without stirring the sort of incredulous fuss that had arisen both in Australia and in the United States), as well as more recently by Carol Berger, an Oregon special-education teacher, and Arthur Schawlow, a Stanford University physicist and Nobel laureate, both of whom were in attendance at the Denver conference.

Berger had been using hand and arm support to assist students with autism and other disorders with both handwriting- and typing-based communication for five years prior to learning about Crossley's work. And Schawlow and his late wife had happened on the technique when their son Artie, a young adult with autism, had shown interest in typing at a computer keyboard one day about two years before. With tears streaming down his face, the elder Schawlow described the Saturday when, with his mother's light support at his wrist, Artie straightforwardly had typed I WANT TO GO TO PIZZA HUT as his first attempt at facilitated communication, a request that also signaled the first linguistic communication of his life.

The fact that facilitated communication did indisputably work—in some if surely not in all cases—Schawlow commented, had to be hard to believe, of course, if you began, as many people did, with the assumption that people with autism lacked not only personality but intellect as well. If you were a professional whose educational, psychological, or medical career had been built around the belief that people with autism were severely mentally disabled, then a suddenly demonstrated ability to produce grammatical, often eloquent statements obviously would seem preposterous—surely the facilitator's unwitting work rather than some sort of communicative breakthrough. But for individuals who were willing to challenge their assumptions about autism, as well as those who knew from firsthand experience that people with autism indeed were *in there*, cognizant and capable behind their oddly solitary masks, the viability of facilitated communication seemed no stranger than a blind person's use of Braille or a deaf person's fluid speech through sign.

Biklen acknowledged, following Berger's and Schawlow's presentations, that his own thinking about autism had changed dramatically in the years since he had begun to observe much remarkable communication made possible through facilitation. Rather than being principally a personality deficit—an inability to recognize the self and its interactive relationship with the world—autism, he now believed, was more fundamentally a sensory and neuromuscular disorder, one in which people with normal and sometimes even sophisticated intellects, as well as commensurate linguistic abilities, are trapped inside bodies they can't control. In that context, he argued, there is nothing remotely mysterious about the way in which facilitated communication allows meaningful words to find their exit. A supporting hand placed beneath a trembling and awkward palm is analogous to the training wheels on a child's bike that remain reassuringly important long after they still are absolutely needed, he suggested, analogous too to a nonsinger's ability to successfully sing in a choir. "It isn't a Ouija board and these are *not* the facilitator's words," he insisted. "Facilitated communication at its root is simply a form of physical and emotional support."

The room was packed with parents and teachers who had come

to the meeting from all over the western United States and Canada
eager to try the technique with their own children and students,
incredibly keen, you could sense, to ascertain just who the person
was who had lived in their midsts so privately for so long. Yet
apprehension also filled the air. Few dared to raise their hopes too
high, and after twenty or even thirty years, some also were afraid,
understandably, of the words they soon might have to read, of the
several unsettling explications they might be forced to face. For her
part, although she knew, of course, that Ian was at ease with computers and keyboards, Claudia worried whether his severe ritualization
would mean that—presuming one day he *could* type successfully—
he would be able to do so only in a single, specific setting or at a
precise time of the day, or both. It was common, she understood,
for people with autism to be able to communicate successfully only
with the facilitating assistance of a single teacher or sibling or friend
with whom they shared a special rapport; Ian, she could imagine,
might similarly need to have every detail in his life precisely arranged—akin to some sort of rare celestial alignment—before he
could grow calm and secure enough to attend to typing. She knew
that for people with autism who possessed some echolalic speech,
that communicative skill surprisingly tended to be still one more
hurdle in the way of successful facilitated communication. And she
still really couldn't imagine Ian sitting still long enough to type
anything for more than a second or two before he would be frantic
to be left alone. But nonetheless, by the time the conference closed,
Claudia was determined to try it, to see whether this technique
would suit her son, to determine for herself and perhaps for him as
well whether there *were* words and sentences inside him that wanted
a way out.

Educators and scientists like Biklen, Schawlow, and others were
risking their professional reputations in championing something that
appeared to so many of their colleagues to be either a folly or a hoax.
They were aware, for instance, that Gina Green, director of research
at the New England Center for Autism, recently had visited several

facilitated communication programs in Australia and had labeled them "an insidious cult." They knew that Eric Schopler, editor of the *Journal of Autism and Developmental Disorders*, maintained that facilitated communication's proponents were guilty of "an especially pernicious form of sales technique [that] may well succeed in setting autism services back forty years," although he did, in fact, acknowledge that some people with autism clearly *could* communicate with the technique. They had read—and Biklen had responded angrily to—the work of Australian educators Robert Cummins and Margot Prior, who had claimed in the *Harvard Educational Review* that "on not one single occasion has a systematic investigation of assisted communication [they refused to use Crossley's own terminology] revealed consistent and valid evidence that such communications emanate from the client. Rather, all relevant investigations have revealed that in each instance studied the assistant has, wittingly or unwittingly, been responsible for the recorded response." Similarly, they knew that Howard Shane, director of the Communication Enhancement Center at Boston's Children's Hospital, had recently conducted tests of his own design in which *no one* among more than two dozen people with autism who were tested had been able to correctly type the name of an object he or she had been shown unless the object had also been shown to the facilitator. And they were sadly aware as well that Bernard Rimland, who had made the courageous case back in the 1960s that autism was a neurological rather than psychological disorder—and who had even proposed at that time the use of a "talking typewriter" for communication—now was loudly warning that only very few young people with autism could possibly succeed with facilitated communication because, he maintained, the majority of them remained prelinguistic throughout their lives. "We are asked to believe that one hundred percent of the mute autistic population can express themselves in writing," he wrote, "even though there is little evidence that the vast majority of these individuals can *read*."

Rimland's vocal entry into the dispute, it seemed to me, highlighted the slow and ongoing evolution of informed attitudes toward autism, which once, of course, had centered on the outlandish conviction that cold and emotionally cruel parents were responsible for the onset of a terrible dishevelment of the psyche. Only after decades had Rimland and his contemporaries succeeded in convincing the medical, psychological, and educational establishments that autism had a neurological basis, that it beset young brains in unpredictable and insidious ways, precluding speech and distorting sensory receptivity and perhaps even cognition and personality in the process. And now, nearly thirty years later, yet another way of looking at autism was being demanded of anyone who believed that facilitated communication was something more than a mirage.

If even a very small percentage of people with autism (no one ever had suggested *all* of them, as far as I could ascertain) could indeed type intelligibly with some assistance, then several new and often uncomfortable assumptions necessarily had to be made: some people with autism possessed at least basic intelligence; some were quite cognizant of and curious about the world around them despite the behaviors that made them appear they were not; and some of them *were* linguistic. Regardless of their proficiency with speech, those who were capable of writing when finally offered the proper writing tools obviously were proficient readers also, a skill many had somehow acquired without formal training. Yet for far more than a few professionals and interested lay people, these remained outlandish assumptions well into the 1990s, and I think you can appreciate why they did.

Imagine for a moment that for ten years, or even for twenty, your interaction with your own child or with a student had been based on the assumption that he coiled and uncoiled a rope for hours on end because he possessed few, if any, abstract thoughts; that she seemed to utterly ignore everything in her surroundings because she lacked the simplest concept of herself or a basic understanding of her interface with the people and objects around her; that surely she beat her head repeatedly because she was terribly retarded; that he didn't speak because toilet-training, let alone language, was far beyond his skills. These common kinds of perceptions about the capabilities of people with autism remained current even as people much like these had begun to type, and the eloquence of their words often seemed utterly incompatible with the realities of their behaviors. What were parents to make of a child who tried to eat his feces, say, or to gouge his forearms with a nail on the same day that he typed IMN NOTJH STUPID LIKE TYOU THIKNK IAM? What were teachers to think when faced with similar behavioral dichotomies? What sorts of responses realistically could be expected from the weedy field of experts other than skepticism and indignant outrage?

But then assume, on the other hand, that your first introduction to facilitated communication has come from a source other than prime-time television, that it initially has been presented to you as a communicative tool rather than a miracle cure incapable of explanation. Assume as well, as I think you should, that autism's etiology is somehow parallel to the etiologies of multiple sclerosis, Parkinson's disease, or the several aphasias—in which sometimes subtle physiological abnormalities in the brain lead to disparate, often profound, motor deficits—and remember too that someone without speech doesn't necessarily also lack language. With those several suppositions in hand, it seems to me, a modest sort of account of the way in which facilitated communication actually might succeed depends less on synonyms for *mystery* than on words that work at describing movement.

It is neurobiologist William Calvin who envisions an important neural network linking the site in the left temporal lobe that controls the motor-sequencing skills of the hands and arms with an associated site that manages movement of the orofacial muscles, and Calvin believes it is likely that human speech indeed evolved from throwing skills that once were essential for successful hunting. In his investigation of Broca's aphasia, Calvin's colleague Philip Lieberman separately but similarly notes how often Broca's speech deficits are associated with inabilities to regulate and control intricate movements of the hands and fingers, and that people who cannot speak or who have difficulty speaking—for whatever mix of reasons—tend also to encounter problems with using their hands. And from my own limited tenure at a neurologist's side, I know that patients with Parkinson's disease—its motor-initiation problems rooted in structural damage to the basal ganglia and an associated deficiency in the production of the neurotransmitter dopamine—often have difficulty not only with slurred speech but also with initiating a spoken string of words.

People caught in Parkinson's cruel complex of symptoms, whose hands tremble rhythmically, ceaselessly, side to side when resting in their laps, are momentarily tremor-free when they reach to grasp a glass or to take a coat from a hanger. Some Parkinson's patients who must walk tortuously slowly as they cross a floor, each step a willful and concentrated act, can descend a staircase fluidly, perfectly normally, once that first step down is under way; some who simply cannot initiate the movements involved in rising from a chair or in taking a first step can, quite curiously, at last succeed in doing so when a companion's hand is placed on their shoulder or when the companion's fingers are intertwined with their own, the companion somehow *facilitating* the initiation of a motor sequence by providing pressure, tactile sensation, and emotional support.

It is Lieberman's conjecture that a bundle of projection fibers normally connect and integrate the deep-brain basal ganglia with the prefrontal cortex, their concerted functions making possible the smooth initiation of every manner of movement, from pointing an index finger to the pronunciation of a word, and after reading him, I began to wonder whether some sort of damage to Ian's prefrontal cortex or to the circuitry that links it with separate brain structures plays a role in his inability to deal with newness as well as in his faulty speech. It didn't therefore seem to be too tenuous a leap for me to imagine, at the close of that Denver conference, that a supporting hand wrapped around the wrist of someone much like Ian could indeed calm erratic movements, that it could provide the kind of reverse-direction pressure that allows a movement to commence, that it *could* make possible the sequential pecking of keys without controlling which keys were, in fact, pressed. I already accepted with some confidence the notion that just because someone much like Ian keeps a vacuous expression imprinted on his face doesn't mean that the brain behind that face cannot observe or understand what surrounds him; already I was convinced that the fact that words from an autistic mouth may be scarce or nonexistent doesn't prove that thousands of words aren't, nonetheless, alive somewhere inside, trapped in faulty neural circuitry. Facilitated communication, it seemed to me that icy February, as Claudia and Mary Lou returned to Woodland Park eager to draw keyboards ever more extensively into Ian's day, differed only a little from the kinds of supportive techniques that physical and occupational therapists had employed successfully for years in neurological rehabilitation. Didn't this procedure simply attempt to transmit communicative information by novel and supportive means? Didn't it simply affirm that meaning can be conveyed through open conduits of several kinds?

The question of insuring message accuracy is far more problematic in the context of facilitated communication, of course, than it is with speech or other kinds of written communication. In addition to the possibility that the meaning of a given message may be distorted by strange word selection or odd, rule-breaking syntactic arrangements, as is always possible in any informational system, facilitated communication obviously poses additional barriers to understanding: the use of keyboards by people with poor motor control virtually assures the occurrence of a noisy and confusing number of typographical errors in every series of letters typed; people who have never before expressed themselves linguistically are likely to employ obscure turns of phrase as they begin to do so; and typed statements and responses, which tend to be rather brief, can be quite misleading, the few words with which they are composed often interpretable in contradictory ways.

But despite the recurring strains it places on message accuracy, the aspect of facilitated communication that can lend its messages a kind of quaking profundity is the reality that people who use this technique are communicating expressively, *linguistically*, for the first time in their lives. You and I take our abilities to say "I love you," "Do you understand me?" or even "I'm kind of nervous," so entirely for granted that I doubt we can truly imagine what it must be like to lack speech or sign or the ability to write for five years, for ten, for twenty-five, then to be able at last, come one incredible day, to reach outside yourself with words. Imagine the surge of fear you surely would feel, wondering whether your words were as good as anyone else's, the doubt that surely would flood you about whether *you* really had something to say. Imagine the wonderful sense of accomplishment that would accompany your first words, the frustration you would feel at how slowly, tortuously you had to type them. And once you do so, it quickly seems unsurprising that emotional as well as physical support tend to be critical components of the process. Imagine how amazed you would be by finally becoming complete, a person capable just like any other of producing words and sentences as well as receiving them, someone who at last could say what you mean and also revel in the understanding that what you mean truly matters.

Language is about nothing so much as the emergence of meaning, of course. Whether its fundamental role is communicative—the successful expression of meaningful information between otherwise isolated individuals—or representational—a symbolic system that orders and makes meaningful the world and its experiences as they are perceived—language's symbols are ultimately inseparable from the things they *mean*. Although conventional dictionaries are organized around the notion that meaning is the province of the single word, it is impossible in practice to separate *semantics*, the study of the meaning of words, from syntax. Other than the forceful *no* or the willing *yes*, we almost never use single words in isolation, and even when we do come close to sequestering a word from its syntactic context, it is often difficult to distinguish its *denotation*, its normal or commonplace sense, from the sorts of associated meanings that are called *connotations*. *Sex* is such a word, for example, one that variously denotes gender, desire, instinct, or copulation, but which for most of us is rife with dozens of connotations, associated sorts of meanings that are attractive or repellent depending on the individual and the context in which "sex" is spoken. *Autism*, I suppose, is also illustrative, a term that might well have possessed a single, rather restrictive meaning, but which, in fact, denotes drastically different things, and its connotations range from some haywire thing that turns children into eerie automatons to a disorder that somehow mirrors much about the sum and substance of living.

The spectrum of connotations of these two words, as well as a million more, also points to a peculiar irony of language: although it is language's purpose to infuse communication and cognition with meaning, with order and explanation, language's symbolic structure and its ceaseless creativity often act, in fact, to broaden the sense of what is intended rather than to delimit it, to draw connections and blur distinctions rather than to clearly delineate and distinguish, and we speak and write in metaphor with such constancy that we seldom are aware we are doing so.

By the time a word is spoken—let's say the word *Ian*—it is three levels of representation removed from the being it denotes. On the primary level, one we must boldly call reality, there is the blond boy with blood in his veins who screams and giggles and runs. Secondarily, there is our perception of this boy, distinct and separate from the reality, a symbolic representation of him shaped and necessarily limited by our senses and our complex brains. On a third and at last linguistic level, there is the morpheme that represents the perception that in turn represents the being: *Ian* linguistically symbolizing "Ian," which is a mental construct of Ian, as Derek Bickerton would visually, orthographically distinguish the three. And *Ian*, in that regard, is very nearly as metaphoric as *The kid across the street who always runs along the fence line* or even *The lad who lives inside himself*. To tie metaphor solely to poetry or to orators is to mistakenly assume that there is little symbolic distance between words and the vivid ideas or palpable objects or persons they represent. That distance instead is ineluctably, happily large, one that lends language its scope and its malleability. Just as syntax serves to insure accuracy in linguistic communication, metaphor fuels language with energy and imagination, with the kinds of creative leaps that trigger fresh ways of associating and perceiving, and that sometimes transform meaning into something akin to transcendent understanding.

—

Ian typed his first tentative words in early March 1992, at first simply adding the final word to sentences Claudia had typed on a laptop computer, the kind of "set work" Biklen and his colleagues had recommended as an introduction for both assistant and "speaker" to the process of facilitated communication. WE DID NOT GO OUT FOR RECESS BECAUSE THERE WAS TOO MUCH, Claudia typed before Ian, his small right hand wrapped in hers, his index finger strongly extended, followed with SNOW, a process not unlike the language exercises with which he was well accustomed at school— Ian carefully duplicating the proper placement of a word in a sentence otherwise typed for him by a teacher. AT SCHOOL TODAY, MRS. ROSS READ A POEM ABOUT A PURPLE, Claudia prompted next, and Ian followed quickly with COW.

A week into this new routine—brief typing sessions attempted once or twice a day, Ian occasionally quite willing but often flatly refusing to approach the keyboard—Boyce suggested that Ian explain to his mom what the two of them had seen on the morning's drive to the research station. Claudia, who hadn't yet heard what they'd encountered, typed TODAY DAD AND I SAW A, before bringing Ian's hand to the keyboard, steadying it, pulling it firmly back following each sharp keystroke that soon spelled COYOYE. It was the first time Claudia had not known what the appropriate final word would be, her initial proof to herself that she was not subconsciously willing the proper keystrokes. Yes, they *had* seen a coyote, Boyce confirmed, and although Ian's expression remained unchanged, his parents were little less than stunned: this was something very different from the kind of word-placement exercises Ian often completed at school. He had not simply supplied a word he already had seen used properly in a sentence; it wasn't a word like *cow* or *bear* that he had often practiced before. *Coyote* was a word that theretofore hadn't appeared to be in his vocabulary, and, to be sure, it was *Ian*, not his mother, who had sought out the keys that corresponded to the letters that spelled the word he wanted.

As Ian began that spring to type more unpredictable and indeed surprising words each day, Claudia stopped typing her questions and prompts and began simply to speak them aloud in conversation with him, his words alone now entered into the computer, words that were often flushed with elucidation and information. SCARED OF FAQLLING, he finally had explained by typing late one warm afternoon near the end of March, answering the plaintive question *why* hours after he had begun to scream and thrash uncontrollably in the car, the whole family en route to the nearby Royal Gorge, a canyon he never had visited before, a place he'd first heard de-scribed—by way of Sarah's excited and animated conversation—only moments before his tantrum had begun. By the time they finally had surrendered to the continuing screams, turned the car around and returned home, the experience had been exhausting, crushingly traumatic for the four of them: Ian hadn't screamed so long and ceaselessly, so perplexingly, in a very long time, and his parents and sister, like everyone who was close to him, of course, had hoped—had secretly been *certain*—that this remarkable new means of ex-pressing himself would tend to quiet his all-too-regular distress, and now it seemed plainly probable that that never would be the case. Yet it had been a day of epiphany as well. Ian *had* answered their query. He had explained in only those three words why an outing he normally could have happily contended with had suddenly in-duced in him such fright.

As they replayed in memory the moments in the car that had preceded his tantrum, they remembered that Sarah had suggested to her parents that they would have to be sure to keep Ian's "friends"—the plastic figurines he was never without—safely inside their bag as the four of them walked across the high bridge that spanned the gorge. "What would we do if one of his friends fell over the edge?" she had asked, and only seconds later—it all fit together now—Ian had begun to shriek. By the close of that draining day, Ian's single, rather simple, explanation had become a vivid confir-mation of the way in which facilitated communication could begin to provide a clear channel for statements of many kinds that he still could not verbally express, a means at last for him to send messages marked with urgency or to offer important clarifications, and the outing had illustrated too how important it henceforth would be to keep the computer or some sort of keyboard close at Ian's hand.

But the day none of them ever will forget, one flooded with equal measures of astonishment and anguish, was Thursday, April 2, 1992, its events recorded by Boyce late that night in the diary he keeps sporadically, these exegetic words wanting a way out of *him* before at last he could let go of them and sleep:

I'm writing tonight with tears streaming down my face, my chest tight, and my mind reeling from what I learned about Ian today. I'm also exhausted, as is Claudia, who at the moment is sitting stunned in the Dallas–Fort Worth airport. I just finished putting Ian and Sarah to bed. Sheila is lying on the front steps watching car headlights as they occasionally go by at the end of the street. Noelle, Sarah's hamster, is chewing on her cage, desperately trying to get out.

I used to think that's what Ian was trying to do—to break out of the shell of autism that isolates him from much of the world. His anger, rigidity, and frequent tantrums as a toddler and preschooler seemed to underscore his frustration at being unable to express his feelings, desires, and thoughts. Then, after he started school and adapted with some flexibility to new surroundings, interchangeable adults, and a building full of 300 kids, I thought he was blissfully unaware of his differences, unashamed of his inability to hold a pencil, talk, or dance to music. Till now, we have all comforted ourselves in believing that, although Ian is different, he is often happy. This week, and especially today, have proven otherwise. And facilitated communication has changed our lives forever.

We have known for some time that Ian is not retarded—that, in fact, his intelligence is high, his memory good, and his problem-solving skills adequate. As he began to say a few words in early 1991 and gradually express himself more and more, teaching us what he knew and could learn, we were delighted but not surprised, proud but not incredulous—but we kept wishing he could tell us how he felt. He had learned to say he was mad, sad, or tired at appropriate times, but this week, using the laptop computer, we have gone way beyond one-word confirmations of what we could already see he was feeling.

At the end of spring break, he refused to go back to school this week. With patience and perseverance, Claudia managed to get him to type why he didn't want to go to school and why he was so upset at the prospect of going back. We learned that he was worried about having a BM in the morning—how could he let his teachers know he needed to go if he was in class?—that he wanted to keep his friends (Tigger, et al) with him all day; and that a boy named Jason upsets him by fighting with his best friend Eddie. So, together with Ian, we worked out solutions to these problems, and at last he seemed eager to return to school.

These revelations about what concerned him were mind-boggling enough, but today was the real shocker. Today he begged Claudia—on the computer—to help him go to school, to give him something to make him calm so that he could go to school. But all the while he was typing these desires he kept kicking and screaming, "Stay home! Sick! Stay home!"

He finally explained that contradictory behavior by typing that he cannot rest unless he has things the same. So, now we know that he understands that he sometimes wants to do things his body won't let him—that there is conflict raging inside him sometimes. The old truism that "all communication is behavior" no longer seems precisely true. I recently heard at a conference that many autistic children and adults have begun to explain by typing that they simply can't control their actions—that some spinning, kicking, screaming, hitting don't mean anything, that they just can't help themselves. Now Ian is telling us exactly the same thing.

And now the other shoe to hit the floor: When Claudia tried

to encourage Ian this morning by telling him, "Eddie needs you at school to be his best friend," Ian typed, NO I AM NOT EDDIES FRIENMD.

"Why not?" she asked.

I HAVE AUTIXSM, he typed in response.

Ian *knows he is autistic* and believes that it makes him different, and that's why tears are streaming down my face.

Tonight after supper, I showed Sarah what Ian had written today. We have been sharing his other sessions with her and it seemed natural to share this one as well. But we were soon both in tears, awash in emotion, overcome by the realization of what Ian's typed statements mean—aware of how profoundly this will change all our lives. The full impact didn't hit me until then, as I shared this with Sarah and tried—ineffectively I'm sure—to explain it to her.

I had spent the day at Willow Ridge near Morrison, chairing an ICC meeting—reworking a full-day agenda into a 4-hour slot. I arrived home in time to find Claudia collating handouts for her presentation, packing, and attending to Sarah in the minutes before she had to leave to catch a plane for her ASCD education conference in New Orleans tomorrow—at the same time that she was trying to explain these incredible things that Ian had typed. I was focused more on helping her get ready and out the door on time than on the typing sessions, the import of which certainly did not sink in then. Sarah told me tonight that learning this has made her sad and scared for Ian as well as happy, and I know how she feels.

We are on the sharp edge of the unknown now, knowing we can't go back and yet unsure how to proceed or where we're going to end up. It is scary—and exciting—and heartwrenching. My mind jumps back constantly to past events, trying to reinterpret them in light of this astonishing news of Ian's prescience. And then it leaps to the future and whether we will be able to help him be more secure, successful, and happy.

—

I cannot explain better than Boyce the profundity of those few facilitated words. But in my mind I can vividly imagine those dramatic minutes that morning—Ian alternately writhing on his bed and running shrieking from his room, screaming "Stay home! Sick! Weekend!"; apparently desperate not to go to school, yet typing words that starkly contradicted what he said, Claudia poised behind him and clutching him around the waist to hold him steady, to try to quiet his violent thrashing, supporting his flailing hand above the keyboard, its keys only visible out of the corner of his eye as he twisted his head to his shoulder, his voice a sort of whine as he wrote, I BIREEER READY.

"You mean you *are* ready to go to school?" she implored.

4READY TO GO, he replied on the laptop.

"To school?"

YES.

"Do you want me to make you go to school today?"

I KWANT TOO GO TO SCHOOL.

"But why are you still kicking and screaming and saying 'Stay home,' when you type that you want to go?"

BECAUSEI CANNOT RESTH UNLESS IHAVE THINGS THE SAME.

"So what should we do?" Claudia asked him at last in exhausted desperation.

HEL;P ME TO TO SCHOOL, he answered. GIVE ME SOMNE THING TOB HELP NME NBE CCCALM.

But there was nothing that she could give him that morning, of course, nothing that might make autism disappear or suddenly allow him to contend with change. There was nothing she could do but hold him as he screamed "Stay home," and as she realized too how much he wanted to go to school. As it became clear that Ian could not settle down that morning—he was too upset to go to school but neither could he ease into his weekend routine at home—Claudia finally took him for a drive, the single sedative that almost always calmed him if they traveled far enough, Claudia driving automatically, almost unaware as they made their way to the village of Deckers, still shocked by what Ian had expressed, her mind a whirl of emotions as she drove, her vision blurred by tears. She called me once they had returned home and Ian, at ease at last, had retreated to his bedroom to watch his midday movie. She explained the events of the morning in anguished and, it seemed to me, harrowing detail, her exhaustion evident in the way she spoke, her reactions still a mix of astonishment and deep sadness. "He really is in there," she told me before we said good-bye. "He understands everything. He knows how trapped he is."

It was not new for Ian to have difficulty returning to school following a break of several days; and even Monday mornings often were difficult—the two-day weekend capable of creating enough of a pattern, a dependable enough routine, to make the shift to the weekday schedule problematic. But prior to that early April day, his parents simply had accepted his verbal protestations, sure that they reflected his true feelings and desires, and they normally had endeavored to get Ian off to school, or to begin some other activity, only until it became clear that he could not settle down and that his continued screaming was not worth their shared distress. But suddenly now—night turning to bright day, noise giving way to information—they knew that Ian's outward behavior, his apparent contentment or pleasure as well as his rage, was not evidence they could depend on.

WE SHOULS FIX MY ASCHEDUL, Ian proposed at the keyboard a day after Claudia's return from New Orleans. How so? she asked. CHANGE MY MOVIESD EVERY DAY. And this too was amazing news. For almost seven years, no constancy in Ian's life had seemed more important than the repetition of his movies. Always his family had assumed that he found great security and reassurance in watching them time after time after time. But what he wanted, he now was saying instead, was *please* to see some new stuff. The movies he had watched every day for six months, some for a year or more, had long since become DREAFFULLY VBORING, as he put it, using an adjective his sister liked to use. And soon he began to type that he wanted to try a dozen things that were new and that previously had been impossible even to contemplate: I WOULD LIKE TO MAKE A FEWQ SUGGESTIONS, he announced one day. I WOULD LIKE TO READ ANEW BOOK TONGIJHT. IWANT TOEAT KIN THE DINING ROOM. IWOULD LIKE RO EAT SOKKME HIONEY. I WANT MYHAIR TO LOOK LIKWE EDDIESHAIR. Yet with each acquiescence, each obviously empathetic attempt on his parents' part to comply with his request, Ian responded by screaming, by fighting the new experience as if it were likely to be lethal, his typed words always antithetical to his physical reactions, Claudia and Boyce always surrendering in the end, the kicking, biting, and shrieking too much for anyone to bear, his wishes seemingly unfulfilled, yet even that often was uncertain: as Ian's requests for honey had continued, Claudia decided to experiment and offer him a teaspoonful one afternoon. He had assured her by typing that she should put it in his mouth even if he fought her, and fight he did—shrieking, kicking, biting her hand hard enough to draw blood before a bit of honey finally made its way into his mouth. "We shouldn't try that anymore," she said to him, crying, Ian too still distraught, but his response suggested otherwise. YES YES RREALLY REALLY GPOOD, he typed.

Repeatedly now, Claudia and Boyce pressed the question: Should we believe what you say or what you type? And his response, like this one, always was unequivocal: YOI SHOULD DO WHATT I TYPE. But it was an anguishing dilemma. Ian longed for new experiences of every kind; he desperately wanted to do the things his sister did, and to be like all the other kids, but each attempt to introduce him to new foods, new activities, new books and movies at unusual times of the day, was met with nothing less than a kind of physical terror at the prospect of the impending change.

But although he continued to express a steady stream of desires his body simply could not consummate, he could, at least, successfully sate his curiosity, and questions too began to tumble from the keyboard, seven years and more of wondering and wanting to know now finding an outlet, finding words: I WANT TPO TALK ABOUT SDEER. I WAMTT TO KNOW IF THEY HAVE FCRIRNDS, he typed on a day when Claudia had asked Ian to lead the conversation, an opportunity he tended to seize when she asked him what he wanted to talk about or what was on his mind. KKI WANT TO TTALK ABOUT THE SNOOPY MOVIE, he typed another time. IS SNOOPY A DOG OR A CDHILD? UI WANT TO KNOW HOW MARYLOUS MOTTHER DIED. UI WANT TO KNOW WHY MOMS ZND DADS SLEEOP TO-GEYHER. I WANT TO KLNOW HOQW THE WIORLD GOT HWERE. I WANT TO ASKJ YOU WHY YOU ARE FASXCINZSATED ABOUT ME. Then, on an evening when both his mother and father were present, he asked a new series of questions that were far harder to answer than those they had responded to till now: I WAZNT TO KNOW WHY I HAVE AUYTISM, he typed, in what was emerging as his own straightforward and disarming style. I WANYTG TO MNOW IF I WILL ALWAYSS HAVE IT. I WANT TO KNOW IF THERE ARE ANHY OTTER CHILDREN WHO HAVE AUTUISM.

Cradling Ian in his arms, Boyce was equally direct, explaining to him about a suspect pertussis vaccination that surely he didn't remember, saying too that there were thousands of children and adults with autism, and many of them had autism for other reasons, for reasons no one knew. Claudia told him that scientists were trying to find drugs that would make autism better, but, she also confessed as she fought back tears, hardly anyone ever got totally over it. Nonetheless, she wanted Ian to know, lots of people with autism were happy, and things like learning how to type had made their lives much better.

I M HAPPY, Ian responded.

"Will you tell us when you have good ideas about how we can help you?" his father asked.

YES.

"Is there anything else you want to say right now?" Claudia asked as she steadied his wrist.

I LOVE YYOU, he typed, words he had never had means to say to them before.

It was early May before Ian next astounded his father and mother, his amazed and still rather uncertain sister, as well as all the rest of us who had begun to eagerly anticipate the sentences he next would type as further introductions to *Ian*, the regular kid who till now had been hidden inside himself, one who, so it seemed, could be alternately comic and melodramatic, forthright and sentimental, one who knew very clearly what interested him and what he wanted to do. It was May before Ian announced, I WZANT TO TYPE ASTORY.

Sarah wrote stories, *good* stories, Ian knew. Kids at school wrote stories; people whose names he didn't necessarily know wrote the stories he liked to read; and even an uncle of his wrote stories, although those he hadn't read. So it wasn't *that* surprising that he too had stories he wanted to tell, but you can imagine that uncle's delight in hearing that storytelling already was a kind of communication Ian wanted to try. During most of his typing sessions, he couldn't stand or sit calmly enough to type an extended string of words without interruption, normally needing to pull away after several words and dart across the room as if to release the energy the enormous effort entailed, but this time he persevered, and the story quickly, almost magically, emerged:

THERE WAS A SBOYH WHO HAD AUITISM. HE HADF A HARTD TIME DOIMG THINGS THAT OTHER KIDS DID BUT JHE HAD F5RIENDS. HE LIKED EDDIE AN TRISTAN AND ALL THE MKIDS. THEY WERDE HAPPY TOGETHERY.

Another story followed in a week:

THERE WAS A BOY NASMED IAN. HE HAD AUTIISM BUIT HE HYSAD A LOT OOF GFVRIENDS, VERJY GFOOD FRIEEMNDS. HE WAS HAPPY AT SCHNOOL. ONE DAY HE SAID I WANT TO GO TO SCHOL AND HIS DAD TOK HNI,M TO SVCHOO;L.

He typed many more tales like these as spring gave way to the mountains' brief summer, almost all of them concerned with issues of autism and friendship, many about a boy named Ian. As was the case with his other typed responses and statements, the stories seldom, if ever, contained incomplete sentences. Despite the physical difficulty involved in doing so, he seemed to want to type as correctly and precisely as he could each time. Instead of typing AT KING'S CROWN, for example, in answer to the question of where he would like to hike that day, he invariably would type a much more formal response: IWANTT TOP HIJKE AT KINGSD CRROWN TO-DAAY; and just as soon as his parents began to end each typing session by asking whether there was anything more he wanted to say, it had become his habit to respond, YES, I WANT TO SAY . . . , prefacing what came next with words he didn't really have to write, words that weren't expressly needed, except perhaps by him—a means of making each sentence familiar and predictable by making it grammatical, Ian facilitating his own communication, in effect, by expressing himself in a formal way.

Ian's language skills, still so limited, so *proto*linguistic in terms of his verbal speech, were completely—I think I can call them impressively—grammatical as he began to type. The same boy who still pronounced something that sounded like "Eesha" as he tried to say his sister's name, and whose verbal expressions concerning her were limited to statements such as "Sarah go school," was, nonetheless, capable of typing this when he was informed that Sarah remained both frightened and intrigued that summer about what he now could say: I WANT TO TTRELL HER THAT I HAVENT BEEN ABLE TO TALK FOTR 8 YHEAARS AND I FINALLY CAN, SO SHER SHOULDF BE EXCI5YTED ABOUT IT. What could explain those sharp distinctions? Were spoken language and written language quite distinct processes, as it turned out? How had Ian so successfully learned grammar without undergoing a period of trial-and-error practice? And what possibly could explain the way in which his typed language sometimes differed so drastically in content and in meaning from what he said aloud?

One easy way to explain it all, of course, would be simply to contend that it was Ian's mother or father, in fact, who did the typing. And if you chose to do so, you wouldn't have to look far to find a reputed autism expert who would affirm for you that these people simply didn't have the minds for such stuff, that sophisticated language skills were among the several cerebral capabilities they sadly lacked. But if, like me, you had become vividly aware that not every person with autism was an idiot by any means—that some, in fact, could make the experts seem like simpletons—then your search for answers would take a broader tack.

Ian's strange concentration as he typed—his body contorted, his view of the keyboard often limited to his peripheral vision, his mouth emitting sounds he never otherwise made—was, I remember, my initial indication that he indeed was directing what he typed: *watching* him type was itself a sort of proof. I was aware as well of the myriad times he had referred to events his facilitator could not have been aware of; I had observed that his typed suggestions for ways in which his parents might help calm him were ways that truly *worked*; I knew that particular words he liked to use—*dreadfully, killingly, pleasant, so really really*—emerged regardless of who was supporting his hand; and I knew too (and perhaps most remarkably) that a friend of Ian's from school, a special-education student I'll call Clara, whose ability to read and write was severely limited, had nonetheless learned how to facilitate single words for him, always eager to ask a nearby teacher to read for her what it was that she had helped Ian type. Assuming therefore that this blond boy was indeed the generator of those many remarkable sentences—messages whose meaning sometimes took your breath away—then those questions pertaining to the genesis of his linguistic excellence and his deficits do become intriguing indeed, and their answers—such as I can attempt them—seem to say something not only about Ian's language, but yours and mine as well.

Foremost, it seems to me, Ian offers a remarkable confirmation of Bickerton's contention that protolanguage and language are distinct, that the former is not a precursor of the latter, and that the sites where each is localized in the brain are likely quite distinct. Given his inability to conjugate verbs in his spoken speech, to employ pronouns or link clauses or utter more than four words at once, Ian's verbal output is a vivid example of the kind of primitive linguistic ability that Bickerton describes as being comprised solely of lexical (vocabulary) elements and lacking discernible grammatical structure. Describing the linguistic abilities of Genie, the Los Angeles "wild child" whose case captivated him and other linguists in the 1970s, Bickerton wrote, "[She] acquired protolanguage because protolanguage is more robust than language (having formed part of the hominid endowment for much longer) and it does not have a critical period. . . . Genie's acquisition ceased because the faculties of protolanguage and of language are disjoint, and acquisition of the one in no way entails acquisition of the other." And surely the same holds in Ian's case. "Robust" spoken protolanguage was able to emerge from him despite substantial damage to essential speech-producing neural circuitry, damage that made sophisticated, grammatical speech impossible. Yet during Ian's critical period—years that corresponded with his years entrapped by autism—he had, nonetheless, internally acquired *language*, and he had done so without the ability to *test* it aloud. He had learned language by hearing it—and by applying to what he heard the innate, genetically derived mechanisms of universal grammar, I can hear Noam Chomsky shouting—rather than by mimicking.

Ian was able to acquire true language, I have a strong suspicion, because those brain centers responsible for it were not compromised by his disorder and because the acquisition of language, very surprisingly indeed, does not appear to be dependent on expressive practice. The multifaceted syndrome labeled autism affected, in Ian's case, the expression of language—verbally or manually—but its equally complex preliminary symbolic formulation in the cerebral cortex somehow went unscathed. His early bombardment with symbols and their manipulation, his massive exposure to the intricacies of language in his movies and his books, plus, of course, the speech that shaped the days within his household, had been catalytic enough to let his brain begin to make sense of language, then to claim it as his own, and surely sentences had swirled inside Ian's brain for years before his parents' hands began to steady *his* hand enough to allow them a way out.

The quality of the linguistic skills that Ian began to demonstrate in the spring and summer of 1992—his ability, for instance, to type this farewell message to his classmates as the school year closed: YHOU ARE ALL MY FRIENDS AND IK LIKE YOU VERRY MUCH.

HAVE GOOSD SUMMWERS ANDD I WILL SEEE YLOU IN 5THE
FQALL. GFROM IAN—was evidence not so much of miracle making
or prodigious talent, it seemed to me, as it was explainable instead
by his mutism and his isolation. If you could not speak, you would
marvel at and surely envy, wouldn't you, the way in which others
could turn words to spoken sounds. If words, however unfairly,
could not find a way out of you, wouldn't words themselves and
their manipulation inevitably take on a massive and focal sort of
importance? Wouldn't you understand better than anyone how wonderful expressive language was? Wouldn't you at least shape impressive sentences and tell splendid stories to yourself?

But the question that fairly begs for an answer, of course, is
why Ian's protolinguistic, verbal expressions—"Stay home! Sick!
Weekend!"—often were the semantic opposites of his typed and
grammatical desires: I KWANT TOO GO TO SCHOOL. Although he
implored his parents to believe what he typed rather than what he
said, didn't his explosive reactions, the flailing and crying as well as
those shouted and desperate words, communicate something that
was far more convincing in contrast? Regardless of what he typed,
didn't his whole being seem to be saying in that instance that he
really *had* to stay at home? I can't pretend that this paradox truly
can be reconciled, or to know *whether* it can be, but I do, nonetheless, have some suppositions, ideas grounded in current research
into the etiology of autism as well as in Ian's own comments, *his*
perspectives, ones to which I obviously tend to pay some attention.

By the summer of 1992, Massachusetts General Hospital neurologist Margaret Bauman and her research colleague, Dr. Thomas
Kemper, had extensively examined at autopsy the brains of six children and young adults whose lives had been beset by autism. Despite the evidence that at least some autism was vaccine-induced,
their studies continued to persuade them that a subtle, *prenatal*
malformation of the brain stem's cerebellum played a significant role
in causing the disorder's disparate symptoms. But their focus had
broadened by now as well to include the adjacent limbic system,
known to play a significant role in aspects of memory, learning,
emotion, and behavior. However, unlike the loss of neurochemical-

producing Purkinje cells, which Bauman and Kemper previously had encountered in the cerebella of autistic patients, nerve cells in the autistic limbic systems they examined were increased in number when compared with age-matched controls. But curiously, those limbic cells were sharply reduced in average size—a finding that was consistent with Bauman's hypothesis that the syndrome is normally, if not always, set in motion by some sort of curtailed brain development that occurs prior to birth.

In none of the six brains they examined microscopically did Bauman and Kemper find signs of structural abnormalities in the cerebral cortices, although in an interview published in the newsletter of the Autism Society of America, Bauman did caution that "we cannot be certain that there are not abnormal connections between the limbic system, the cerebellum, and the cerebral cortex, in fact there probably are, at least at a neurochemical level, and perhaps also at a structural level which is beyond the capability of our method of study."

Three contemporaneous studies, each of which employed magnetic resonance imaging of living brains instead of postmortem microscopic examination, have indeed noted subtle cerebral abnormalities. In separate MRI studies undertaken at the Western Psychiatric Institute in Pittsburgh in 1991, researchers, in fact, found *no* differences in cerebellar structure between thirteen autistic individuals and thirteen controls matched for age, sex, race, and verbal and nonverbal IQ. They did discover, however, abnormal high-energy phosphate and membrane phospholipid metabolism in the prefrontal cortices of eleven autistic adolescents as compared to eleven closely matched controls. In the Pittsburgh study that focused on the cerebrum, a series of MRI "pictures" of the prefrontal cortex were taken as subjects attempted a variety of standard cognitive and linguistic tests. As test performance deteriorated, levels of high-energy metabolite compounds decreased and levels of membrane breakdown products increased in all eleven autistic individuals studied, but similar processes were noted in *none* of the controls.

Correspondingly, Dr. Joseph Piven and his colleagues in the Department of Psychiatry at the Johns Hopkins School of Medicine reported in a 1992 issue of the *American Journal of Psychiatry* the results of their own MRI study of the structure of the cerebrums of thirteen male subjects with autism and an equal number of matched controls. Seven of the thirteen young men with autism evidenced abnormal bilateral convolutions, grooves, and clefts on the surface of the cerebral cortex, while the cortices of the thirteen control subjects appeared entirely normal. Piven was careful to note that although the cortical abnormalities encountered were unlikely to be the cause of autism in those cases, they did, nonetheless, point toward the likelihood that the disorder is produced by abnormalities located in several parts of the brain.

Studies like these—vital, obviously, to a better understanding of and, one day perhaps, successful treatments for the disorder—likely will continue to appear contradictory for some time to come, not only because their methodologies tend to vary but because the disorder is surely several disorders disguised as one, disorders initiated by a wide variety of neurological abnormalities that are precipitated at various stages of prenatal and postnatal development. Yet it seems to me that as clearer and more complete scientific information continues to be amassed, it is becoming almost certain that abnormalities in *both* the cortex and one or more deep-brain structures play major roles in the kinds of behaviors and deficits with which most people with autism must contend. And although they don't concur, the Massachusetts General and Western Psychiatric studies together lead me further toward the conviction that, in Ian's case, his brain stem and his basal ganglia, as well as Broca's area and the prefrontal region of his cerebral cortex, are all involved in the concert of symptoms that makes him who he is. And I take Ian at his word as well when he explains that his brain cannot control, oftentimes, the things his body does.

It had become Ian's unfortunate habit during that summer in which his typing first flowered to take hold of his mother's hair with his left hand as he pressed the keys on a keyboard with the index finger of his right hand. Despite her repeated attempts to tuck his left hand under his leg and to ask him, *please*, to stop it, the incessant pulling of Claudia's hair had become a painful and constant casualty of the typing. When she finally pulled *his* hair in exasperation one day and said, "See? This is what it feels like. This is why I really don't want you to do it anymore," Ian was abashed, typing IAM SOR SORRYU, yet even as he typed those words he continued to pull her hair.

"Why do you keep doing it then?" she implored.

BESCSUSE MGY BLDY DOES IT, he answered.

"Can't you tell your body not to do things?" she then suggested.

YES BUJT MHY BODY DOESNT LOSTEN, he explained, continuing her metaphor.

Although Ian's brain and his body are inseparable—as is the case with all of us—I suspect he often simply cannot, willfully or otherwise, extinguish the pulling of hair or the flapping of book pages or the endless repetitions that comprise his daily schedule. Surely he, most of all, would love to limit his tantrums, to end them after seconds, if only there were some way he could. I suspect that his verbal speech, linked as it is to movement-initiating mechanisms in his prefrontal cortex and basal ganglia, is often involuntary as well. At times when he is under crescendoing stress, his vocal speech curiously tends to be at its best, pushed out perhaps by the same involuntary mechanisms that send his flickering fingers to the corners of his eyes. I suspect, although, of course, I cannot know, that in the same way that he responds in physical terror to the prospect of impending change, a kind of physical—vocal—speech that he can't control tends to respond in chaotic kind. And I suspect as well that in a wonderful, quieting kind of counterpoint, the physical touch and reverse-pressure support provided by someone at his side as he types, together with the emotional support that dauntlessly assures him he can *do it*, are often enough to override those involuntary movements, that involuntary speech.

In that manner analogous to the way in which Parkinson's patients who seem frozen in space sometimes can begin to walk with only the aid of someone taking their arm, I think that Ian—and many people like him—similarly can suppress erratic movement and initiate intentional movement with a kind of assistance that is not high-tech but rather high-touch. I think that Ian's spoken speech and typed speech are often as distinct as expletives are from whispering, and I think it makes much semantic sense to pay attention to what he types.

Two particular words caught Ian's parents' attention early on—words he typed often and about whose connotations they were curious. *Scared* was a word with which he described his reactions to everything from the possibility that one of his "friends" would fall into the Royal Gorge to the noise a vacuum cleaner made, and as Ian employed it, it seemed to connote not so much a straightforward or simple fear but a kind of complete coming unstuck, a disintegration of any semblance of order, a sensory overload, or perhaps all of those in a single nightmarish mix. When Ian was *scared*, things were horrible for him indeed, and little by little his parents tried to draw out of him a fuller understanding of the word. *Calm* was the other word he regularly used that seemed to mean something about which they needed to know more. Ian had pleaded with Claudia on that overwhelming day in April to give him something to make him calm, and many times subsequently he had typed the word again— explaining that riding in a car was so essential because it could make him calm, noting that the constant presence of his plastic friends offered similar quieting assistance, asking in the midst of yet another episode of screaming for one of his parents to rub the soles of his feet to help him settle down.

The notion of Ian longing to be calmer was intriguing too because he recently had explained that he could try to break certain routines—and sometimes succeed—when he was calm, but that those same rituals were virtually impossible to abandon when he was not. Calmness was the crux, he had clarified by typing, and this was critically important news. Although Claudia and Boyce could spot many subtle signs that indicated those times when Ian was verging toward trouble, and although they knew he perseverated far more intently when he was under stress, they heretofore had assumed that the key to ending one ritual was simply to replace it with another, and they had long believed, of course, that the routines themselves were activities he somehow loved rather than ones he was desperate to be rid of. If only Ian could feel far *calmer*, it now appeared—and it did so solely because of the information he himself had been able to convey—then wouldn't that be the first step toward adding the diversity to his days that he so craved? Could calming Ian conversely open him to far more activity and to a richer life?

Among the first meaningful things Ian had been able to type in the middle of his ninth year of life had been HELP ME, the plea for some sort of calming medication so impassioned that you can imagine how somehow tracking down an effective drug quickly had become a paramount concern. A variety of sedatives and antidepressants had shown various levels of effectiveness in treating autistic symptoms in recent years and Claudia and Boyce had been well aware of their availability, but because of Ian's allergic hypersensitivity they had been leery of their listed side effects and had doubted whether his system could tolerate them. But now in light of his pleas, they felt they owed it to Ian at least to try, to test one or more of the most promising drugs in hopes that it just might offer him some relief.

During the year that I had spent at Dr. Sternberg's side, I had met many patients suffering a grim assortment of obscurely labeled movement disorders—Parkinson's disease, of course, as well as choreas, palsies, and dystonias with names like orofacial dyskinesia, spasmodic torticollis, and the visually arresting syndrome named for the nineteenth-century French physician Gilles de la Tourette—all of them basal ganglia diseases in which abnormalities in that critical deep-brain structure spawned a spectrum of symptoms that ranged from paralysis to wild and irrepressible twists and jerks. I remembered one patient in particular who had contended all his life with Tourette's syndrome—constant and utterly uncontrollable facial, shoulder, and limb jerks, sudden snorts and bizarre vocal sounds— and how he had spoken too about the awful sensation of *never* feeling calm, and I had asked Patrick whether it seemed conceivable to him that a drug used to treat Tourette's or other movement disorders might offer Ian help.

Although he had never met Ian, Patrick had heard my many astonishing stories about him, to be sure, and he was quickly engaged

by my question, explaining that in the six years since I had clung so
cloyingly to his heels the drug of choice in the treatment of Tourette's
syndrome had become clomipramine, marketed under the trade
name Anafranil, a drug that also—and quite intriguingly, now that
I mentioned it—had shown remarkable success in the treatment of
obsessive-compulsive disorder. And there *did* seem to be a connection between the two disparate symptoms—Anafranil successfully
countering uncontrollable movement as well as obsessively repeated
behaviors—that made the notion of treating Ian with the drug seem
compelling indeed. Then, within a week of my mentioning Anafranil
to Boyce and Claudia, a newsletter to which they subscribe arrived
bearing a brief mention of a recent study that had found Anafranil
to be quite successful, in fact, in the treatment of autistic children.
The coincidence—as well as the promise of the drug itself—therefore seemed to demand a trial. Following a quick but convincing
investigation into the study's findings on Claudia and Boyce's part
as well as Patrick's, Ian became his official patient, responding enthu-
siastically when asked whether he would like to try the drug, typing
I LIKJE HIM ALREADDY when told that his new doctor was a close
friend of mine, one, like him, about whom I had written a book.

Fatigue and dehydration that led to constipation were the two
most common side effects of the drug, everyone knew as the experiment commenced, and although he began to take it at a low dosage,
Ian quickly encountered both of them. But they were worth it, he
typed, bearable because IT IS HELKPING ME MORE EVERYYDAY.
And so it seemed to be: over the course of the following weeks, Ian
was able to experiment with a few new foods and to return again to
some he had eaten in the past and then abandoned; he began to eat
at the dining room table rather than in his room (something he'd
never been able to do before); he could go to several new places
and, once there, could successfully engage in novel activities. It had
been unthinkable previously, but it wasn't too long before Ian even
could lie on a lawn or a bed of needles beneath a tree and do *nothing*
except watch the fat white cumulus clouds scud across the summer
sky, something he could accomplish, he was certain, simply because
he was REALLYREALLLY CALMER THHAN BERFORE THE MEDU-

CINE. As Ian's Anafranil dosage was steadily raised, his increasingly dry skin began to madden him with itching, but that too was tolerable because by now, he reported with relief, even the FRIRENDS INM MY HEASD had gone away.

"Friends in your head?" his parents asked, startled yet again by some new thing that he announced, an occurrence that had become by now virtually commonplace. "What do you mean? Were they like dreams or like voices?"

BVOICES.

"What did they say?"

TRHEY SAID REALLKY BAD THINGS.

"Tell us what they said, Ian," Claudia encouraged him as she bent over his shoulder, holding his right wrist in her palm. "Can you tell us what they said?"

YESD THEY SAID YOUU WERE DEADD. THE FRIDENDS SAID YOUARE GERTTING A DIVORCE. THEY SAUY IM STUPID.

With repeated questioning over the course of several days, it became clear that Ian indeed had heard voices inside his head, periodically at least, for many years. Apparently, they were akin to those voices that schizophrenics often hear, as do some Parkinsonian patients and sufferers of a wide range of other disorders—voices which may be accounted for neurologically by the brain's tendency to "fill in" for absent stimuli, yet which are as seemingly real as any others. In Ian's case, they were loud, strident, and demanding voices, and they had insisted to him several times that he must run away.

I had arrived for a short visit on the balmy afternoon during which this incredible conversation continued—our speculations about the voices only hunches at best, but his comments full of clarification, Ian seeming comfortable and at ease as he briefly sat with us outside.

"You don't hear the voices at all anymore?" his mother asked as he joined us at a picnic table.

I HAWVENT HEARRD THRM SINCE ISTASRTED TAQKING THE MEDFICINE.

"But before, it really was the voices who told you to run away?" Boyce asked.

YESD.

I asked him whether he remembered the first time he ran away from the research station.

YESD I REMMEMBER. ITWAS SO SDCARY. ITHINK IT WADS THE FIRST TTIME IGOT LOST.

"Did you really want to run away that day?" I inquired further.

OF COUURSE NORT, he responded to me quickly. IHJUST DIDF WHAT THE VOICESW TOLD ME TODO. DONT WRITE ABOUT ITH THOUGH BEDCAUSE IT WS TOO SCARY.

I told him I really didn't need to write about it, but that the reason I had wanted to was to help explain how frightening it is for everyone when a little boy who can't talk suddenly disappears. I wanted to tell him too that at long last his disappearances made astonishing, if alarming, sense, and to say as well that, good God, he hadn't deserved to hear hateful and malevolent voices in addition to everything else with which he had so long had to contend. But, in fact, I said nothing more in the seconds before he reached for the keyboard again and typed with his mother's help, YOUU CAN WRIRTE ABOUYT QWHATEVER YOU WAAZT RUSSSELL. YOUI ARE A GOODD UNCLE. ITRUST YOU. And then he was off to his room.

All of that amazing summer seemed to unfold in the way things did that day—Ian growing progressively calmer, more at ease, ever more game to give new things a try, able to sit comfortably with people for some minutes and directly converse with them for the first time in his life, to tell them much that brought both sadness and delight, to express repeatedly how very happy he was. And by the time his August birthday approached, *he* was sure, as were those of us who loved him, that he had made some impressive gains. At the end of July he had been able to share his sister's excitement as they attended a pioneer day celebration, the two of them dressing in early-day garb—Ian in *costume*, can you imagine?—wearing a fringed leather jacket and a cowboy hat, spending a few hours in the comfortable company of strangers, typing when they had returned home tired and sunburned that ITWAS UNBWELIEBVABLY FUNB AND IAM GEYTING SO MUCH BETTER, informing his family too

that I AMN HSAPPIER THANI HABVE BEEN IN MYT LIFRE BE-
CAYUSE IWAS A REGYULAR KID TPODAY.

Ian came close to being a regular kid on his birthday as well,
trekking with his family to Denver on August 2 for visits to the zoo,
the botanical gardens, and the natural history museum at his request,
spending the night at Claudia's close friend Ann Lacy's apartment
(complete with swimming pool)—each activity accomplished by
weaving it into the necessities of his schedule, VCRs, plastic
"friends," and other essentials dutifully packed from place to place,
the four of them drained and exhausted before the birthday goals
were met but thrilled, nonetheless, to be out in the world *together*.
And Ian arrived home the following day in great anticipation of the
fact that his best friend, Eddie, was coming to spend the night.

Six months before, it would have been difficult to imagine Ian and
a friend—even the remarkable Eddie—spending hours together in
Ian's room, interacting successfully on their own terms, Eddie talking
nonstop, Ian talking not at all, Ian's routines novel enough for Eddie
that they were fun, after all, the boys rolling on the bed in their
pajamas, seeming determined never to go to sleep, Claudia finding
them still awake near midnight when she opened the door to Ian's
room to check on them, the lights bright and Ian trying in a kind of
pantomime to show Eddie how to hold his hand above the keyboard
so he could type a message to him. IQWANTED TO TUYPE TO ESDDIE
THAT ILIKE HIM SO MUCH AND I AM HGLAD JHE IS MY FRIEND,
Ian was able to type at last with his mother's help, communicating,
before they finally slept, precisely what he hoped to say.

"What I am pointing out," wrote Robert Frost, "is that unless you
are at home in the metaphor, unless you have had your proper
poetical education in the metaphor, you are not safe anywhere.
Because you are not at ease with figurative values: you don't know
the metaphor in its strengths and its weaknesses. You don't know
how far you may expect to ride it and when it may break down with
you. You are not safe in science; you are not safe in history."

Nine years old now, Ian could express himself at last, and it seemed that his remarkable linguistic abilities—his ease not just with words but also with story and with metaphor—had freed him in a profound and wonderful way, and in Frost's sense, I think, had even made him safe. He appeared to understand uncannily—and perhaps it was because of the wordlessness that so long had limited him—that words were very distinct from the objects and ideas they represented, at once ethereal and paltry yet incredibly powerful as well, capable of framing experience in ways that made it something more than it otherwise was, words wily and supple symbols that enlarged life as they explained it, made sense of it, and told its many stories. And the stories Ian told that summer continued to help him, I also had to presume, define precisely who he was, what his complicated circumstances were, and what his future held in store—those fundamental elements of his life still utterly bound by concerns about normalcy and its alluring form of anonymity, about the validating importance of family and friendships, and about the way in which relationships really are the only things we own of any value. Read this story, for instance, and listen to the several things it means:

ONCE THERRE WASX A BOYU WHO LIKED TO VGO TO SCHOOL. HJE HADM ALOT OGFF FRIENDS. YYOUJ CPOULD NOT BELKIEVE HOW MANY FRIENDS HE HAX. ONE DAY HE CAME TO SDCHOOLL WITH A BAD XCOLD AND A;LL THE KIDCS MADE HIM FEEL BNETTER BUT HE HAD YTOO GO HOME BERCAUSE HE WAS SICK. ABOUGTR A WEEK LATER HE WENTG VACK TO SCHOOLK. ALL THE KIDS WERE HUJAPPY.

It is not a story about a boy named Ian this time, and neither does it mention the disorder whose name he says he has known since he was very small. But like most imagined stories, it reflects nonetheless its author—his trials and his tentative conclusions. It examines them from the distilling perspective that comes with a bit of distance and it addresses them with metaphor. The protagonist of this story is someone who is not characterized by disability or disease but rather by what he cares about and what he possesses: school and supportive friendships. Its action, its plot, the pivotal event that it plays out, is not a coming to grips with abstract trouble labeled autism but rather with the far more universal distress of a deadening cold, one that has to be surrendered to, yet which is overcome in time, surmounted with patience and the support of friends.

It is the metaphoric aspect of Ian's story that most intrigues me, the way in which—at nine and only just now at last past infancy— he was able to examine his own story by telling someone else's, employing narrative not only to help order his experience but to learn its lessons as well, Ian telling metaphoric tales because he is *normal*, in fact, because normal people are driven to tell them without cease. "The whole nature of our language is highly metaphorical," insists C. Hugh Holman in *A Handbook to Literature*, a battered copy of which I have packed and unpacked innumerable times yet have kept close at hand since 1970, a book that, despite its concessions to academic orthodoxy, succeeds in making the strong point that it is only in the attention to words themselves in the context of storytelling that language ever approaches art. "Most of our modern speech, which now seems prosaic enough, was once largely metaphorical," Holman suggests. "Our abstract terms are borrowed from physical objects. Natural objects and actions have passed over into abstractions because of some inherent metaphorical significance."

Words, whether grunted sounds or scribbled shapes, have no significance inherent in themselves. They are necessarily arbitrary, meaning nothing until we attach a tattered meaning to them. Yet the meanings of words *can* be inherently significant. Words like *friendship*, words like *love*, are filled with far more substantial stuff than we can ever define, and metaphor—the identification of one object or person with another in a way that emotionally, imaginatively enlarges both—is the means with which Ian, and all of us, seek relationship, understanding, and a kind of connection that at its heart is very calm.

Ian could travel overnight to three separate destinations now. Presuming the route was the proper one, he could venture to Ann

Lacy's Denver apartment, where a room was briefly transformed into a facsimile of his own; he could be driven to my parents' house in the far southwestern corner of Colorado, as long as the three-hundred-mile trip unfolded in the way it had long been designed and carefully carried out, and once there, he could be comfortable for a week or more; and now too with his family in tow he could visit my parents' cabin at Trout Lake, near Telluride, where a canoe sat at the icy lake's shore and where he could hike to near the top of a pristine and magical world, a place where the four of them and an aged dog at last could come close to having a true holiday.

They were en route to Trout Lake in mid-August, the Subaru packed high but cresting the Continental Divide without undue distress, the hours passed by surveying the endlessly unfolding vistas, by playing Twenty Questions, spotting silly road signs, telling stories. With his father behind the wheel and his mother beside him in the backseat, Ian at last could join their carbound conversations, and it was his typed suggestion that they give one another appropriate Indian-style names.

One of Ian's favorite books that summer had been *Knots on a Counting Rope*, the tale of a young, blind Navajo named Boy-Strength-of-Blue-Horses and his elderly grandfather—a sage who agrees to retell the story of the boy's birth and the origin of his name—and Ian had been intrigued as he got to know the book by the possibility that names could be so evocative, so full of stories themselves. Sarah, they collectively decided as they drove, ought to be called "Girl from Time" since she was so fascinated by eras that preceded her own. No names they could conjure, however, seemed just right for Claudia or for Boyce; Sarah had suggested "Woman Who Crosses Mountains" for her mother and "He Who Laughs at the Wind" for her father, but although they were appropriate in several ways, they weren't as wonderfully on target, they all agreed, as was Sarah's new name.

"Do you know what your name would be, Ian?" Sarah asked from the front seat, far more at ease than she had been three months before in directing questions toward her brother, at ease now as well with his answers.

MYT INDFIAN NAME WWOULD BE BOYY WHO LIVES IN TUN-
NEWL YERT STILL SEESS VERTY FAR, Ian typed determinedly, so
quickly that surely the name already was one to which he had laid
a kind of claim.

As Claudia read the name from the laptop's small display, Boyce
and Sarah were as suddenly dumbfounded as she was, equally
stunned to realize that *yes*, Ian truly had identified himself with that
metaphoric chain of words. He did live in a tunnel, they all knew
far too well, yet more and more, it seemed, he *could* see beyond
the summits of the nearby peaks, and that summer, it seemed, he
had learned to see—and to shout—even beyond the ridgelines of
the distant ranges.

9
A LABOR OF
LANGUAGE

Words have been our birthright across the generations, stories our inheritance.

This morning I sifted through a bundle of letters my mother treasures but seldom unfolds and reads, each written in a clear and practiced cursive script on lined correspondence paper now yellowed, stained, and becoming brittle. They are letters my grandmother, the woman we knew as Dandy, wrote a very long time ago; they reflect eras and attitudes starkly different from these contemporary days, and they are eloquent only in their direct expression of the kinds of sentiments our clan too often leaves awkwardly unspoken, a trait I carry with me like a useless limb. "Dear Dad," she wrote to her husband nineteen days after the bombing of Pearl Harbor had set the world on end, even in a snowbound corner of Colorado:

Christmas is gone for another year and in its place is a bitter cold, with a biting wind and awfully low, gray skies. Bob just got back from Lewis with the mail: He got his classification card and is IV-A, which bothers him a lot. And now he has to leave to try to get to camp. He's leery about the roads and the weather, but he has to check on the sheep and says he will make it as far in the car as he can, then will try to borrow a horse from someone and go horseback the rest of the way. I pray he doesn't plow into trouble.

We have been telling everyone that you are down on the winter range. When George told Bob he wanted to go see you, Bob had to fib again and say that Roy Akin had come along last night and taken you to a meeting of the Utah grazing department in Moab. It's sure quite a task for all of us to keep telling these lies. But only one more week. If you need to send a wire once you know how you'll travel home, address it to yourself and just sign it "Bill," and we'll know it's you. You know, you *are* Bill, if your folks had just called you that instead of Griff.

Won't you please write to me too? Every night I reach over and put my hand on your pillow and say to myself, "Sometime soon he'll be here and everything will be all right."

She gave him all the family's news before she closed, as well as what she had heard, relayed by telephone and her infrequent visitors, about the holiday festivities in their tiny farm community. Then she announced that she quickly had to seal the letter and find a stamp because the girls—my mother and her twin sister, the two teenagers still living their lives as one—had the new horse saddled and were sure that, even riding double, they could negotiate the snowdrifted road to the post office in the minutes before the outbound mail would be on its way. "Much love to you from me and all of us," she wrote.

More than fifty years later, it is difficult for me to fathom the critical need for secrecy my grandmother imagined, the desperate importance she assumed in keeping from friends and neighbors the truth that instead of being away in Utah or stranded at his snowy Colorado camp, my grandfather was in temporary residence, in fact, at the Mount Airy Sanitarium in Denver, undergoing treatment for his disposition to indulge in periodic drinking binges. I am betraying that secret as I write this, I know, but I'm certain as well that in doing so I'm betraying neither her nor him—people who met much hard work and recurrent times of trouble in their lives, yet who confronted both optimistically and with the sense that you simply did whatever you could do, and it saddens me that their society seemed to demand keeping covert what was nothing more, in my grandfather's case, than the taking of the bull by the horns, a time-worn country metaphor I'll employ even though Griff Rutherford was a sheepman and never held a high opinion of bovines of either gender.

But Ian Drummond had an eye for cows, of course, and in a kind of generational comparison, I can't help but be very thankful that by the 1980s, personal challenges of several sorts—as well as the myriad ways in which people had to contend with physiological or psychological abnormalities—no longer needed to pose embarrassment or shame. Had Ian grown up in rural Colorado in the war years of the 1940s, his parents almost certainly would not have known that a psychiatrist named Kanner away in distant Maryland had begun to see many young patients whose behavior was much like his. They would not have had a name with which to describe his concert of symptoms nor any clue about their cause, and no doubt neighbors would have whispered with a mixture of sympathy and uneasiness in their voices about how terribly he was "disturbed," the poor boy "a mental case," an "idiot," a few surely gossiping that all he really required was the discipline induced by a father's razor strap. Although contingencies of distance and expense probably would have precluded Ian from being placed in an institution, he might well have lived his life exclusively in an upstairs room, and almost certainly, he would not have gone to school. Language skills of any kind might well have been lost to him, and surely he would not have learned to type and to tell the world what was on his amazing mind.

But we *do*—haltingly, little by little—make medical, even cultural advances, and Ian had had the great good fortune to be born in a time and place in which irrational fears about anyone who was "different" finally had begun to fade, in which scientific inquiry had led, at least, to a rudimentary knowledge of autism, if not yet to anything approaching choate understanding, or a treatment, or a cure. But foremost, of course, it was Ian's enormous luck to be the

progeny of his particular parents—two people remarkably capable
of weaving insight and intelligence into the enveloping fabric of their
care and concern. Right from those first days and months of Ian's
incessant screaming and eerie withdrawal—and mirroring, it often
seemed to me, my grandparents' earlier resolve in the face of recurrent adversities—Claudia and Boyce had laced their love for him
with a steely and nearly inexhaustible determination, with a sober
sense of what the future might hold, yet also with the unwavering
conviction that their son deserved, above all, opportunity and support—words synonymous with love, I now know.

Those of us in Ian's larger family—although necessarily removed
from the horribly deflating daily struggles that he, his sister, and
his parents endured—nonetheless, and certainly unheroically, had
succeeded in a similar way in communicating to him early on that
he was at once extraordinary and simply one of us. Just as my parents
had made clear to me long ago that I could make anything I wanted
of my life, so had all of us in turn said the same to Ian, acknowledging
that his hurdles were very high, but marveling too at how this boy
could leap. Ian had grown up comforted and encouraged and always
accepted by those of us who shared his names, and as he began to
eloquently express himself, the idea of family began to appear as
quietly important to him as did the more demonstrative significance
of friendship.

In early May, on the occasion of my parents' first visit to his house
since facilitated communication had begun to offer him a channel for
his words, Ian had inquired whether he could help make a Mother's
Day card for his grandmother, surprising Claudia and Boyce with
his awareness of that impending holiday, then typing a special statement he wanted the card to include. TRHRERE WSAS A BOY WJNHO
HAD AUTIS,M, my mother read as she opened the handmade card
on a sunny Sunday morning—Ian appearing uninterested, however,
where he lay nearby on the floor, rapidly flapping the pages of a
book—AND HE COULDNT SAY I LOV3E YOLUI TLO HIS GRRAND-
MOTHER DSO HEW TYPED IT TO HER, her tears quickly as fluid
as his words. And for my father, he had divined an Indian name he
wanted to bestow: YOURT NAAME SHPOULD BE MANN WUITH

KIND FSACE, he typed as Claudia took the keyboard to him and held his wrist—the typographical errors imposed by his awkward movements and his wandering eyes still constant, his sentiments, his personality, his *presence*, overwhelming them nonetheless.

With his Colorado grandparents on hand, it wasn't surprising that Ian's paternal grandparents were on his mind as well. They lived away in Arkansas—his father's boyhood home, a place Boyce would have loved to introduce to Ian, but one he probably would not be able to until perhaps some distant day when Ian might have surrendered his demand for daily sameness. Boyce's parents had come to Colorado once a year since Ian had been small, yet his need for solitude and his verbal silence heretofore had limited their interaction, and now he wanted his dad to know that IAM GLAD YOIU ARE SEBNDING MYY TUYPING TO TYHEM SOI THYEY CAN GET TOKNOW MRE BETTER.

When Claudia asked Ian if he understood that the grandmother he and Sarah called Nana—the woman across the table from him now—was *her* mother in the same way that she was his, his answer was a matter-of-fact ODF COURSSE. Next she wanted to know if he remembered who Dandy was: NSANA ISD MY GRABNDMOTHER AND DANDY WSAS TYOURS, he automatically explained, and, had he been able to, surely he would have rolled his eyes at the silliness of these questions. But Claudia wanted to know something more: What exactly did he—just a three-year-old the last time he saw her—remember about Dandy?

Ian had typed too much already and was restless, yet he wanted to answer, to *prove* how much he knew. He began to make the high, whining sound that by now had become commonplace as he typed, twisting his body into a taut and energized knot as he negotiated the keyboard: IREMEMBER THSAT SGHE LIVEDS OUT IN THEE COUNTRY AND SGHE WAS KUIND OF FAT AND SHE JHAD A CAT ANDS SHEE TOLD US STORIRES AND WSHE IS DEAD. He was correct on every count, of course, and although I wasn't there to witness it, I'm sure those who were seated round the table laughed at what he'd typed with that blend of pride and bemusement that every child and grandchild so often engenders, and I know

that Dandy—*there* was a fitting name—would have been heartily
tickled too.

The statements and stories Ian now was typing tended to be composed rather formally, and there was often something startlingly
poetic about them as well: they were cast in words that seemed
carefully selected, not solely for what they represented and described but also for the way in which they rhythmically related to
each other, for the way in which his strings of words sometimes
seemed like songs. Words and eloquent strings of words seemed to
be things he highly valued and I couldn't help but wonder how he
had come by this budding poetic sensibility.

For as long as I could remember, I had been as readily interested
in the way words sounded as in what they seemed to mean, but I
was surprised to discover that nine-year-old Ian seemed to share this
interest in what is probably easiest to label lyricism—the linking of
words as melodically as you can muster them. As I did when I was
young, Ian loved stories written in rhyme and stories borne by lilting
language, but was that the sole source of the literary timbre of much
of what he typed? Did he—did I—somehow inherit this specific
interest, or did it come from our separate exposures to books so
beautifully written that they had survived for decades, some for
centuries even? Was my interest in lyric language simply an attempt
to be showy or needlessly effusive? I wondered from time to time.
And there was another question that intrigued me: Did Ian seem to
carefully craft so much of what he wrote simply because he still could
write so little, or would his words remain poetic even if he could
type for hours on eloquent end?

I do not come from an academic clan and, for reasons that are
broader than that fact alone, the very word *literature* is one from
which I tend to run. In its most basic denotation, I'll admit that it
does seem innocuous enough: a kind of writing regarded as permanently important because of its intrinsic excellence. But too many
associate professors of English for too many years have unnecessarily
attempted to justify their trade by casting literature in the most

dusky and inaccessible of lights, trying to convince their students that it is as thorny a subject as political theory, as dense and impenetrable as particle physics. Yet just because it is the most venerable and surely important subject taught at any school doesn't mean that it therefore must appear impervious to modest minds, and simply because we currently classify those language-focused academic enclaves as *English* or *literature* departments doesn't mean we can't someday come round to actually calling them what they are: *departments of narrative and poetry, departments of storytelling, departments of reading the really good stuff.*

But the issue that inevitably turns a quick look at the subject of literature into something rather sticky is how in the world one goes about defining excellence. Is identifying the good stuff simply a matter of taste? Is one person's *Love Story* likely *Romeo and Juliet* to other eyes? Is *Moby Dick* marvelous solely because it has been claimed to be for so long? Was Ernest Hemingway a master or a macho pig, or was he both at once? Is the work of a writer like James Joyce—or Thomas Pynchon, let's suppose—essentially artful because of its lushly upholstered obscurity, or does it so often seem impenetrable to regular guys like me because—*yo, fella*—it's art? I try my best not to try to answer these tricky kinds of questions, but they intrigue me nonetheless, and when absolutely pressed, I suppose I do agree that some writing is art indeed, but surely it is so for a wide array of reasons.

As particular pieces of writing are commonly categorized in academe, they tend to be shuttled into one of several polar types of composition: the thing in question is either poetry or rhetoric, description or argumentation, narration or exposition—and fiction or nonfiction, of course—and it is the former type in each dichotomous pair that normally is accorded the literary label. To help clarify those polarities, let's define *rhetoric* rather too simply as the presentation of ideas and facts in clear, logical, and convincing language, while *poetry* is a linguistic expression rooted in rhythm, imagination, and emotion. *Argumentation* tries to convince by establishing the certainty of a proposition, while *description*, on the other hand, is content to paint a picture. *Exposition* attempts to elucidate things as well, but its sharpest tools toward that end are definition, classification, comparison, and analysis, while the hammer and nails of *narration* are the recounting of events and a kind of bringing them to life through language. *Nonfiction* is reportorial—these things happened in a particular place and time—while *fiction* is imagined: let's suppose they happened this way.

Although these categories are employed only for illustrative purposes—nothing is written just to fit a niche, in other words—they do shed some light on the range of written endeavors and they also highlight an element or two that are common to most artfully rendered language—Ian's or anyone else's—those devices and styles that are, perhaps, the linchpins of literature. "Show me, don't tell me," writing instructors have implored their students for generations, and it is a plea meant to draw them away from the didactic end of the spectrum toward a kind of writing infused with the power of words themselves, their cadences and rhythms, their ability to limn sharp images and incite emotions, to shape amazing stories out of meager scratches, out of simple sounds. Students who are certain that they have something to say will likely be better preachers than poets, it seems to me, and theirs is a pitfall of which every apprentice literary writer probably should be warned. Regardless of the subject, its questions are almost always richer than its answers, and it is in the asking of those questions that something artistic infrequently and somehow magically emerges.

On the occasions when I have returned to The Colorado College, my alma mater, to try—with sweaty palms and sweeping trepidation—to offer something of some import to students in the English department, I have attempted to clarify this distinction between showing and telling, between the playfulness of inquiry and the audacity of answers, between poetry and preaching, by quoting the late Richard Hugo, a poet haunted by haggard Rocky Mountain towns and haunted too by words. "When you start to write," Hugo proposed to his writing students in *The Triggering Town*, "you carry to the page one of two attitudes, though you may not be aware of it. One is that all music must conform to truth. The other, that all truth must conform to music. If you believe the first, you are making your job very difficult . . . [but] if you feel truth must conform to music, those of us who find life bewildering and who don't know what things mean, but love the sound of words enough to fight through draft after draft of a poem, can go on writing—try to stop us."

All music must conform to truth. All truth must conform to music. Dichotomies again: paired statements, each expressing in just six words the essence of two utterly distinct and polar approaches to language, neither one *better* than its opposite, but the two separated by something of a sheer-walled canyon, the former fundamentally concerned with writing as an avenue of expression leading toward specific kinds of products—ideas, facts, persuasive points of view— while the latter is focused foremost on the avenue itself, a line of words headed somewhere, its direction oftentimes unknown. In a given piece of writing, if its music must conform to truth, then the lyrical nature of the language is necessarily subservient to what is expressed. But if its truth is at music's mercy, in contrast, then nothing is so important, so veritably *certain*, that it can be said in harmonic dissonance, out of rhythm, its cadences all wrong. Writing in which truth conforms to music is writing that cares more for sensuous sentences than it does for erudition, and it is writing that tilts toward art—melodic language you might even label literature.

Babette Deutsch, the American poet and novelist who died in 1982, the same year of Hugo's passing, was mindful of music too as she attempted to define language transformed and transcended into art. Poetry, she wrote, is the "art which uses words as both speech and song to reveal the realities that the senses record, the feelings salute, the mind perceives, and the shaping imagination orders." Words as order, words as song, words at once constrained and set in motion by their beating rhythms—and Deutsch's definition pertains as readily to lyric prose as it does to forms conventionally called poetry, of course, simple words encouraged to strut their stuff and sing in either genre, to create an eloquent, if internal, music.

In the same way I'm convinced that prose and poetry ought be considered closer kin than they are often credited to be, I also

believe fictional and nonfictional forms bear much more in common
than the literary taxonomists often try to convince us. It is of some
substantial importance, of course, to create a kind of contract between writer and reader—to announce dependably, assuredly,
"These events indeed unfolded as I have described them to you,"
or to suggest on the other hand, "These events possess their own
reality, if perhaps they never actually occurred." Each is a contract
that should not be broken, and the two are merged into the murk
and mire of the "docudrama"—"maybe it happened but, well, just
assume it happened anyway"—only at great peril.

But apart from the importance of making amply unambiguous
that distinction between whether a piece of writing is reportage or
imagination, there is little that *necessarily* distinguishes the two.
Writing that incorporates a certain didacticism, that attends to a
convincing or clarifying task, is almost always nonfiction, I'll admit;
and it is also true that fiction, with its myriad imaginative possibilities, is much more often created out of rich, orchestral language than
is nonfiction. But those are generalities rather than literary rules,
and fine novels are sometimes written out of drab, sackcloth kinds
of language, just as essays—even those that rashly answer the very
questions that they pose—often sing instead of speak. Meditations
and memoirs, their subjects drawn from memory rather than fantasy,
histories transformed into stories flush with consequence and flourish, homely journalism dressed up in its Sunday best, even simple
letters laid out in labored longhand and sent to friends and loved
ones far away—all are often more intent on music than on truth,
assured somehow that music makes its own truth in the end.

At the close of the school year in May 1992—the end of Ian's second
grade—he had received a letter from his teacher, one he was very
proud of, which his parents had tucked away to safe-keep for themselves and for him. Barbara Ross had requested—and the school's
administration lately had approved—a transfer to third grade in the
fall, the move allowing her to teach the same group of students

for a second year, one precipitated in large part by her desire
to work with Ian again, his new ability to type presumably connecting him still more valuably with his classmates and with her
in the year ahead. "Dear Ian," she had written on the final day of
school:

> Once there was a teacher named Mrs. Ross who was blessed
> to have a boy with autism in her class. She was constantly
> amazed by all the things he knew and understood, and by the
> problems he had learned to live with. She was in awe of his
> sensitivity and love and friendship with other kids. She wanted
> to help him in any way she could, but he actually helped her
> to gain some understanding of what true courage and love are.
>
> Thank you for the green bookmark with the dogs on it. Your
> picture and the story on the back are incredibly wonderful to
> me. I will value it forever, and I'm so excited about next year.
>
> Love,
>
> Mrs. Ross

The gift of the bookmark had been Ian's idea, and he had helped
his mother make it—a photograph cut from a magazine of dogs that
looked like Mrs. Ross's own dogs pasted on one side and a story by
Ian pasted to the other, this one a brief tale about a boy whose
teacher helps him to make friends.

Ian was equally delighted that Barbara Ross would still be his
teacher, and he eagerly looked forward to school beginning again as
his renaissance summer came to a close. He could express himself
now—he could tell stories and ask questions and answer them as
well; he could demonstrate how smart he was and could tell his
classmates how much he cared for them. And although he still could
not stand in front of the class and tell his friends how remarkable his
summer had been, he *could* type that news now with his mother's
help, and on the first day of school in September Barbara Ross read
aloud for Ian what he had wanted everyone to know:

DEATR KIDS.,

IHAD AMN AMAZIBNG SUMMER. I ASTARTED TTAKING A
NEW MREDICINE AND I AM GWWETTING WELL. I XCAN
DSO ALL SOERTS OF THINHGS I COUKLDNT DO BEIORE,
LOIKE I WENT TO HORNBECK HOMWESTEAD AND I WPORE
A COSTUME AND I ASCTED KLIKE A SREGULAR KID. AND
EDDIE SSOPENT THRE NIGHT AND IAM EATING ATT THE
YTABLE WITH MY FA,MILY. I CVAN PLAY MORE TOO.
PKLEASE P;LAY WITH ME LOTS. BUT RTHE MOST EZX-
CVITING THUING IS MNY PET SNAKE. I NSAMED HIM JOHN-
NYO. ISNT RTHAT A GREAT MNAME? IGOT HIM ON AHIKE
WITH MY DAD SAND SISTER. IAM SO HAPPUY TO BE BACK
QAND IGREATLY HOPE YTO BE YOOUR FRIEND.

IAN

Ian surely listened carefully as the words of his letter briefly filled
the classroom, and he must have been buoyed by his classmates'
applause and eager cheers, yet he did not appear to be: instead he
simply sat on the floor with a book between his legs as he often had
in other years, his face bent over the pages that he busily flapped
from side to side. And as successive school days unfolded, Ian's
internalized excitement and his heady optimism in fact turned starkly
sour. He had imagined that now he would be a regular, communicating kid at Gateway Elementary, and the realities he encountered
instead come that September were hard for him to bear.

Unlike previous years, when Ian had remained at ease and comfortable at school during the part of the day when Mary Lou Krueger
was working at another school, this year he seemed to need her with
him every instant, in part because of the stability and constancy she
provided but also because she was the only teacher at school with
whom he could try to type, and he felt stranded, disoriented, and
terribly mute without her. Although a few classmates like Clara were
learning too just how to hold his wrist and pull his hand away from
the keyboard after each quick stroke, they were often busy with
their own work. Despite a decision to shorten his school day, Ian's

new frustrations, anxieties, and the drowning of his hopes combined to alter his attitude toward school. He began to vigorously resist the routines that pointed him toward school each morning; he often arrived late and only after he had worked his way through yet another chaotic episode. He would cry inconsolably for hours at Gateway if either Mary Lou, Barbara Ross, or his friend Eddie was absent; and clearly this year—*this* year of all years—he would require the same kind of rigid and unwavering sameness at school that he long had needed at home.

On a warm Saturday when the leaves of the aspen trees had begun to turn, Claudia broached the subject of school with him, hoping to draw out of him the issue that was at the heart of his discontent, and she began by telling him that Annie Carter, a teaching assistant who worked with Ian often throughout the day, had mentioned to her recently that he didn't seem interested in math anymore. "Why aren't you?" she asked.

BEXCAUSE ITS TOO EASSY FOR ME, he replied.

"That's what I was afraid of," Claudia responded. "I talked about this with all your teachers at our meeting. I wasn't sure if you'd rather do the same math with all the kids and just practice using a pencil or if you should do harder math with just you and Annie."

IWANT TIO DO HARDEER MATH BEXCAUDSE I NEED TO LEARTN SOME HARDER STUGFF BUT IWANT TOBE LIJKE THE OTHER KIDSS TOO, he explained, unsure himself about what he wanted. Then he began to whimper, slumping on his bed.

"What is it?" his mother asked.

I ASM JUST SO SAD BWECASUSE I CAN MNEVER BE LOIKE THE OTHER KIDDS.

"Because you can't talk like they can?"

I DONBT CARE IGF I CAN TALK OR NOT BUTT I HATE TGHE ROUTINRES. I CVAN TY[PE WHEN I MNEED TO TA;LK BUT EBVEN WITH THE MEDUICINE I CANNT DO THE TTHINHGS THEY DO. PLESASE MAKE MY LIFE NBETTER.

That final plea was wrenching enough for her to read, but no more so than the blanketing realization that Ian's sky-high hopes had collided head-on with far grimmer grounded circumstances, and

although she could remind him that he *was* still getting better—the
voices in his head were still quiet, at least, he was sleeping through
the night, and he was still much calmer than before—they both
were very much aware that the medication that had been such a
breakthrough over the previous months now increasingly bombarded him with untenable side effects. Ian often complained of
headaches; urination was painful; and his terribly dry skin now itched
in ways that nearly drove him mad, his fingernails tearing sores along
his legs and arms. A dermatologist had prescribed oatmeal baths and
a topical medication for his skin, and in consultation with Patrick
Sternberg, Boyce and Claudia now would begin to lower Ian's Anafranil dosage in hopes that the several side effects would abate, but
they were anxious and concerned nonetheless about the possibility
that it might have to be abandoned—the drug that had been such a
boon now appearing to pose two new problems for every one it
curtailed or diminished.

I REALLY HATEE THE ITCHING AND I YUNDERTSTAND
ABOUYT ,MAKING THE MEDUICINE LOWER, Ian explained once
the slow dosage reduction was under way, BUT IAM A LKIYTTLE
SAD BEXCAUSE I WAS HIOPING FOR MOTRE FOODS AND
FQEWER ROUTINES.

Autumn winds had stripped the last of the leaves from the aspen
trees and Ian had grown still sadder by the time I came to visit at
the end of October. I had intended to go to school with him, as I
had several times before—to observe his interaction with his peers
and teachers as well as the impressive way in which he could adapt
to the vagaries of that environment despite his incessant needs—
but more and more these days, Ian could not bring himself to begin
the morning routines that eventually would lead him to his classroom. He would awaken and quickly become distraught at the realization that school was part of that day's plan—fussing and crying,
sometimes screaming at the slightest inconsistency, repeating a
video he normally needed to see only once seemingly to stall for
time. To his parents' repeated queries about why he was having so

much trouble getting back into school, Ian offered several answers: He loved his friends in Mrs. Ross's room, he said, but kids he didn't know from other classes made fun of him on the playground; he desperately needed quiet time at school, but the resource room where he went twice a day to help him relax away from his classroom's commotion was for SDUMB KIDS, he explained; science still excited him but the reading and math he did with his peers was DFREADFULLY BOERING; and foremost among his complaints was the fact that ITIS RWEALLY HARD NOT RTO BE ABLE TO YTYPE THERE. I FWEEL ALL AKLONE AND LOIKE THERE ISNO ONE TO GHELP NME.

Ian's several teachers were, in fact, making concerted efforts to learn how to "facilitate"—how to properly hold his wrist and briskly pull his hand away from the keyboard following each stroke. Still, neither Mary Lou nor anyone else at school was nearly as successful as his mother was at helping him type, and it was at school, most of all, where he hoped to express himself as often and eloquently as he could. It was at school where the prospect of successful typing seemed sure to make him both a bona fide student and a regular kid, and if he had to remain effectively mute at school, then he didn't want to be there. CANT RUSSRELL TAKE VCARE OF ME INSSTEAD OF SVCHOOL TODAY, he asked in his bedroom—still in his pajamas, still refusing his meager breakfast—aware, certainly, that his proposal had a good chance of being positively received.

"Wouldn't it be good to have Russell go to school with you?" his mother inquired instead.

ITT WOULD VBE BETTWER TO GO TO MUELLER SRTATE PARK WIUTH HIM ABND SGHOW HIMN MY GFAVORITE TTRAIL.

It was a clear, crisp, and inviting day and neither Ian nor I really *needed* to be at school, both of us having already mastered our multiplication tables, both of us reading rather well by now, and it remained exceedingly difficult, I'm sure you can understand, to say no to a boy who only recently had become able at last to make this kind of request. If Ian and I played hooky that Monday, his father could still work as he had planned, Claudia could surrender the morning's struggle and, with Sarah in tow, she could get off to school on time. If we were absent that day, I could visit a place I'd never seen before and spend more time alone with Ian than I ever had. I liked the idea, but I didn't lobby for it until both Claudia and Boyce had acquiesced, and by nine-thirty or so, Ian had completed the series of "weekend" routines that otherwise set his day in motion and we were ready to go—his juice and snack packed, notes duly scribbled down on the route we *must* adhere to, the garage door ceremonially opened by Ian once he was dressed in boots and jacket, his verbally spoken "Mozart" his request for the music we would listen to as we drove.

This was the kind of outing each of Ian's parents had made thousands of times with him, the kind of drive they surely made on a sort of autopilot on most days, yet it was new for me—something of a small adventure and certainly a responsibility—and I remember feeling rather like a teenage baby-sitter trying to live up to the adult demands of my first employment as we drove away, first winding through their hillside neighborhood as Ian always required, then circling back to the house as if on something of a shakedown cruise before we ventured out to the highway and truly were under way.

Since he had been small, Ian, like many children, had listened to Raffi songs as he traveled in a car, yet he, of course, long had needed to listen to *particular* Raffi songs at particular points along the routes he regularly traveled. But among the many things Anafranil had made possible during the preceding months was Ian's new and continuing ability to listen to different music from one day to the next, and classical music—Mozart and Vivaldi were his current favorites—by now had replaced Raffi's "Down by the Bay" and "Ever Green, Ever Blue" as the music that accompanied his mountain tours. So we listened to a Mozart violin concerto as we drove west out of Woodland Park—Ian buckled into the right side of the backseat where he always sat, his uncle his chauffeur, one who periodically reminded him to sip his juice, the slender highway almost empty as we crested Ute Pass at midmorning on that Monday, the park too all but deserted as we arrived, not a single car but ours parked at the Outlook Ridge trailhead, the setting ours alone to wander in and explore.

Outlook Ridge, THE OBNLY PLACE TTHAT IS REAALLY QUIET, was one of Ian's favorite places in the Pike's Peak region, one of several idyllic spots where he seemed particularly content, where, as he put it, ICAN PRETEND THAT I ANM A PATRT OF NATURE. It also was a place where an ability to talk seemed subordinate to seeing what lay beyond each bend in the trail, where the brisk pace he kept as he hiked was ritual enough for him, where the wilderness ironically seemed ordered, perfectly arranged, its sounds melodies instead of noise, its sole language the occasional words of birds and the high, bugling calls of elk in their autumn rut. And although I chatted with him as I helped him zip his bright red jacket and don the sunglasses that made him look like a Saturday morning TV star, telling him how excellent his suggestion to come here already seemed to be, neither of us then said anything more. Ian hiked ahead of me as we made our way along the trail, his head held slightly cocked in that manner that had become his signature— something that seemed to allow him to glimpse the upper branches of the trees as he passed beneath them—the crisp breeze tousling his fair hair and soon reddening his cheeks.

We were high on the Pike's Peak massif where we walked, the summit of the mountain hidden by its humped and rocky northern shoulder, but the views in other directions were open and pan-oramic—the timbered slopes of the Tarryalls visible in the north, the peaks of the Mosquito and Sawatch ranges rising majestically in the west and already dusted with new snow, the sharp summits of the Sangre de Cristos off to the southwest seeming surprisingly close at hand. The ground around us lay littered with aspen leaves, their bright yellow color only just now beginning to fade, and ahead of us—our destination—huge and sculpted granite boulders, some as big as seagoing ships, rose up at the tip of the winding ridge, seeming to cap it, to offer it some punctuation, and we wound our way toward them like climbers intent on a long-sought summit.

Ian had enjoyed heights since he was very small. He always had been at home on ladders and slides and assorted pieces of playground equipment as well as outcroppings like these, and with me trailing him—a little uncertain about whether I should let him do so—he scampered to the top of the first knot of boulders we reached. The view from their rounded crown was even better than it had been below, and there was enough room for both of us at the top to sit and simply drink it in, Ian calmer for a few minutes, more nearly motionless, than I think I had ever seen him. But he wanted to look out into the gaping canyon that dropped suddenly and sharply away from us, and he continued to scoot himself toward the sheer-sided edge of the rock until I told him not to go farther, Ian turning to look at me as I admonished him, and I thought I could see the hint of a smile as I explained that his parents would be a bit cross with me if I returned from the trip without him.

It soon became clear that Ian's plan was to climb to the top of each of the granite knobs that lay scattered along the end of the ridge, each one easy enough to access along its gently sloping back side, each also high enough and sheer enough on its southern and western sides that I issued him a brief warning each time we sat and surveyed what spread below us. The final cluster of boulders, truly enormous now and rising still higher than those we had already scaled, stood at a spot where the ridge abruptly ended and beyond which lay nothing more than five hundred vertical feet of autumn air, the chasm that opened below us appearing splendid and utterly still until a single black bird lifted from its perch in a tree far below and began to climb in a series of lazy spirals. I told Ian that I could not tell the difference between crows and ravens, and I wondered if he knew which bird this was.

"Raven," he said aloud and surely correctly, his enunciation easily clear enough to understand, *raven* the only word he spoke through-out our trip.

Both of us stayed comfortably silent then as we sat at the top of the granite promontory, and I casually moved close to him, close enough that I could take hold of the tail of his jacket without his notice, a poor but reassuring means of keeping him back from the brink, and we did nothing but observe that bird and a sizable chunk of Colorado for thirty minutes or so—for what seemed like a longer stretch than he possibly could have kept still. I wanted to tell Ian what a fine time I was having, how much indeed I liked this place, but the silence somehow seemed preferable. I wanted to assure him that he *was* a part of nature and of this particular place, that we all were, despite the fact that we so often conducted our lives as if we weren't. And I wanted to let him know too that although he might never be able to describe aloud this place and the sense of peace it engendered, he *could* render it with written words if he wanted to, and that fact freed him as surely as the raven was free to fly. I wanted to tell him that the fellow seated next to him was perfect proof that *anyone* could write, and to make sure he knew too that he was as normal as any of us as he typed, turning words into information, into music. I wanted to try to tell him that labors of language surely are the best work we ever do.

Like Ian, I had grown up charmed by stories, and I always had simply assumed that stories were the best ways for any of us to offer explanations. I had grown up steeped in the grand, melodic English language of the sixteenth century as well as the pliable and vivacious American vernacular of the twentieth. Like him, I had had the great good fortune to be applauded by my parents and challenged by my teachers. I had had the audacity to write stories of my own simply because so many people had said for so long, "Of course you can." Whether it was the alliterative and rhythmic Anglican liturgy that set the first example, or perhaps the simple way in which my grand-mother encouraged us to imagine with her nimble words, I think I always understood intuitively that whatever truth pretended to be, it ought to be couched in verbal melodies. And even approaching adulthood, once I had completed college it had been my bit of luck to need to make a buck, and I had discovered in the process that it was as easy—and for me as essential—to stay cognizant of aesthetic sound when I was writing reportorially as when I was writing out of my own lumbering imagination. Whether I was making it all up or attempting an approximation of how things actually had happened, words and the songs they sung when you set them down in certain patterns always had been what seemed to matter most.

As I sat with Ian on that wonderfully exposed spot, the weather surrounding us stirred by subtle warnings of the coming winter, I couldn't help but marvel at my good fortune and even, somewhat

surprisingly, at the fortune that was his. I had been lucky to be born
a snoop, nosy enough that nothing ever had seemed safe from my
need to take a look at it, to listen in, curiosity certainly not the thing
that killed the cat, but rather, it seemed, the kind of questioning
that brought the cat to life. And there had been great good luck as
well in my unstudied eagerness to pass along what I had encountered—as if I ever really *knew* anything, for heaven's sake—my only
real certainties arriving on those rare occasions when I was briefly
sure that I had rummaged exactly the right words to limn a given
bit of gossip, information, or amazement. "Can you imagine?" my
grandmother always had asked as she spun her simple stories, and,
yes, I had been able to imagine with young and naive delight. But
I have a hunch now, half a lifetime later, that *telling* stories is perhaps
the greater pleasure, the enterprise of creating whole worlds out of
words one that is enormously seductive despite the work and
worry—beginning in the beginning full of a faith you can't define
and ending only as you reach a place you know you've never been
before.

In the summer of his tenth year, Ian had become a different boy,
one who had been fundamentally transformed. For all of his life till
now, sounds, symbols, words, and stories had been his great and
stalwart allies in ordering a world his brain perceived as chaos. Until
early in the summer just ended, the repetitions of those stories and
the rhythms of those sounds, coupled with the loving constancy of
his family and friends, were all he had to help shelter him from his
neural storms. But now—and imagine for a moment the profundity
of that change—he had means to shape whole worlds himself, to
sing instead of only listen. If miraculous words now were things with
which he too could create, if he, like the rest of us, could unravel
stories and sing a sort of order out of his surroundings despite his
life's enduring complexities, then mustn't he be mightily capable
and important after all?—not just a regular kid but too, a regular
raconteur, fortunate for the ability, at once simple and astonishing,
to describe how things had happened once upon a time.

Perhaps I should have said aloud to Ian as we sat on that high
rock, "You know, I think I can begin to understand what it meant

for you to start to type, and I can imagine too how you've felt this fall at school when you haven't had a dependable way to get your words out." I could have told him that I knew more than a little bit about what it was like to have them stuck inside you, impeded for reasons that were mechanical, emotional, or simply unaccountable—stories like Ian's impossible to tell perhaps until words and subject at last had begun to merge.

But before I said anything at all to him, Ian was standing again, his face turned toward the far southwestern ranges, that curious distance in his expression for once perfectly befitting the scene he quietly surveyed. I stood close and was poised to grab him, but whatever caution he needed to heed I let come from him this time. For a few moments, he seemed to take real pleasure in that alert flirtation with danger—and that was a pleasure I knew too—then he bounded down from the rock and made his way toward the trail, that solitary raven still high in the breeze-swept sky.

"When you write," Annie Dillard has explained, "you lay out a line of words. The line of words is a miner's pick, a woodcarver's gouge, a surgeon's probe. You wield it, and it digs a path you follow. Soon you find yourself deep in new territory. Is it a dead end, or have you located the real subject? You will know tomorrow, or this time next year."

As I began to lay out the winding line of words that at last has become this book, I knew little about either autism or language, and it had been my intention to inquire into both—the cruel complexity of the disorder and this most astonishing of our human capabilities—and, in doing so, to try to gain some substantial sense of how autism, in fact, had left a boy I knew named Ian Drummond desperately bereft of language. But the route I followed in the end—its signposts often shrouded, the roadway sometimes suspended when there simply were no words—led me in a direction I could not have imagined as I commenced: Many circuitous miles into this linguistic journey, I discovered—dumbfounded as were all of us in Ian's enveloping extended family—that language was indeed alive in him, and that it

had been since that distant spring when he began to speak, then
stopped. I discovered, at least in Ian's singular case, that, yes, he
had been robbed of normal verbal expression by this concert of
maladies unfortunately known as *self*ism, but that his brain had been
fully patterned, nonetheless, by language.

Had I begun this book shackled with a nascent thesis about the
nemesis that is autism or the nature of language—theses I not only
had to detail but to defend—had "truth" been my distant destination, that astonishing discovery surely would have wrecked the trek
and landed me in a writer's muddy ditch, the words dead-ending
without any consolation. But all I really had hoped to accomplish as
I got under way was the telling of an often difficult and occasionally
jubilant tale—that and the asking of questions set to simple music.
When you understand right from the outset how little you know now
and perhaps can ever know, you're wonderfully free to concentrate
on which are the best queries, to focus your often faulty cognition
on the digging, the probing, as Dillard puts it. And when music is
the thing that foremost sets your course, when you trust language
itself enough to let it seek its own sort of order—meaning emerging,
when it does, out of the phonemes' and the words' serendipitous
arrangement—then dead ends tend to offer little trouble and you
discover, one year, two years hence, that in the end you cannot
separate the subject from the singing.

Yet although it is my nature to shy away from answers and to
claim little as true creed, I do hold to some hunches and even strong
convictions as this line of words comes near its close. It makes plain
sense to me that language is the offspring of physical activity, of our
ancestral ability to link a series of subtle movements that first allowed
us to accurately throw a stone or chip a spear point. Once our
brains proved adept at those serial sorts of organization, I believe it's
probable that speech and the neural networking that we call abstract
thinking proceeded rather side-by-side, language at once a communicative *and* a representational system, our budding abilities to symbolize and analyze making the desire to communicate far more
urgent than it had been before, while what we spoke and what we

heard spoken began, in turn, to allow us to generalize, to universal-ize, and to *imagine* far beyond our reach.

I suspect that these symbiotic processes—communicating as well as ordering with language—became so valuable over the ebb of time, bearing so elementally on virtually every other human activity, that much of the neural circuitry in our left cerebral hemispheres is now, in fact, predicated by language, its phenomenally intricate patterning providing not only the rules we call syntax but also the structure with which our brains attempt to make sense of every sort of sensory input. I also have a hunch that each of us must acquire language early in life or not at all because young brains are necessar-ily ravenous for whatever kinds of patterning they can imitate and replicate, those patterns ultimately forming the neural framework with which we interact with the world, our brains forfeiting their ability to construct that framework at a time that signals the end of creative childhood as surely as does puberty.

Children give language its verve, its heady voice, and it seems to me that language belongs to them in ways we barely begin to understand—idioms evolving over generations and occasionally even emerging new from pidgin stews through the playful voices of children. The acquisition and manipulation of language in childhood is a kind of wonderfully unconscious creativity, one capable of defin-ing syntactic regulations that are simple for virtually every language user to employ and obey, yet which nearly defy, nonetheless, our best attempts to set them down in rulebooks or pedantic catalogs. It is a sublime sort of creativity that delights in attaching meaning to arbitrary symbols as well as loosing symbols to shape their own realities. And it is a kind of creativity that takes lucid note of the way in which words often seem most meaningful when they are borne and buoyed by rhythms. I suspect that work and play are not the polarities we tend to make them out to be, that both, in fact, are kindred forms of a fundamental human enterprise, as essential as our seekings after food and sleep and sex, and that labors of language are simply the work that most miraculously makes us who we are.

—

There remains, come the close of the day, little in my understanding of autism about which I can announce such confidence. In the half century since Kanner gave the disorder its deceptive name, the only truly definitive progress in understanding its etiology has been the now universal acceptance of the fact that autism is *not* a psychosis, that it is set in insidious motion instead by one or more structural or neurochemical abnormalities of the brain itself. It is a malady that makes its appearance in early childhood and that lingers for a life-time. It assaults the integration of information from the five senses, the initiation and coordination of subtle movements, and the verbal expression of creative language.

Not very long ago I might have written with the most complacent sort of confidence that autism inhibited or indeed made impossible the acquisition of language itself; I might well have claimed that the disorder was chiefly characterized by the *absence* of language and that those who suffered its vexing symptoms lacked language's ability to shape the stuff of personality and to forge meaningful, communica-tive connections with others; I might have tried to persuade you that people with autism were incapable of abstract thought, given their obvious lack of words with which to organize and think. But those suppositions would have been as dramatically incorrect, I now know, as that daffy notion from the 1950s that autism itself was the rueful outcome when modern parents grew too icy and aloof.

Hoping to steer clear of a similarly specious trap, let me be careful to contend in contrast that autism's origins likely are as numerous as its several symptoms. I am not disposed to argue, for instance, with neurologist Margaret Bauman when she proposes that, based on her own postmortem studies, the disease is rooted in prenatal malformations of critical deep-brain structures, and surely its deficits *are* predetermined by birth in many cases. Yet in the case of a boy I know in Colorado, as well as hundreds of others round the world, I am indeed persuaded that autism's onset has been medicinal—the culprit a virulent vaccine unwittingly administered to hyperallergic children in an ironic effort to help them avoid a dread disease.

And autism has other antecedents, almost certainly—genetic, congenital, environmental—causes too veiled still to recognize, yet which somehow set to stir early in life the same mix of symptoms and bizarre behaviors that collectively prompt this joyless diagnosis. Whatever its source, autism inevitably emerges as a disorder in which brains are cruelly and chaotically bombarded by the same sensory information with which we otherwise investigate the world and our relation to it—sight, smell, sound, taste, and even a mother's touch often disturbing, frightening, nonsensical. It is a disorder in the most elemental meaning of that word—one in which the brain's inherent need to order, to represent, symbolize, and arrange—is terribly and surely maddeningly impeded, order subsumed by hideous disarray. And it too is an entrapment, rendering brains incapable of controlling the bodies they inhabit, repetitive movements often impossible to suppress, desired motion of many kinds impossible to initiate—flapping an object in front of your eyes something you do for hours because you *must*, feeding yourself with a fork or speaking a serial string of words things you long to do but never can. It is a disorder of Dantean horror, I know from my familial proximity to it, and it stands in the starkest contrast to those abilities and attributes that otherwise endear us to living.

As Ian and hundreds of other people with autism began to type in recent years, not only did they begin to shout their linguistic competence and even to dazzle with their eloquence, they also began to respond, often disarmingly, to the kinds of rudimentary questions that theretofore never had been put to them: *What do sounds seem like to you? Are your words vivid in your mind but simply stuck? Why do you need such sameness day to day? Is autism something you are aware of, or it is simply who you are?*

PPEOPLE DIONT UNSDERSTAND THSAT AUTIXM IS LIKE HABVING A BAD DREAM, Ian explained metaphorically one day during that autumn that was etched by his sobering sadness, his mother still the person whose facilitating touch most reliably helped him express himself. YOU HACVE TO LLEARN EBVERYTHINGG THE HAERDEST WAY POSSSIBLE AND RTYPING IS THE GFIRST TUIME AMNYTHING HASD BEEN EAASY FOR ME. ITIS EASY TO

POIMNT TO LETTRERS ABND IT IS SO GHARD TODO EVERTHING E;LSE.

I asked him if he had been able to understand what his parents and his sister were saying even when he was very little, and he assured me that yes, he had been able to for as long as he could remember. He said he had been about four when he learned to read, JIUST BY LPOOKING AT WPORDS UNTI;L I FUIGURED OUT WHAAT THEY NMEANT, and he added that he could read all the words in his picture books even as he flapped their pages in front of his eyes.

Over the course of several months, Claudia had periodically asked Ian questions taken from the Slossen Intelligence Test, one of the tools with which her gifted students are evaluated, and his reliably accurate responses had seemed to startle him as certainly as they caught her attention and his father's. I DISDNT RESALIXZE HOW SSMART IWAS YUNTIL YOU TTESTED ME ANBD THEN ISTARTED TO REALIZRE IT, he typed, and when she asked whether autism might actually help make him smart, he had this to say: AUTIXSM MAKESME EZXTRA SMARRT AND IWOULD GHGAVE BEEN SNMART TOO. Similarly, he seemed to remember precise details from years gone by and could, without question, repeat many books and movies word for word, and I inquired why he supposed his memory was so good: ITHINK IT IS VBVECAIUSE I HAVE NMORE RTIME TO THIMNK BECAUSSE ICANT DO OTGHER THINGS.

When it came to Ian's explanations—those of a nine-year-old, we sometimes had to remind ourselves—of his demand for repetition, he repeatedly referred to his need, to his quest, you could say, for calmness. Keeping virtually everything dependably the same, he explained, HHELPS ME BE CAKLM ABND IT HELPS MEE COPE WUITH AYUTISM—*cope* a word his mother often used, one he had added to his vocabulary in the imitative way that every youngster does. And music too was his ally, he told us as he typed, BECAUUSE IT HRELPS MNE GWET CALM. ICAN GET CAALM IFI LIDSTEN TO NMUSIC BECAYUSE ITIS SO SOOTHUIING. Lately, he had discovered the music of Beethoven, in fact—initially inquiring whether his parents owned any he could listen to because Schroeder, one of the characters in the Charlie Brown cartoons that mattered immensely to him, played Beethoven on his tiny piano, and by now Beethoven's Fifth Piano Concerto was Ian's particular preference: ILOVE IT. IT IS TGHE NBEST OF ALLTHE MUISC SIO FAR, he opined assuredly.

There was one more question I had wanted to ask him since long before I ever had imagined I might be able to, one I wasn't sure he or anyone actually could answer, but I asked it nonetheless: Did he think there was a connection between not being able to talk normally and needing to have everything the same?

Ian had typed longer already than he usually was able to, yet he didn't screw his body into a knot now, nor did he try to pull away. Claudia supported his wrist an inch or two above the keyboard, but instead of immediately beginning to reach for specific keys with his forefinger, he held his hand motionless for a moment, as if he were mulling the question over before he answered it. At last he began to peck out his considered answer: I THUINK THERE ISA CONNWECTION BWECAUSSE I NEEED TO GHAVE THINHGS THE SAME NMORE NOW THATI CAN TALK.

Yes, it was true, although no one else had yet made that observation: Ian *had* become even more ritualized, if that were possible, in the two years since his primitive, protolinguistic speech had commenced, and if that link were one he plainly sensed, then it very probably existed, although what it implied neurologically surely would remain obscure for some time. Would a connection between the two suggest that the initiation of even the crudest verbal speech tended to induce a kind of chaotic stress in him, stress that was mitigated a bit by sameness? Was motor initiation of every kind inherently disordering or stressful for Ian—whether speaking or any other purposeful sort of movement? Was commencing anything antithetical to calmness?

As it had for some time by now, the question of calmness and its counterpoint—call it chaos, or better perhaps, simply call it stress—seemed to be the key to a story still unwinding, to explanations unapparent. But a few hours later on that gray and blustery day, one that seemed to welcome winter, Ian did offer a vivid answer to an

old and far simpler riddle: The game was Twenty Questions, one
the four of them readily could play and in which company too could
be included, and Ian had begun his turn this time by announcing,
IAM A NMAMMAL. His responses to the queries that ensued soon
made it clear that the critter in question lived on farms and provided
meat, and Sarah, not surprisingly, now knew what it *had* to be.
"You're a cow!" she proclaimed, but she was wrong, and Ian was
delighted that he had stumped her. HAHA, he typed, IKNEW YIOU
WOULDD TYHINK I WAS A COW BUT IMA PIG. I NBNEVER
RWEALLY LIKED COWWS THAT MUCH. IJUST NEEDED RTHEM
FOR MTY ROUTINE—his personality, his humor, this boyish ability
to tease still new to all of them, still astonishing, and although it
seemed certain that routines long would rule his days, perhaps next
to nothing now remained a sacred cow.

The question of whether the words that appeared so often on the
laptop's small screen actually were Ian's had been settled long ago,
and it didn't cross his family members' minds during that tumultuous
autumn. His startling, often elucidating statements and responses
unquestionably were his own, and he reinforced that proof in one
way or another almost daily. But although the same held true in
hundreds of households—people around the world vividly, doubt-
lessly aware that neither this comment nor that one could have come
from *their* fingertips, too many people with autism too eager to
return to their keyboards *every day* for the phenomenon to be,
in fact, a colluded and carefully orchestrated worldwide hoax—it
nonetheless was also clear that facilitated communication did *not*
work for everyone. Surely more than a few therapists, teachers,
and parents—possessed of the best intentions—were unwittingly
helping to type words that they themselves had authored. A number
of professionals whose careers had been spent in autism research or
in its clinical care did remain skeptics or incredulous and outraged
opponents of facilitated communication, its efficacy challenging too
many fiercely held presumptions about the nature of autism itself,
perhaps, to make it possible to accept. And the same television

newsmagazines that once had heralded the technique as some sort of curative miracle now were titillating their viewers with accusations and "proofs" from several quarters that it was nothing more than the chimera of the Ouija board.

In the United States, Douglas Biklen remained an easy target for those who maintained that large numbers of people with autism could not possibly have the brain power to reason, reflect, and express themselves, contending without saying so overtly that Biklen had personally hoodwinked the many hundreds of people who regularly held their flighty hands close to keyboards, tricking them into believing that, with help, their hands and fingers could say what their mouths—and their brains—could not. Biklen had grown irritated and, understandably, a bit combative in response to the attacks, and his own efforts these days were focused on ways in which facilitated communication could more readily be "validated" by those who successfully employed it, as well as on his conviction that the goal in every case should be for the autistic individual to type independently one day, free from the possibility of any kind of controlling touch. Yet he remained sanguine about the long-term outcome of the debate over the viability of the technique. "We're on the right side, there's no question about that," Biklen was sure when he returned to Denver a year following his initial workshop. "It's real, it works in many cases, and the people who use it know it works. We just have to be patient and continue to offer proof."

Empirical proofs derived from experiments performed in carefully controlled laboratory settings by individuals unknown to the autistic typists being tested would be slow in coming, however, in large part because those settings tended to induce demands and stresses that drastically inhibited performance. But inductive and observational investigations into facilitated communication, on the other hand, performed in those places where the subjects in question actually lived and worked and went to school, already had provided a wealth of persuasive data. And physicians, scientists, and educators in several countries, most of whom only recently had begun to examine the phenomenon, now were finding it easy enough to accept—not as a salvation or panacea, but simply as a kind of occupational therapy akin to helping a stroke victim relearn the process of tying shoes or using a fork, yet one that also demanded new ways of looking at the very nature of autism.

"I am convinced that for some children and young adults with autism, [facilitated communication] can be an extremely useful mode of communication," Margaret Bauman commented early in 1993 in an interview with the newsletter of the Autism Society of America.

> Some students who are using FC successfully indicate that they have no trouble organizing their thoughts, but have trouble getting their "body" or "brain" to do what they want it to do, particularly in a demand situation. If we assume that the students are correct in their analysis of their difficulties it might imply that the processing of internal cognitive information is substantially easier for them than the verbal output of that same information. . . . My own personal observations suggest that, in many cases, the autistic individual has trouble with initiation, most especially on demand. I have wondered whether the touch of the facilitator offers the student the physical "cue" to begin. Further, part of the facilitator's job is to provide resistance to the hand or forearm which prevents impulsive, repetitive pointing to a particular letter. The resistance seems to allow the student time to "regroup" and consider his next choice. Assuming that this observation is correct, it may be that some autistic persons not only have trouble with initiation but also with inhibition, which is, in this case, provided by the external structure of the facilitator.

Similarly, University of Florida psychiatrist Ralph G. Maurer, also an autism researcher, had become convinced of the technique's viability and recently had focused his own attention on whether facilitated communication had begun to demonstrate, in fact, that autism was largely a motor disorder. In comments to the Autism Society's recent national convention, Maurer noted that his personal observations of facilitated communication had seemed to make newly relevant research he had done back in the 1970s with University of

Iowa neurologist Antonio Damasio, whose theory that a variety of cognitive, memory, and language processes were facilitated by "convergence zones" in the cerebral cortex had received much attention and acclaim in recent years.

After he had observed a class of autistic children with Maurer in Iowa nearly two decades before, Damasio had commented that he had seen similar kinds of gaits, arm movements, and body positioning in adults who suffered disorders of the basal ganglia, particularly Parkinson's disease. Intrigued by the seemingly remote yet nonetheless conceivable connection between the two, the physicians had enlisted physical anthropologist Joel Vilensky in a project that compared the movements of autistic children and Parkinsonian adults using high-speed film, and the results had confirmed what Damasio believed he had recognized. Neither Maurer nor Damasio had further compared autism and Parkinsonism in the intervening years, but facilitated communication lately had linked them once again in Maurer's mind: People suffering from both disorders, it now was obvious to him, could often manage to initiate movement with the touch-based prompting of another person. They could, with some small and supportive help, make their unruly bodies obey them at last.

I remembered from my neurological apprenticeship at Patrick Sternberg's side how patients with Tourette's syndrome, Parkinson's disease, and a variety of other movement disorders whose pathogenesis lay in the basal ganglia often had confessed that they never felt relaxed, that they were never calm or entirely at rest—a sensation, of course, which we lately had learned that Ian encountered constantly. And now there was additional information: Early in 1993, David Hill and Martha Leary, speech and language pathologists in Toronto, Ontario, published the results of their wide-ranging survey of the contemporary medical literature on autism and a variety of movement disorders of the basal ganglia. What they found in comparing the several disorders' symptomologies was arresting and it seemed far more than coincidental: "The overlap or co-occurrence of symptoms between autism and the neurological syndromes affecting movement was remarkable. Although the age of onset and the course of these syndromes were clearly different from autism, the descriptions of the symptoms were very familiar and characteristic." Hill and Leary argue for a shift in the focus of autism research to the growing likelihood that it is indeed a movement disorder, and I was struck by their statement that it is the rare malady known as postencephalitic Parkinsonism—the result of severe brain swelling in response to an influenza virus, not unlike the allergic response to the pertussis virus that set Ian's symptoms in insidious motion—that perhaps most closely mirrors autism's syndrome of movement abnormalities and its often bizarre behaviors.

My family and friends consider me normal enough (despite several sticky issues that they tend not to discuss), yet I often do these things when I'm under substantial stress and am anything but calm: I bite my upper lip and the tips of my fingers, and I tear at my fingernails with masochistic abandon. My eyes dart everywhere, looking *for* nothing but looking *at* everything as if I'm taking a manic census. I have been known to check an alarm clock a dozen times before I can assure myself that it is set, and when I'm truly on an anxious edge, the dishes get washed in a wink and everything else is promptly put in the place where I decide it rightfully belongs. I sometimes make bizarre, breathy sighs as I try to determine what to write, what to say, and when I truly can't think of something I occasionally give myself a rap on the head as if to shake it loose. When Karen reminds me that we're about to miss a plane and says, "We've got to get out of here," I tend to echo her prodding words right back to her. And when I'm standing on skis at the top of a slope that is far too steep and impeded by far too many monstrous moguls for my liking—my stomach crawling up my esophagus as I survey the snowy scene—I sometimes shout "There's no freaking way I can do this!" as I go ahead and try, saying one thing yet oddly doing just the other.

It is an unpleasant truth that you too probably act peculiarly from time to time, and I raise it not to pester you but just to try to make the simple point that the characteristic behaviors of people with autism—presuming that indeed they are made under an intense and constant sort of stress—are not necessarily that outlandish or inexplicable when compared with the stress-induced behaviors of those of us who claim a certain normalcy. And together with those several other issues and concerns about the roots of Ian's imprisoning condition—the possibility (the likelihood, in fact) that his brain stem cannot properly filter the sensory information it receives; the possibility that demyelination or other damage to nerve pathways inhibits the flow of information between his brain stem and interpreting and organizing centers in his cerebrum; the possibility that he endures similar demyelinating damage to those several cerebral centers themselves, particularly his prefrontal cortex, whose job it is to make sense of new experiences; and the possibility too, of course, that those abnormalities all exist in concert—a new one now emerges. It now seems very possible to me as well that the function of his basal ganglia is faulty: It may be that one or more of the four small structures that comprise the basal ganglia is malformed. Or perhaps the collective structures do not produce as they should one of the critical neurochemicals that a normal brain depends on. Perhaps specific nerve pathways leading from the basal ganglia to motor centers in his cortex are impeded. Or, of course, his basal ganglia may be involved in his neurological predicament in ways about which I still know too little to imagine. Whatever the etiology of Ian's autism one day proves to be, a drug widely used in the treatment of a separate basal ganglia disorder already has demonstrated its ability to offer him some relief, some semblance of calmness, and I can't help but wonder whether other drugs used successfully to treat a whole spectrum of motor disorders might someday prove far more efficacious for him and for others—people whose autism is at once characterized by too much and too little movement, by constant and explosive stress.

As Ian's Anafranil dosage slowly but steadily was lowered as that fall gave way to winter—in the hope, primarily, that the severe headaches and the awful itching and subsequent bleeding sores it induced would subside, then disappear—Ian's sense of calmness commensurately began to wane, and occasionally the voices in his head began again to call his name. IFEEL KLIKE I AM GOOING TO EXXPLODE, he typed repeatedly now, and when he did so his parents could do little more for him than to rub his feet and legs in ways he found comforting, as well as hold him tight and tell him that they hated this almost as much as he did.

The deflating sadness that had succeeded Ian's summer euphoria now seemed nearly constant, and it was a sadness that spread, of course, to the other members of his family. As heavy snow began to blanket Pike's Peak, lying deep as well on the winding trails that were Ian's brief solace each afternoon, he, his sister, his father, and his mother each had to confront in his or her own fashion the reality that Anafranil probably would not be able to bring him the kind of quantum improvement that had seemed possible, even probable, only a few months before.

As the weather began to confine Boyce to his office in the house, and as the demands of his consulting work in early childhood issues drew him still further from the science that truly invigorated and sustained him, the long depression that had lifted nearly two years before now seemed to slip back inside him—the humor that so long had been his ready ally and release now emerging less frequently, the fact that a fellow 1964 Arkansas All-State Band member recently had been elected to high office not the occasion for southern celebration that it otherwise surely would have been. Sarah grew quieter as the winter commenced—not withdrawing so much as simply becoming ever more cognizant and surely suspicious of life's vagaries and mean uncertainties as she continued to mature, her eleven-year-old spirits still often bright and buoyant, but a crushing disappointment also often etched across her face.

Ian had been trapped in recent months by insidious new routines that *demanded* that his mother be outside as well as he played in the yard each afternoon and that she be with him as he awoke in the morning and when he went to bed each night—literally trapping Claudia as well as Ian, keeping her energy and attention focused so constantly on him that her emotions simply had no time or any means to escape, and I couldn't help but wonder how long she could continue without igniting somewhere inside herself a similar explosive charge. Ian's shackling morning and afternoon routines, plus her mounting exhaustion, had made it increasingly impossible for her to work, and recently she had seen no alternative but to take a five-week leave of absence, getting little real rest in the process but at least briefly lessening the myriad demands of her days. For now, Claudia simply functioned on automatic pilot, and she increasingly built a high wall around herself, infrequently letting friends or even Boyce inside it, feeling increasingly, guiltily, out of touch with people she cared about, yet completely lacking the energy to contact them, to explain it all in deep detail, to let down her rugged guard. But there were times too when she was visibly battered by the setbacks—her exasperations with school bureaucracies, with uncomprehending or inarticulate colleagues and family members, and with the periodic publication of still-one-more book touting a sure cure for autism sometimes flashing into vivid and vocal disgust. She and Boyce recently had been able to buy the house they initially had rented in dog-driven desperation two summers before—the former house since sold and now forgotten—so at least they were settled again, but as the December days grew very short they also certainly seemed to lose any luster they previously had had, any of the recent polish that had been buffed by their bold hopes. As Claudia's grandparents had done decades before in the face of assorted troubles and, at times, despair, she, her husband, and her beloved children would simply have to do what they could do.

Aged, arthritic, increasingly immobile Sheila, the canine companion that Ian seemed to depend on more and more, had grown very frail that fall yet was giving her final days the good fight. Noelle, Sarah's hamster, had died soon after Thanksgiving; it wasn't long before it had been replaced by one whose tan mane and courtly manner seemed to deserve the name Charlemagne. Then Johnnyo, Ian's treasured garden snake, also suddenly died, but with Sarah's recent example to follow, Ian was able to deal with that loss in ways that engendered his parents' pride as well as other pent-up emotions—each animal given a proper burial behind the house within the span of only weeks, tears shed and the grieving unashamed each time, both deaths opportunities to discuss death's meaning, the reality that it was at once natural and woeful, its role, they collectively discussed, one that punctuated life's brevity and its importance.

As had been the case since he was small, Ian once again tended to follow a good day with a bad one, appearing outgoing and at ease and entirely happy for perhaps two full days, then screaming for hours on agonizing end during the three successive days that followed. One day he would return from school flushed with the news that they had begun to study space in Mrs. Ross's third-grade class and that SSPACE ISSO REA;LLY REALLY COOL, explaining too, as though he simply could not type fast enough to let the words out, I ;LIKE SSATURN VBEST OF WALL THE [PLANETS BVECAUSE ITHAS TRINGS. I QWISH I COULD GO TO SATURN TTRTHEN I COUULD SEE TYHE RINGS FOR MYSDELF. IF YOU ARE WONDEERING HOQW SATURN GOT TRINGS IT GHAPP[ENED THIS WAY. GFIRST ALOT OF GASES EZXPLODED WHEN ITWAS GFORNMED AND THEN THHEY COO;LED AND BEVCAME RINGS. But only an hour later, he too would catastrophically explode when a plastic figurine was misplaced, or if the telephone rang too often, or if he found the garage door open as it simply could not be.

On a day like December 19, 1992, Ian had been buoyed by the fact that it was his great buddy Eddie's birthday and that Eddie was again coming to his house to spend the night, and Ian had been eager that evening to type this story before Eddie arrived:

ONVCE THEERE WWERE TQWO FRIENDS WWHO WERE DIRFFERENT BRECAUSE ONE HAD ZAUTISM ANND ONE DIDNT VBUT THEY GFOUND WAYS TO NBE HA[PPY TPPOGETHER. EEVERYONE YTHOUGHT TTHAT THEY WERE TOOO FDIFFERENT TO BE GFRIENDS BUT YTHEY WERE ALLWAYS NBEST FFRIENBNDS AND THEIR BNAMES WERE WEDDIE AND IAN.

But by the following day—despite his delight in how normal he had seemed the previous evening and how happy he had been while Eddie was with him—Ian was wrapped in maddening, maniacal knots again, surely because out-of-the-ordinary experiences like the one he had shared with Eddie often were followed by a kind of uncontrollable crash, Ian becoming terrorized again as Claudia tried one more time to break his bizarre afternoon need for her, a ritual demand that both of them were desperate to do away with, Claudia steeling herself not to go outside where he simply *had* to have her, Ian subsequently coming wildly unstuck, screaming for hours even after she relented, and as she struggled to console and control him, typing these words as he continued to thrash and wail in complete despair: I HATTE AUTISM. ITIS A NIGHTMATRE. SSOMETIMNES I WANTTO DIE. IT QWOULD BE BETYTER FOR EBVERYONE IF IWAS DEAD.

As it had fifty-one years before and every year in between, Christmas once again had come and gone, and as my grandmother had done in 1941, Claudia sat down on December 26 to write a letter, not to a distant spouse or family member this time but rather the letter she and Boyce often composed at Christmastime to mail en masse to friends. This time she felt that she could write many pages about the peaks and valleys of the year just past, and she hadn't been sure just where to begin their winding tale till Ian, aware of what she intended to do, announced at the keyboard that he wanted to type his own message for the holiday letter. DEEAR EVRERYONE, he began, YYOU MAY NOT JKNOW IT BUT I CAN TYPEW NOW AMND TELL THE WORKLD QWHAT IAM THINBKING. IT HHAS VCCHANGED MY LIFE SOMUCH. QWE ARE A GFAMILY NOW AND WRE CAN FFIND JOY THIS SSEASON.

He meant the words he wrote, of course, just as he also had meant those he had typed in agony a few days earlier. And at the close of that year, these daily ups and downs, euphorias and desperations, improvements and their attendant setbacks, seemed to be

what the future held for him and for them. Ian's remarkable mother
and father and his loving sister—the three people who had kept him
from a life of utter isolation early on and whose persistence also
had surely played a fundamental part in patterning his brain with
language—certainly remained by his side. He had his larger family
too to support him, as well as sensitive and stalwart friends like
Eddie who seemed, somehow, to be better people than people
usually are. At his ready reach were whole mountains of books to
engage his prodigious intellect, movies to help him make it through
each tortured day, and close at hand lay pristine and quiet alpine
country that let him glimpse, at least, a world where everything
seemed ordered, and which, deep in snow, seemed very calm. Yet
he also had autism and it would endure for him and for his family—
a disease much like a nightmare from which you cannot awake, as
Ian had described it, a bad dream that does not end, that shatters
rest and splinters sleep.

I arrived for a short visit on New Year's Day, the weather cold but
brilliantly clear, and Sarah ran out to greet me in a mood more
exuberant than I expected it to be. "I've got a surprise for you!" she
informed me as she hugged me. "It's a present. It's a story I just
wrote!"

More than a year before, I had asked Sarah if she would like to
write a story that would help me explain who her brother was and
what life with him was like. She had wanted to initially, but as she
tried to write it, the words simply wouldn't come. She continued to
worry about how people who didn't know him would react to Ian's
endless distress, and she wasn't sure how successfully she could
describe the way in which he was difficult and wonderful at once; so
she had told me in May, her soft voice diluted by defeat, that
although she really had tried to, she couldn't write about her brother;
she just couldn't find a way to shape his life into a tale. I assured her
that I understood her trouble, and I explained that for far too long
it had visited me too. But I thanked her nonetheless and I assured

her not to worry. Her mother told Sarah she was proud that she had tried to write the story but then had been assertive enough to give it up and let it go, then we spoke of it no more.

But on the same day that Claudia, Boyce, and Ian began to compose their Christmas letter, Sarah sat in the sunlight that poured in from the house's bank of southern windows, and in her careful handwriting she unwound a line of words that offered more about Ian and her family than she ever had written before, more too than she had ever said aloud, and she called her story "The Wished-For Christmas Miracle":

It was Christmas morning! There were many wonderful presents, although the gift I wanted more than anything was not there. It was the gift that our whole family had wanted ever since Ian had learned to type and before.

Later, when all the gifts were opened, I leaned back with a contented sigh. But then something under the tree caught my eye. It was a long, tube-shaped gift with a ribbon at each end. My eyes twinkled. Mystery gifts always interested me. But even that did not prepare me for what was inside. The package was addressed simply to the Drummonds. Usually either my father or mother opened presents that were addressed in such a manner, but I was going to open this one.

Slowly I removed the wrapping paper and was surprised to find a large, shiny bottle. It had a label on one side. I turned it over and read it. I gasped and read it again to make sure I hadn't made a mistake. This is what it said: "A Cure for Autism and Other Diseases."

I turned and called across the room to Ian. He turned at the sound of his name but only answered with something that sounded like "monkey, monkey." Ian couldn't say much else because he has autism, which is a disease that makes him not be able to talk and have to follow boring routines.

Mama and Boycie (what I call my father) came over to see what it was. Oh, the joy that came to our family that day! It

was all so wonderful that we cried. It felt so good to cry that
I almost couldn't stop. But in spite of all this, we lost no time
in giving Ian the medicine.

Late that afternoon I looked at Ian. He looked so real, so
wonderfully real, that a force inside me willed me to get up
and run to him. I stood up as though pushed by invisible hands
and ran across the room to Ian. But it was slow, somehow, as
though I were moving through water. When I finally reached
him, I threw my arms around him in a tight, loving hug.
But suddenly everything changed. Ian's arms hardened into
carved, wooden posts. His body shrank back behind them and
also became hard and cold. The Christmas tree and the light
from the windows disappeared into blackness except for the
tiny nightlight which brightened only the area beside the
wardrobe in my bedroom.

Slowly I unwrapped my arms around the two bedposts,
crawled under the covers and turned over. My pillow was wet
before I slept again.

The long winter wears on as I write these words but surely spring
will soon supplant it, and I believe that mine has been a story
much like Sarah's, in the end. The writing of each one has seemed
impossible at times, words refusing to give either story shape or
destination till the time was right perhaps, till a tune had come to
mind and finally there was some linguistic music. Sarah's story and
this larger one both attempt to acknowledge the elemental importance of hope, but to acknowledge too a grounded reality that often
is hard and cold and inexplicable. Both affirm, I trust, that Ian has
come to all of us as a gift we somehow don't deserve, and there is
conviction in each story that love, like language, is probably too
much at the heart of everything for us to truly understand it, too
endlessly creative to contain. Both contend, and surely you should
too, that although miracles seldom happen, they are well worth
wishing for.

None of us can know with any certainty what Ian's future will hold, but it seems certain that he will long to be normal in the coming days and years as he plaintively does now, and surely he will suffer many bitter disappointments. Yet in the same way that Saturn already is his to claim despite the fact that he cannot truly reach it— out there for the clear imagining in books and photographs as well as in the vivid eyes of telescopes—so too will his quest for normalcy be one he steadily continues in his own singular and wonderful way, his life exactly like every other life as it progresses toward its end: animated by curiosities and incremental understandings, sustained by love and friendship, described and made meaningful by words. IF YYOU QWONDER GHOW IKEEP GFROM GOIMNG CRAXZY ILL TEL;L YOU, he explained only the other day, specifically for me and for this book. I YTRY TO HOPPE FOR QA CURE WEVERY DDAY. IHAVE ;LOTS OF GFRIENDS AT SVCHOOL AND MYY YTEACHERS ;LOVE ME AND IAM ,LUCKY THAT NMY FQAMIILY IS SO AMAXZ-ING BUT I VCANNOT BARE MY LOIFE SOMEETIMES. VBUT IHAVE SO ,MUCH TO BBE GHAPPY ABOUT TOO. I ;LIVE H3ERE IN THE MOUMNTAINS ANDIT IS B3EAUTIFFUL. I;LIKE TO 5READ ABND LEARN AVBOUT EVERRYTHIBNG. IHAVE SO NMUCH ;LOVE I RREALLY CANNOT BE UBNHAAPY ALLL THE TIME.

From his early years of picture cards and naming games to his slow and tedious introduction to linguistic symbols; from the small machine that first spoke on his behalf to the day he murmured "cow" out of silence that second time; from his oral recitation of *The Farm Concert* to the first time he typed I LOVE YYOU, Ian's life till now has been a labor of language—difficult, exacting, impossible, yet made significant simultaneously by ideas, interactions, and senti-ments wrapped in words—words electrically envisioned, arranged and ordered by neural rules, then set to singing rhythms. And as his future days unfold, surely language will similarly chart their uncer-tain course. Ian will encounter much, endure much, and along the way he will imagine a million stories. Like his great-grandmother before him, for whom stories were life's best benevolence, he will set some of them magically in motion, as he already has begun to do, his typing a rich voice in its own right, full of range and emotion. Like her, like his sister and an uncle he humbles, he will offer his

stories not so much to instruct or to advertise his sanguine explanations, but simply in an effort to connect, to try to make some sense,
to marvel. They will be stories, it seems sure, about people who
struggle and yearn yet who somehow persevere, stories borne by
the wonderment of words, tales set to Ian's melodies.

   Can you imagine?

FOR THE BEST IN PAPERBACKS, LOOK FOR THE

In every corner of the world, on every subject under the sun, Penguin represents quality and variety—the very best in publishing today.

For complete information about books available from Penguin—including Puffins, Penguin Classics, and Arkana—and how to order them, write to us at the appropriate address below. Please note that for copyright reasons the selection of books varies from country to country.

In the United Kingdom: Please write to *Dept. JC, Penguin Books Ltd, FREEPOST, West Drayton, Middlesex UB7 0BR.*

If you have any difficulty in obtaining a title, please send your order with the correct money, plus ten percent for postage and packaging, to *P.O. Box No. 11, West Drayton, Middlesex UB7 0BR*

In the United States: Please write to *Consumer Sales, Penguin USA, P.O. Box 999, Dept. 17109, Bergenfield, New Jersey 07621-0120.* Visa and MasterCard holders call 1-800-253-6476 to order all Penguin titles

In Canada: Please write to *Penguin Books Canada Ltd, 10 Alcorn Avenue, Suite 300, Toronto, Ontario M4V 3B2*

In Australia: Please write to *Penguin Books Australia Ltd, P.O. Box 257, Ringwood, Victoria 3134*

In New Zealand: Please write to *Penguin Books (NZ) Ltd, Private Bag 102902, North Shore Mail Centre, Auckland 10*

In India: Please write to *Penguin Books India Pvt Ltd, 706 Eros Apartments, 56 Nehru Place, New Delhi 110 019*

In the Netherlands: Please write to *Penguin Books Netherlands bv, Postbus 3507, NL-1001 AH Amsterdam*

In Germany: Please write to *Penguin Books Deutschland GmbH, Metzlerstrasse 26, 60594 Frankfurt am Main*

In Spain: Please write to *Penguin Books S. A., Bravo Murillo 19, 1° B, 28015 Madrid*

In Italy: Please write to *Penguin Italia s.r.l., Via Felice Casati 20, I-20124 Milano*

In France: Please write to *Penguin France S. A., 17 rue Lejeune, F–31000 Toulouse*

In Japan: Please write to *Penguin Books Japan, Ishikiribashi Building, 2–5–4, Suido, Bunkyo-ku, Tokyo 112*

In Greece: Please write to *Penguin Hellas Ltd, Dimocritou 3, GR–106 71 Athens*

In South Africa: Please write to *Longman Penguin Southern Africa (Pty) Ltd, Private Bag X08, Bertsham 2013*